Safety in the
Ceramics
Studio

How to
Handle
Ceramic
Materials
Safely

Jeff Zamek

© 2002 by
Jeff Zamek

Published by

**krause
publications**

700 East State Street • Iola, WI 54990-0001
715/445-2214 • FAX: 715/445-4087   www.krause.com

Please call or write for our free catalog.
Our toll-free number to place an order or obtain a free catalog is 800-258-0929.

Library of Congress Catalog Number: 2002105107
ISBN: 0-87341-922-7

Printed in the United States of America

To my wife, Lauren, and my children,
Ben and Maya, who gave me the time to write.

A fine teacher attains a kind of immortality because it is
impossible to know when, or if, their influence stops.

—Henry Adams

Table of Contents

Introduction

Common Sense in the Ceramics Studio

When I first contacted my publisher about writing a book on ceramic toxicology, they thought it was a very good idea. It would address issues that potters always want to know more about when handling raw materials or working in their studios. I had actually assembled a body of information, which was to be another book titled *More About What Every Potter Should Know*. This text would be an additional study of ceramic materials, which was partially covered in my first book, *What Every Potter Should Know*. After researching the material for *Safety in the Ceramics Studio*, I had almost decided to drop the whole project. There is a great responsibility in being accurate, especially with the written word. If I write that a certain glaze formula will work in a kiln firing and the potter uses that formula and it runs down the pot and onto the kiln shelf, aside from a mess and expense, no one is hurt. However, if I write something about a ceramic raw material being safe to use and I am incorrect in my statement, the potter could potentially be exposed to a health risk.

Why even write about this area of ceramics when other topics are so interesting and less controversial? I was drawn to this topic many times and since December 1999 have started and stopped writing a number of times as I felt an obligation to assemble the current information and state it in simple direct terms for potters to read, think about, and then go on to make their own decisions on the safety factors they wish to incorporate into their own working conditions. A famous author once said, "Easy reading is hard writing." I hope this book reads easy and is useful in explaining the options open to potters.

When we think of ceramic toxicology, a vast unknown area of raw material dangers comes to mind. I have used the term in this book to describe a wide range of potential health hazards in the ceramics studio, from kiln firing, cuts, burns, physical stress, psychological stress, raw material information, and, significantly, how other potters are using the materials they come in contact with on a daily basis. Much has been investigated and written about the effects of clays, feldspars, flint, and other ceramic raw materials. There is a vast amount of health related documentation concerning miners' and industrial workers' contact with clays in the workplace. However, there is very little data or health studies on how potters as a group use ceramic raw materials.

As potters, we are all concerned with our own safety in the ceramics studio. We also care about the health of fellow potters and customers who buy and use our pots. In the past few years, the ceramic arts community has been warned with increasing alarm about the dangers of working with ceramic materials and kiln emissions that we come in contact with on a daily basis. The numerous health hazards associated with clay are now the common themes of articles, lectures, publications, and workshops. "Experts" with their own agendas have claimed the safety issue for their exclusive territory in order to educate potters on the correct way to handle ceramic materials. In many instances, the advice on raw materials has taken the form of "when in doubt, throw it out." Who can logically argue with the statement, "Wear a respirator when opening bags of flint, as high exposure levels can cause silicosis"? Every month we read or hear unconfirmed reports (gossip) about the dangers of exposure to raw materials. Which poison of the month will be added to our list of *problem* materials? Exactly how many *safe* raw materials will be left to make a glaze? What is so wrong with warning potters of potential health risks they face or might inflict on their pottery-buying customers? How can this type of message cause a problem or be anything but constructive?

The sum total of all the dire health warnings has been to cause more confusion and anxiety than clarity. We are in the season of a ceramic toxicology witch-hunt. Any mania will intensify as long as the relevant facts are not discovered, published, and communicated to the people who use the material. Is it possible that studio potters, students, and teachers have been dying or seriously injuring their health for years without our notice? Has anyone just put down the latest article on the toxic effects of raw materials and wondered why there is a potter still left standing in their studios to read such news? Simply stated, while the articles on potential health risks to potters are sometimes issued with good intentions, they are based on studies that do not pertain to potters. The medical literature and industrial health studies concerning raw materials used in moist clays and glazes do not relate to the concentrations and exposure rates that potters experience in their studios. Often what is inferred from the information can be skewed and distorted based on the individual authority's vested interest in promoting a specific point of view.

Does this mean all the information is invalid or irrelevant and we should run into our studios and dump flint on the floor? No, not at all. The other side of the argument is just as unacceptable. It is possible to damage one's health by the improper use of ceramic materials. However, the gray areas in between scaring people away from raw materials and the materials being considered completely benign have to be filled in more completely than has been attempted to date. The subject is too important to leave in the hands of individual experts. Since we cannot wait for the eventual return of reason, we must try to find a safe and sane way to work with raw materials during this time of hypersensitivity to all things ceramic. Like all excessive doctrines, common sense, education, and balance will prevail at some point. Hopefully this text will give potters a sense of security in their studios. A little knowledge about ceramic raw materials can go a long way in maintaining a safe ceramics studio.

A greater scope of information has to be gathered on how raw materials affect potters. An appropriate professional organization or college would be the ideal place for such research, as they have the capabilities and resources to investigate whether or not potters are exposing themselves to risk with ceramic materials. At this point, no one person or group has come forward to offer an investigative body. A nationally known ceramics college would be the perfect organization to study such an important aspect of ceramics. Unfortunately, many higher educational institutions are more inwardly directed and are not interested in the larger non-academic community of people working with clay. In the end, further investigation is needed to fill in the blank areas in the ceramics-related health field.

The Power of Myth and Ceramics Safety

When talking with many potters about their health concerns and fears, there is always a point where they relate a story about a specific problem or raw materials toxic reaction that happened to themselves or to another person. While these cautionary tales are often very dramatic and sometimes scary, by their nature, they are not based on a scientific gathering of information, which can be subject to independent review. In short, they do not follow the scientific practice and methodology we use in evaluating other important areas of our life such as medicine or biology. Such personal stories can often have a mythic quality to their content, which captures the listener's attention. The teller of the account can also play a dramatic part in its presentation, highlighting certain passages with fear or dread. All of which can alter the accuracy of the facts.

The Oxford American Dictionary defines a myth as "an idea that forms part of the beliefs of a group or class but is not founded on fact." It must fulfill several objectives, some of which are: a quality of common experience that the listener can relate to in his or her life, a cautionary tale (beware of dangers), and a bizarre or out of the ordinary story. Myths that meet these qualities have the power to be passed on from one ill-informed listener to another, without any critical evaluation of the tale. I myself have been captivated (and I think that is the most accurate word for the experience) by a good myth even when I know the actual facts cannot support the myth. I am drawn back to the story with a certain fascination with the myth. However, once the listener knows the factual information, the story loses a considerable amount of its power to enthrall. The power of the myth is potent and unrelenting when the listener does not know or understand the concepts behind this form of communication.

One myth that illustrates a lack of factual knowledge of the natural world is the long-ago belief that the earth was flat. Surely it looked flat when you observed the horizon. While looking back at this belief, we do not believe the earth is flat because it has been proven to be round. In the past, people believed the earth was flat in part because they did not have access to accurate information. While this is a general myth that we all recognize, there are specific myths pertaining to potters. One such myth I found on the Internet, a constant source of misinformation posing as fact, is the tale of the "Alfred Dog." The story takes place at Alfred

University, College of Ceramics (a place of national prominence to most potters). The "pot shop" dog, which lived in the Alfred ceramics studio dies (a sympathetic innocent animal). The owner of the dog decides to cremate the dog (death always gets one's attention in a good story). After the cremation, when the oven is opened, the dog's silica-lined lungs are all that remain of the poor animal (a bizarre cautionary aspect that warns potters of breathing silica or flint found in their studios).

I love this story as it has all of the "hooks" to capture the listener's attention. The tale also allows for a certain amount of embellishment by the storyteller. Can you imagine the horror of seeing just the silica outlined lungs of this unsuspecting raw-material contaminated animal when the oven door was opened? This horrific image stays with me even though I know this event did not and cannot happen. Why do I know that this myth is not founded on fact? My dog "Friday" Silverman (yes he had a last name) died and was cremated by the veterinarian. I received a small container of his ashes, which I made into a very nice glaze, but that is another story (see my book, *What Every Potter Should Know* for details). There was not a silica-outlined lung present in this pot shop dog after he was cremated, only a soft gray powder. I have since asked my veterinarian if it is possible for this event to happen and as I suspected his answer was no. Does this fact prevent me from telling the story of the Alfred Dog? No, in fact I enjoy the story more with each telling. The look on people's faces as they listen to the tale is always fascinating to observe. However, unlike a good magician who will never reveal how the trick is done, I always tell the listener the truth, as disinformation does not serve the greater purpose of ceramics education.

My hope in writing this book is to replace the myths of hazardous ceramic materials with the facts on how to use ceramic materials intelligently and safely. We all know not to go into our kitchens and place our heads in a hot oven or cut ourselves with sharp knives. While these examples are almost too intuitive to question, think about them for a minute. Children not educated in the safe practices associated with the kitchen can often use appliances or tools incorrectly. We as adults know this basic safety information and do not think of the kitchen as a health hazard. The potential for injury is always present, but having the simple knowledge of safety in the kitchen keeps the potential hazards at a manageable level. We must apply the same methods and education to our understanding of ceramic materials. Namely that we can go into our studios educated in the safe and sane use of ceramic materials and related ceramics equipment. At that point, we will have reached the level of competence that we have in cooking in our kitchens or living in our homes.

The information contained in *Safety in the Ceramics Studio* comes from many diverse sources. As in the general wider field of ceramics, the potter must accumulate information from many diverse areas of expertise. Experiential knowledge, or information gained from one's own perception, is an important part of a potter's education. However, it is not the only source of information available to understanding clay, glazes, and kiln firing. Potters frequently attend workshops or enroll in lessons (private, college, craft centers), in an effort to learn more about kiln firing, glaze calculation, and throwing techniques. The same effort should be applied to understanding the safe handling of raw materials.

Unfortunately, there is not one source of safety information. Often what is published applies to larger industrial uses of the material. Some information is simply and plainly inaccurate. It is the potter's responsibility to gather facts from many varied places and then make an informed educated judgment as to the risk involved in using any raw material or ceramics related procedure. I would like the reader to pay particular attention to the recent surveys pertaining to potters' use of raw materials ("The Potter's Health & Safety Questionnaire," page 141), the report by Edouard Bastarache M.D. ("Eye Injuries due to Radiation," page 76), and the Canadian study ("Kiln Emissions and Potters' Exposures," page 58), as they contradict several of the false assumptions on the dangers of raw materials, eye injury, and kiln emissions that are currently given wide acceptance. I believe such studies are just the beginning instruments for obtaining accurate data and observations on how potters react to the materials in the ceramics workplace. There will be more research and medical studies in this specialized area of ceramics, which potters can find and hopefully use to help set up and maintain a safe working environment. I recommend reading this book and then going out and finding other sources of information on health and safety in the ceramics studio. It is only by judging a wide range of information that potters can formulate a rational balanced safety program that will function in their studios.

Chapter 1

Studio Planning

Often the oldest and simplest advice is best. We have all heard the importance of maintaining clean health habits in our living and working environment. Throughout history, people who have not heeded these now "common sense" warnings often developed diseases and suffered premature illness or death. Once microbes and germs were fully understood, the admonition to keep potentially harmful substances away from our bodies and living spaces became even more forceful.

Working safely with ceramic materials, or for that matter operating carefully in the ceramics studio, is a learned task that can be accomplished by following several objectives. Know the materials and equipment you are using, and enact competent housekeeping procedures in the studio on a daily basis. Any effort expended in studio planning will pay off many times over when you are actually in the studio in a working production cycle. Once the equipment is in place and ceramic ware is being produced, it is not the time to find out a ware rack cannot fit through the kiln room door or the moist clay storage is located at the opposite end of the studio from the potter's wheel.

Working with clay and glaze materials is by its very nature a housekeeping endeavor. Taking an overview of the ceramics work area and its associated equipment, it looks like a lot of materials in dry and wet states that have to be labeled and stored in different containers. The pottery equipment, whether it is potter's wheels, clay mixers, pug mills, worktables, kilns, or slab rollers, has to be placed within the work space in a logical and safe position. In any ceramics work area, the idea is to maintain an efficient flow of work-related activates to reduce the amount of duplication in movement. Time and energy are wasted if the slab roller is

placed at one end of the studio and the clay and wedging table at the opposite end. The potter would wedge the clay and then have to go across the studio to use the slab roller. This same reduction of actual steps in moving about the studio can be applied to other pieces of equipment or even to ceramics construction steps involved in making pots or sculpture. In schools or crafts centers, the placement of individual equipment has been predetermined and the potter does not have much choice when walking into the studio set up. However, the potter should always observe the studio operation with regard to safety practices. Ceramics studios, wherever their location, should be well organized, clean, and set up to facilitate the efficient production of pots or sculpture.

While decreasing the amount of wasted effort is a recommendable goal, it also serves a more important purpose in studio planning, namely to make the studio a safer working environment. Fatigue and excess movement can lead to careless operations in the studio. For example, if a potter mixes his or her own clay, there are several things to consider before operating within this situation. Dry bags of clay have to be labeled and stored in such a way that their contents cannot be spilled into the air or onto the floor. Proper ventilation of the clay mixing area is essential. The dry clay has to be stored near the clay mixer to cut down on wasted time and effort, and then a water source has to be within easy access to the clay mixer. Spilled water on the floor of a clay mixing operation can lead to slips and falls around moving machinery. Once the clay is mixed and stored, the clay mixing area has to be easy to clean.

Each step within the process of making clay has to be considered for its degree of personal safety and the ability of the potter to maintain a clean work area. Each segment of working with clay and glaze has to be broken down into individual steps to maintain a safe workplace. One way to think about planning an effective studio layout is the ability to work in a less stress-producing and labor-intensive situation. This in turn will allow the potter to produce a greater amount of work. It is easier to make costly and dangerous mistakes when tired. With this in mind, the end result of studio planning should be safety.

Designing Raw Material Protection Systems

There are three possible methods for ceramic materials to enter the body—*inhalation*, enters through breathing; *dermal absorption,* enters through the skin; and *ingestion,* enters through eating. If we first think of how raw materials can enter our system, we can then go on to devise barrier methods to prevent the three methods of entry.

How a studio is set up in terms of the placement of equipment, supplies, and the general utilization of space can help or hinder the transmission of raw materials into the body. Placing a clay mixing or raw material storage area next to a throwing or handbuilding location can cause problems with raw material inhalation, even under the best of room ventilation conditions. Opening large bags of clay in the clay mixing process can deposit plumes of microscopic clay particles into the air. A glaze mixing room with its potential for spills from dry and wet glaze materials would not be a good room to also use for packaging pots for shipment. When possible, it is best to keep two conflicting production areas separated.

Inhalation

Inhalation is the most common way for ceramic materials to enter the body. When making and firing ceramic objects, there are several processes that can generate airborne particles and vapors that can cause respiratory irritation and eventual illness. Airborne particles can come from clay mixing operations, trimming pots, glaze mixing, glaze spraying, or general studio housekeeping procedures, such as wiping down a table. Airborne particles can also be thrown into the air from scraps of dry clay left on the studio floor or from improperly vented kilns.

Since inhalation is such a major potential source of health risk, potters should make a few relatively small investments in protective equipment. Every potter and every studio should address its own requirements for protective equipment and supplies. Each step in the making of ceramic objects should be studied as to the airborne particles or vapors that are released during that operation. While potters have a finite amount of time and money, studying the inhalation of raw materials and vapors should be a high priority safety project. In terms of health and safety, payoffs for time and money expended controlling airborne materials and vapors will have the greatest effect in protecting the potter's health and comfort in the studio.

Dermal Absorption

Skin is the largest organ in the human body. It protects us from the outside world. The most frequent skin problems encountered by potters are burns from reaching into a hot kiln, dry patches of skin from immersion in water, cuts from sharp edges of pottery shards, and skin rashes and non-specific irritations from clay and raw materials.

Often common sense is the best preventative fix for a potential skin problem. Potters have their hands in water during throwing, handbuilding, glazing, and studio cleaning operations. In the winter dry months, it is often easy to forget proper hand care. Always wash your hands after mixing clay and glaze materials and at the end of the workday. Clays and glaze materials can have a drying effect on hands. Any water-based hand lotion can help treat excessively dry hands. It is a conservative safety precaution to wear rubber or latex gloves when handling dry or wet raw materials. However, some potters do have sensitivity to latex. Cuts or abrasions on the hand should be thoroughly protected from any source of irritation in the studio environment.

Ingestion

Several of the raw materials that potters use in their studios can have toxic and lethal effects if ingested, which is one reason for not eating in the studio. Food might become contaminated if it is misplaced on a raw material. While there are no known cases of this type of event, it can happen. Statistically, not many potters knowingly or accidentally eat or drink ceramic raw materials. In cases where this does happen, it usually occurs in unsupervised small children who lick or rub raw glazes on their hands and mouth.

Sensible Steps for a Clean Studio

The best time to think about studio cleaning practices is before designing your own studio. However, the same practices can be applied to any existing studio situation in varying degrees. A systematic evaluation of each movement in the ceramics studio will help in the formation of safety practices for working with raw materials and equipment.

- Never eat, drink, or smoke in the studio. The reasons for not eating or drinking in the ceramics environment relate to contamination of the substances with dry clays, glaze materials, or any other foreign materials that could come in contact with the food or drink and then be ingested. Airborne particles and vapors can land on or in food or drink. Smoking involves placing the cigarette down on a surface that could be contaminated. Smoking also increases the potter's general susceptibility to respiratory illness.

  While these restrictions might be hard to adhere to in a daily work schedule, they are conservative measures to ensure that what's in the studio stays in the studio and not in your body. The degree of compliance with these restrictions relates directly to the individual potter's ability to assign relative risk to such activities. Will eating a sandwich that is carefully packaged and then eaten on a clean plate cause serious harm to the potter? Potters do not report such situations as having caused health problems, but why take unnecessary risks?

- Never store food in the studio. Any food located within the ceramics studio does have the opportunity to become contaminated with materials within the studio. Storing food in the studio encourages eating in the studio. It also sets up a situation where people working in the studio who are not informed on safety procedures can eat or drink under conditions that might cause food contamination.

- Place all dry glaze and clay materials in sealed double plastic bags or lidded jars. Open bags of clays or dry glaze materials can be easily spilled, or dry particles can be released into the studio atmosphere. Clearly label all materials to ensure accurate clay and glaze mixing. Place raw materials, such as clay, in a clean accessible spot near the area where the potter will use them.

- Wear a separate set of clothes in the studio, and clean your studio clothes frequently. During the workday, many articles of clothing and shoes can become saturated with either dry ceramic materials or moist clay.

The potter's wheel should be placed near a source of natural light when possible, positioned under good artificial lighting, and set in such a way as to prevent shadows on the ware during throwing operations. Having a source of artificial light is important for working in the studio in poor natural light conditions or at night. Good illumination will prevent eyestrain and reduce stress. Floor mats can be installed in front of studio exits to stop dry clay from leaving the studio. Work tables and floors should have smooth non-absorbent surfaces for effective cleaning. They should be constructed of non-absorbent material for easy cleaning (wood table polyurethane sealed).

Frequently, moist clay becomes stuck to the shoes. It later dries and falls off at another location. Metallic coloring oxides used in glazes can easily become embedded in shirts and pants, rubbing off on furniture or dusting onto other objects.

- Promptly clean up any raw materials spills on the floor or tables. Any liquid material that dries can become airborne, and drafts can carry it about the studio; or someone may inadvertently step in the material and track it through the studio. As often happens when scooping out dry materials or clays from their bags or containers, some material will fall on the table or floor and be spread around the work area. It is through careful attention to individual small safety practices that the overall environment is improved.

- Wipe down worktables with a wet sponge before leaving the studio each day. A wet sponge will pick up and hold more dry or liquid spills than a dry cloth or broom. The idea is to remove the materials from the spill area and not to just move them to another location within the studio. This is essential for removing materials that float in the air and eventually fall to any surface within the studio. While many of these clean up procedures seem time consuming, if done consistently they become more efficient and part of the work routine.

- Use a fan near an open window whenever mixing dry materials. Ventilation will dilute and reduce the exposure per/unit of time of any airborne particles in the studio. Avoid high concentrations of airborne particles for long periods of time. One of the simplest ways to accomplish this is to open a window and place a fan in the room to create a cross draft. Potters should also wear a respirator whenever mixing clay or glazes.

- Potters who wear glasses should clean them before leaving the studio. Airborne ceramic materials can cling to the plastic or glass lenses. Potters can mix a glaze or work with moist clay and inadvertently touch their face or glasses without thinking about the particles left there. After a day of working in the studio, look at the glasses in sunlight and notice the dry clay particles left on the lenses.

- Place a doormat outside the pottery studio to catch dry materials. While this recommendation seems overly simple, it is most helpful in keeping raw material particles from leaving the studio area. It also catches moist clay that can be deposited outside the studio work areas. The doormat should be cleaned on a regular basis and changed when it is no longer effective.

- Wet mop or vacuum (use a high-efficiency HEPA filter in the vacuum) the studio floor everyday. Wet mopping captures most dry raw materials that have fallen to the studio floor. Using a dry mop or broom will at best only move dry particles within the studio. While many of the particles can be seen and thrown away, it can leave a false impression of cleaning, as the unseen particles are still in the studio environment. The unseen particles are the size that can cause potential respiration difficulty. The HEPA filter is specially designed to hold micron size dry particles, while regular vacuum filters are too coarse and blow dry material into the studio.

- Never sand bone-dry clay pots. This procedure can release micron size particles of clay into the air, which are potential health hazards.

- Any cuts or open wounds on the hands should be thoroughly protected to prevent raw materials from entering through the skin.

- Household kitchen tools or appliances should never be used in the ceramics studio without the understanding that they can never be used again for the preparation of food.

- Wash hands before leaving the studio. Moist clay and dry materials can remain on the arms and hands in unseen amounts during and after working with clay and glazes. Common sense dictates a thorough washing of the hands after using any ceramic material, and this washing procedure should be done whenever leaving the studio. Clean towels or disposable paper towels will prevent raw materials from being reintroduced onto the hands.

The Ceramics Studio

There is no existing perfect studio, and most likely there will be no perfectly built future studio (at least not in the near future). However, thinking through the various steps in the production of pottery or sculpture will greatly improve existing and new studios. While it may not be possible to incorporate all of the suggested recommendations for a clean and safe studio, it is possible to use several specific ideas to improve the working conditions in an existing studio. Often small changes in the physical working place can have significant effects on the operation of the studio. In new studio construction, many of these recommendations are more easily achieved. Keep in mind that any time and money spent in designing venting systems and safety equipment in a new studio space will have significant payoffs in efficiency, production, and the health of the potters who work in that space.

All areas where forming operations take place are subject to moist and dry clay scraps. When working on the potter's wheel, the centrifugal forces of the moving wheel can throw slurry clay (water and clay mixture) up against the wheel splash pan, or the liquid clay can be thrown onto the floor. The clay forming areas of the studio should be thoroughly cleaned at the end of each workday to ensure that clay scraps are not crushed underfoot or moved about the studio.

During trimming operations, scraps of clay can be thrown to the floor as the wheel spins. Always remove the clay trimmings from the floor when the trimming operation is completed. If left on the floor wet, trimmed clay scraps can become lodged in shoes and carried throughout the studio and into living areas. Dry clay trimmings can release microscopic particles of clay when crushed underfoot. Those particles can remain airborne for days.

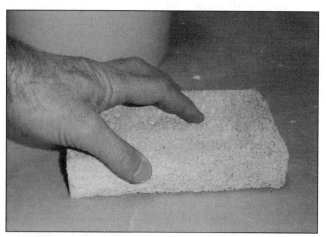

A wet sponge is a very effective cleaning tool for removing dry raw material spills from work tables. Often dry wiping raw materials will just move the particles onto another work surface or send the light density dry materials into the studio atmosphere.

Eating or drinking in the studio can lead to accidental contamination and ingestion of raw materials. To prevent this type of accident, do not bring food or beverages into the ceramics studio.

Potter's wheels should be located in a well-ventilated area. The height of the wheel head (see the aluminum head in the photo) should beat the same level as the seat of the chair. The level alignment will prevent back strain as upper body leverage and not total muscle power can be brought to bear on the moist clay during centering. The wheel area should be kept clean and well organized before and after throwing operations.

Often the simplest cleaning procedures prove the most effective in preventing the movement of raw materials out of the studio. Placing a floor mat either in the studio entrance or outside the studio entrance will reduce the amount of dust or dirt brought in and out of the ceramics studio.

While many kitchen tools are suitable for use in the pottery studio, it is always the best policy not to use the same tools for both functions. All tools used for pottery should be kept in the ceramics studio.

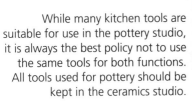

Sanding "bone dry" or bisque pottery can release small ceramic particles into the air. Often the same effect can be achieved by methods that will not cause the potter to inhale micron-size particles of ceramic material.

Adequate studio lighting, both natural and artificial, decreases eyestrain and fatigue. Whenever possible, work areas should be located near natural light. Artificial full spectrum fluorescent lights should be placed as to reduce or eliminate shadows in wheel, handbuilding, glazing, and kiln firing areas.

Chapter 2

Ceramics Areas— Studio Safety

Clean Studios

The storage of raw materials is one of the most important safety considerations when working in ceramics. A truly sterile studio cannot be enacted or maintained, but many common sense steps can be taken to ensure raw materials are kept so that they will not release their contents into the workplace environment.

Dry clay and glaze materials are found in varying amounts in any ceramics operation. Dry clays with additions of water are used in clay mixing, slips/engobes, casting slips, glazes, underglazes, and other ceramics-related processes. Potters who mix their own clay body formulas and glaze formulas need to take extra precautions, as both operations can generate high amounts of airborne particles. Potters who use pre-mixed clays and pre-mixed commercial glazes also must develop a system of protecting themselves in their workplace. Upon first observation, it would seem that pre-mixed clays and glazes will create less dry particles in the work area, as they contain water in either the clay body formula or glaze. In the moist state, airborne particles from clay and glazes are not a problem, as they are contained within the raw material water structure. However, when in the dry state, particles can easily be launched into the studio environment.

The first and critical step is to identify and locate all the areas in the workplace that can generate vapors or solid particles. The main idea is to vent or isolate any materials that can possibly enter the body through inhalation, ingestion, or contact with the skin. Not every potter will have access to a ceramics studio that has a separate glaze room, kiln room, or workshop area, but the same safety guidelines can be applied even if the potter works in one room that serves all pottery-making functions.

Good safety practices in the ceramics studio translate into good housekeeping practices followed through on a daily basis. Specific pieces of safety equipment can make this process easier and more efficient, but the main tool is a dedication to learning about safety processes and the ability to carry them out as a regular part of the ceramics workplace. The potter's dedication to employing any safety measure every time it is needed is the most important safety device.

Workshop Area

In the ceramics studio, all equipment that generates vapors or fine particles should be properly vented. The primary concern in the workshop area is to make sure dry clay and glaze materials are cleaned off of all surfaces, floors, tables, shelves, chairs, etc. Dry clay from wheel trimming and handbuilding operations can often be found in small cracks and crevasses around the studio. The ceramics studio environment contains many other areas of potential airborne particles found in clay, glazes, and common dust and dirt.

There is a rule in protecting yourself when working in the studio. Namely, it is the particles in the air you cannot see that are potentially harmful. We all have walked into a sunlit room and seen particles of clay or dust floating in the air. However, it is the micron size constituent that cannot be seen with the eye that can get past the human body's natural defenses, causing particles to remain in the lungs, throat, and nasal passages.

Potters should wear a respirator during any studio clean up operation. The workshop area should be cleaned with a vacuum (containing a HEPA fine particle filter), and the floor should be wet mopped on a daily basis. An oil-based sweeping compound can also be used to clean the floor. All tables and chairs or worktables should be wiped down with a wet sponge. It is sometimes hard to get potters to follow a daily cleaning schedule when the workplace "looks" clean, meaning there is no visible clay or raw material dust on the floor or work surfaces. However, as stated, it is the micron size particles that cannot be observed that have to be removed from the studio.

Placement of Workshop Equipment

Slab rollers, wheels, extruders, handbuilding worktables, and any additional equipment should be located within the workspace so as to facilitate the flow of production. For example, moist clay storage should be located near the wedging table, which should be in close proximity to the potter's wheel or handbuilding table. After unloading a glaze kiln, storage shelves for the finished work or packaging supplies should be located near the finished pots. There should be a smooth flow of work-related activities with little or no doubling back on footsteps or production processes. Working with clay is a labor-intensive activity. Any effort and planning to reduce the labor part of working within the studio will have significant benefits in less stress and greater productivity.

Stacking kiln posts near the kiln reduces wasted motion and saves time in stacking the kiln. Posts should be arranged by size, so the potter can determine the shelf height as he or she is loading the kiln. Searching for the correct height post is time consuming and frustrating.

Not only does the placement of equipment, tools, and supplies make the production of work easier and more efficient, but it also reduces the potter's mental stress, which results in a safer working situation. In many studios, the ideal flow of materials cannot be completely achieved because of size restrictions or financial limitations. But even in small working areas, the goal should be to reduce duplication of movement within the studio.

Kiln Room

The model situation is to build or have a studio with a separate kiln room. Any type of kiln firing presents a higher degree of risk to the potter, and proper preparation will lower the risk. Kiln firing always has the hazard of someone getting seriously burnt from touching or falling on a hot kiln. Also, adequate lighting for the kiln room is often overlooked. During any kiln firing, it is important to observe all sides of the kiln to ensure the integrity of the structure. Any kiln when heated will expand to some degree, and occasionally kiln bricks can separate and flames or hot gases can be forced out of the kiln.

Observation of the firing kiln will always decrease the risk factors associated with the kiln room. The area around the kiln should be clear of all articles that can cause an obstruction to a potter during the kiln firing. Kiln room floors should always be kept free of any materials that could trip an unsuspecting potter. Many times kiln shelves, posts, chisels, and other related kiln accessories are left randomly stacked against the kiln, which always presents a possible safety risk.

If the kiln is located in a working area, venting is a critical factor and one of the commercial venting systems should be used on each kiln (see Chapter 5 Kiln Venting Systems). Whether the potter fires a gas or electric kiln, it should be adequately vented to an outside air source to reduce vapors and solid particles from the immediate kiln room atmosphere.

Gas kilns require oxygen in the air to maintain combustion, which means the kiln room should be well ventilated to maintain an adequate air transfer in the immediate kiln area. In kilns fired by gas, the kiln stack should exhaust gases, safely removing them from the studio. Each type of gas kiln will have different venting requirements that must conform to the size of the kiln room and local fire codes. When using electric kilns, there should be enough space (at least three feet) around each kiln to ensure the potter can walk around each side of the kiln for inspection during the firing.

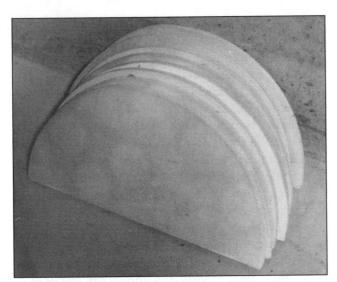

Kiln shelves should be clean and free of glaze drips and excess kiln wash. The shelves should be neatly stacked near the kiln, where they will not cause a safety hazard.

All types of kilns should be located away from combustible materials, studio framing members, and kiln room walls. A common studio hazard in kiln rooms containing gas kilns is physically linking the exhaust stack to a combustible ceiling structure. When the kiln is fired, the hot exhaust gases are transferred through the stack, and they can ignite any combustible material near the stack. Each kiln stack and building should be evaluated individually with this safety factor in mind. Many studios have been damaged or completely burnt down because of a kiln stack design that wasn't well thought out.

Specific firing situations in the kiln room require the use of vapor-rated respirators. For example, luster glazing, where an oil-based metallic particle is fired onto a ceramic surface, releases vapors during application and firing that can cause possible lung and eye irritation. When in doubt as to which type of vapor respirator to use, contact the respirator manufacturer for recommendations.

Glaze Room

Many craft schools, colleges, ceramics centers, and a number of private pottery studios have separate rooms dedicated to glazing operations. In some circumstances, the glaze room also serves more than one purpose, namely it could be used for packing finished pots or accommodating a general storage area for supplies and equipment. Regardless of size or location, the glaze room or designated glazing area should have several elements incorporated into its design. When possible, a water supply and large sink are needed for clean up operations and as a ready source of water to add to mixing dry glaze materials. When mixing glazes from raw materials or when using prepared commercial glazes, wide tables with plenty of room will make the glaze mixing process less haphazard and more efficient. Any glazing operation can leave excess glaze on worktables, studio floors, and glazing tools, all of which have to be thoroughly cleaned to prevent dry airborne particles from being released into the studio. Dry raw materials and wet glaze spills have to be cleaned up immediately. If spills are allowed to remain, they can be disturbed by people walking by and air drafts in the glazing room, causing small particles of glaze material to be released into the air. The primary goal is to gather and dispose of any type of raw material particle before it can become airborne.

Safety Measures in Producing Moist Clay

Clay Mixing Areas

Having a clean well-ventilated clay-mixing environment is critical to a safe work area. Of all the possible work areas to consider separating from the main part of the ceramics studio, the clay mixing room should be given the highest priority.

The process of mixing moist clay starts by weighing out dry materials, which can include clays, feldspars, flint, talc, grog, and other raw materials. After the raw materials have been assembled, they are placed in a clay mixer, usually a large container with a rotating blade. When dry raw materials bags are opened and then dumped into the mixer, clay particles easily become airborne. Good room ventilation will draw airborne particles from the clay mixer and remove them from the clay mixing area. Under the best circumstances, some college ceramics programs (Massachusetts College of Art, for example) have room ventilation systems and dedicated venting systems for each clay mixer.

Traditionally, the mixing of clay has contributed the greatest amount of airborne clay particles into the studio. Many potters have realized this fact and are now starting to use pre-mixed moist clays from ceramic suppliers. Pre-mixed clay offers several advantages in terms of reducing airborne raw clay particles by transferring the clay mixing process to a manufacturer who can perform this service under environmentally better conditions. Ceramic suppliers are economically and technically set up to manufacture moist clay, which can allow potters more time to make pots or ceramic sculpture. Buying pre-mixed clay also removes the safety hazard of working around clay mixing machinery.

If potters choose to buy pre-mixed clays, they should concentrate on finding a reputable ceramics supplier with good quality control procedures in their clay mixing operation. Often the argument for not using pre-mixed clay is a false economy, based on the extra cost of purchasing moist clay versus the potter making his or her own clay. Purchasing good quality moist clay allows potters more time to concentrate their energy into making pots and other endeavors that are more productive than mixing clay. It also removes a potential safety hazard (clay mixing machinery, labor intensive activity, air quality issues) from the studio. If potters are still dedicated to mixing their own clay, which is a valid consideration other than for economic issues, they must think of it as setting up a business (mixing clay) to supply their other business (selling pots or sculpture) with all of the capital expenditures, maintenance, and other associated problems in operating machinery that a second business entails.

Pug mills are machines that compress and de-air the moist clay under vacuum pressure. The moist clay then is fed into a hopper where it is moved along by one or more mechanical screws, at which point it is deposited into a de-airing chamber, where it is extruded out into a compressed moist form.

Clay mixing machines and pug mills are inherently dangerous pieces of heavy-duty machinery with many moving parts that do not have safety guards. It is the potter's responsibility to read and understand all safety and maintenance instructions before operating any pottery machinery. All safety functions on the machines must also be in full use whenever the machines are in operation. At no time are any safety devices on the pug mill to be disconnected to ease the operation of the machine or speed up the pugging of clay. Both pug mills and clay mixing machines are capable of removing hands or arms from the careless potter and have done so over the years.

I have personal knowledge of this type of horrific accident. At one point, I worked for a ceramics supplier who did not train a worker in the safety procedures required to operate the pug mill. The worker's arm was caught in the turning blades of the machine and painfully removed from his body. Surprisingly, the ceramic supplier still has many unsafe conditions in his operation and is still in business!

Before using any machine, the potter should remove any rings, bracelets, or clothing that can be caught in a moving part. Each machine should have a clearly visible and reachable safety cut off switch to turn off the power immediately if there is an operator problem.

If the potter decides to use pre-mixed clay, a pug mill will be unnecessary in the studio. However, some potters do use a pug mill to reprocess scraps of used clay, returning the dry clay into a moist homogenous clay form. While reprocessing clay scraps or trimmings from pots is a widely used procedure in many studios, potters should ask themselves if the time required to reprocess clay could be better used to make more pots and eliminate a safety risk. While this question is economically based, there is a safety consideration in the use of clay mixing and pug mill machines in the studio. The potter should examine this risk before deciding to mix or reprocess clay. Each potter will have to balance the benefits and disadvantages, economically and aesthetically, to their individual working conditions.

In some instances, spreading out a plastic sheet and then dumping dry clay and water together to form moist useable clay accomplishes the clay mixing operation. Mixing clay in this method spews numerous raw material particles into the

Tools can pick up and hold dry clay particles that can later be released into the air. Clean tools after they have been used. Storing clay tools in a logical easy-to-find location can also reduce the stress of looking for a tool when it is needed.

immediate clay mixing area, which causes the micron size component of the dry raw material to remain in the air for days. Small particles can also be taken into other areas of the ceramics studio by drafts and air currents. Studios located in living quarters or physically adjacent to living areas must consider adequate ventilation to remove any airborne particles. Some potters have made the calculation already and have determined it is more cost effective from the safety and actual cost point of view to purchase commercially made moist clay formulas. For those potters who continue to mix or reprocess their own clay, there are many room ventilation systems designed to capture and remove micron size clay particles.

The clay mixing area should have a source of water close to the mixing machines. The best system for feeding water into a clay mixing machine runs the water directly through a hose to the mixer. Filling buckets of water and then moving them to the clay mixer eventually produces back strain and water spills. Many times potters have slipped on a wet floor when mixing clay.

Ideally the clay mixing area should be located close to the clay forming area in the studio. Moist clay is very dense and heavy. Fifty pounds of moist clay encompasses slightly more than a cubic foot of space. Moving moist clay to other locations within the studio is time and labor intensive and can lead to possible back and arm strain.

Moist clay can also present other hazards to potters in the form of mold growth within or on the surface of the clay. When moist clay is stored under the precise temperature, low light, and moisture conditions, mold can be seen on the clay's surface. Some mold looks like fuzzy green or brown particles on the clay. While some types of mold will increase the moist clay's plasticity and workability, some types of mold, if inhaled, can cause respiratory or asthma-type illnesses in individuals sensitive to this irritant. Mold can also cause skin dermatitis or rashes on the hands, arms, or any other point on the body that comes in contact with the clay.

Mold growth on dry clay can cause respiratory distress if inhaled. Clay platelets are a plate shaped structure, and because of their small size and flat dimensions they are perfect "lifting bodies" on which mold or bacteria can become airborne. Bentonite, a very small platelet structure clay (2.61 grams of bentonite, if its platelets were laid end to end, would cover a surface area of 6000 ft.^{2})[1] is often used as a

medium on which to transport bacteria for biological weapons. While the potter will not face such biohazards, it is important to know the characteristics of airborne clay.

Wearing a respirator can reduce the chances of inhaling mold in wet or dry clay. Clay additives can neutralize or stop mold growth in clay, while in other instances changing the clay body formula can stop allergic reactions to the mold.

Dry skin is another common concern when working with clay. Hand lotion can be used to treat dry skin caused by the moist clay's absorbent characteristics. Those characteristics are well known and have been well researched. In fact, many commercially prepared cosmetic creams are clay-based to mitigate oily skin. In the past, moist clay infused with herbs was frequently used as a poultice to draw out "toxins" in the body. Today specific types of clay are used in veterinary medicine as a poultice to draw out fluid from racehorses' knees. For potters, the problems arise when moist clay is in frequent and prolonged contact with the hands; as the clay dries, it draws normal moisture from the hands. If the hands become too dry and cracked, a break in the protective skin barrier can lead to infection.

A related point about working with moist clay and water is the temperature of the water used for throwing and handbuilding operations. Hands submerged in cold water for long periods of time can ache at the end of a workday. Try to use room temperature water in a well-heated studio. Always wash and dry your hands thoroughly after any moist clay forming operations. It is not unusual to repeat this hand cleaning process several times a day when working in the studio. The goal is to recognize and treat any minor ailments or breaks in the skin before they are allowed to progress into more advanced stages of distress.

Moist clay, because of its coarse particle size or the addition of grog (a coarse particle, calcined, filler used in clay bodies to reduce shrinkage and give the moist clay body "tooth" or the ability to stand up in throwing or handbuilding operations), can cause skin abrasions from the friction of the potter's hands on the clay. Frequently, potters comment on how smooth their hands have become after working with clay. The point at which smooth skin becomes overly sensitive because of the abrasion power of moist clay is an individual determination. However, abraded skin is most often found in throwing operations at the lower part of the palm near the small finger. This area of the hand

---

[1]·*Ceramic Science for the Potter* by W. G. Lawrence, published by Chilton/Haynes, 1972.

rests upon the spinning potters wheel head in the process of centering the clay. The solution is to simply use less downward pressure with the hand on the wheel head when centering the clay. As potters gain more experience in working on the potter's wheel, they arrive through trial and error at the appropriate degree of pressure for bringing the clay into a centered position on the wheel head.

A seemingly minor but important point concerning moist clay in the studio is its slick nature. Potters have often slid on a patch of moist clay that has fallen to the studio floor. To illustrate this characteristic of moist clay, bentonite is a very plastic and slippery clay that is used with water as a lubricant in oil drilling operations. The clay slurry mixture reduces friction and heat at the drill bit, allowing it to cut through rock smoothly and efficiently. In "The Potter's Health & Safety Questionnaire" (page 141), high percentages of potters were affected not by major studio accidents but by a series of minor irritating mishaps in their studios. The rates of health injuries such as hand injury, back injury, skin sensitivity, eye injury, and leg injury could have been reduced by following simple but important work related safety procedures.

The details of keeping moist clay and wet glaze off the studio floor are unexciting and repetitive but important for maintaining a safe efficient workplace. Pick up or clean all clay and glaze spills when they happen. If moist clay is allowed to remain on the floor, people working in or visiting the studio can slip or fall; if the clay dries, it can send microscopic clay platelets into the air, causing respiratory irritation or distress. Often it is not a major accident or work related illness that ends a potter's career but many small cumulative injuries and ailments, which, left untreated over the years, result in the eventual syndrome of "burn out." Old potters frequently complain of just being worn out physically. New potters can learn from the history of potters in the past and discover ways of working not necessarily harder but smarter.

Disposal of Dry Raw Materials

One of the central aspects of cleaning the studio of clay scraps, spilled liquid glaze, or dry raw materials is how to dispose of the studio waste. Many studio operations generate materials that have to be taken out of the work area on a daily, weekly, or monthly basis. Do not allow waste material to accumulate in the studio, as this can cause accidents and take up valuable workspace. After working, clean the studio with a wet mop or oil-based cleaning material, and then place the sweepings in a double plastic bag to prevent leakage. The bag can either be disposed of by a commercial waste removal service or it can be taken to the local garbage landfill. While these methods might seem like passing the problem on to a commercial trash removal service or contaminating the landfill, the amount of silica, cobalt, chrome, or other ceramic oxides deposited by potters has not proven to cause problems for local landfills.

Moist clay scraps that cannot be reprocessed or unusable dry glazes can also be placed in double plastic bags and taken out with the household trash. Aside from the weight of such waste clay and glaze, no special precautions have to be taken to remove this type of waste from the studio. Waste liquid glaze or clay slip (a suspension of water and clay) should be set aside and not flushed down studio drains. It will block up septic fields and cause drainage problems in the sewer system. The same precautions should be taken when working with plaster, which is a material frequently used in pottery studios. Liquid waste should be stored in a large container, and in time the solid part of the waste will collect on the bottom of the vessel. The thick consistency material on the bottom can then be scooped out and placed in plastic garbage bags for removal by commercial garbage pick up or to be deposited in a landfill. In either case, the waste will find its way into a landfill.

In terms of the environmental effects on returning raw materials to the ground in which they originated, there are conflicting points of view. Glazes and some clays might contain higher levels of metallic coloring oxides than found in naturally occurring soil. However, this observation by some might not be completely accurate since the chemical concentrations of soils can differ considerably depending on their location. One school of thought states the levels of metallic coloring oxides or heavy metals found in some clay and glazes will contaminate the soil. On the other side of the issue are people who believe this is the "perfect" recycling of raw materials since it returns them to their natural source.

On a practical level, depositing unusable clay, raw glaze materials, or any fine particle waste onto a small front lawn in a residential setting would not be advised for many reasons, the least of which is the sight of raw material "sludge" after a rain storm. However, many potters who have their studios in open fields simply bury or spread the material out over a wide surface area. They have obviously taken into account the possibility of contaminating ground water or adjacent septic fields. While non-porous material such as clays would certainly block a septic field in high enough concentrations, the issue of ground water contamination from raw materials would depend on many individual factors, such as the waste materials' chemical content, the ground water level at the dump site, and the mobility of the waste (seepage) in the specific site. While this procedure for raw material removal is controversial to some people, it most certainly depends on the availability of each site to accept raw materials. As in most issues of ceramic waste removal, there are no clear definitive solutions that can be applied universally to individual waste removal situations.

Physiological Stress

While not generally considered a major health hazard in the ceramics studio, physiological factors can cause stress problems and also exacerbate physical injuries. The physiological aspect of making pottery or sculpture is just one area that has not been researched because of several factors, one of which being that there is no economic incentive for such studies. Potters working in their own studios, schools, or craft centers do not represent the same economic payoff as industrial workers on an assembly line. Less stress on an assembly line can translate into higher production rates. Less stress in the pottery studio, while beneficial for potters, does not economically justify the expense of such research. When working with clay and glazes, physiological stress can come about in many ways, whether it is the student trying to make a few more pots for a final critique or a production potter suffering through defective pots coming out of a kiln. It's normal to have some level of stress in most everyday tasks, but when the level rises to the point where it interferes with daily life, the cause has to be examined.

Making functional pottery or ceramic sculpture by definition involves more unsuccessful attempts at getting the clay and glazes to work and fewer successful pieces. Most people experience a long and difficult learning curve when working in ceramics. Potters frequently fall into the trap of trying to produce a perfect "masterpiece." Many potters enter into the craft having a preconceived idea of producing just such a one-of-a-kind magnum opus. This syndrome is in part due to their lack of an accurate well-balanced art education in today's school system and current stereotypes of artists in today's society. They have not been informed that hard work and knowledge of materials must be accomplished over long years of practice before any single piece or body of work can be considered perfect. In fact, the concept or ideal of perfection is just that and is a goal to be pursued. However, many potters have lost much time, money, and mental effort trying to make the perfect pot or sculpture. Unfortunately, the monetary rewards for this ideal ceramic effort are never enough to keep them in business for any length of time.

Making and selling functional pottery has low barriers to entry, which means the costs of purchasing equipment, supplies, and raw materials are relatively small when compared to capital investments for other more traditional businesses. However, initially most potters do not realize that producing functional pottery by any definition is labor intensive. Both of these economic factors often form a financial trap to the novice potter/business person and undermine his or her profit margin. Often potters start by making pottery on a small scale. When they find that friends and relatives are enthusiastically buying their ware, the next step is setting up a small table of pots at local craft shows. After selling well at several one- or two-day craft events, the next level of enterprise is to set up a pottery business. It is at this point that the financial and business limitations are reached for most potters. Making and selling pots or ceramic sculpture is a business first and an artistic endeavor second. It is one thing to sell at craft fairs and to friends but an entirely different matter to expand a limited sales base into a wider serious business market.

The pressure of producing functional pottery on demand can be at first exhilarating and then eventually overwhelming to someone who hasn't developed exceptional small business skills. Often potters make the mistake of obtaining large wholesale (lower profit margin) orders at craft shows. If they have not done their homework in calculating the fixed and variable costs of production, they could eventually be working for a few dollars per hour. In fact this process can slowly take place over a period of years, during which the potter comes under an increasing degree of financial strain, the end result being someone who is working harder physically and mentally every year for less money. The fact that this downward spiral can take place imperceptibly over time makes it all the more insidious. Potters who have not obtained the basic business skills frequently report they have so many wholesale accounts they can't keep up with production. This group of potters usually reports a low *net* income with "burn out" and exhaustion within five to ten years.

Working for low profits can be one cause of pressure, and working against a deadline is another common stress point for potters. Aside from potters going to craft shows and accumulating wholesale orders from retail stores and galleries, there are also deadlines to meet with special orders from individual customers. The pressure to produce a body of work for show or sale can at times be overwhelming. It always seems like a glaze will fail or a kiln firing will go wrong, which creates a lot of pots that cannot be sold. In some instances, the work does not meet the aesthetic standards of the ceramic artist.

Why is this a common condition in the field of ceramics? Clay and glazes are raw materials that are subject to change in chemical consistency, particle size, and source of manufacturer or mine deposit. The potter is buying inconsistent low cost materials of poor quality and expects to produce a high quality consistent product. This economic expectation cannot be sustained over long periods of time. Something always fails, to the mental anguish of the potter who is under stress and is not knowledgeable in the variable nature of ceramic raw materials.

On the other hand, industries producing ceramic objects such as bathroom fixtures or floor tiles have several economic advantages not open to potters. Industries can often dictate to the mine what grade and specification of raw material they require for production. For example, EPK plastic kaolin mined in Florida is used in the production of spark plugs. The manufacturer of spark plugs requires the mine to produce EPK within specific parameters such as particle size, color, and purity. They are able to set these standards in raw material since they order millions of tons per year from the mine. Potters cannot dictate to the companies that mine raw materials; they do not purchase enough clay to have any economic clout in the market place. Large industries also have the benefit of highly skilled ceramic engineers to monitor and adjust the methods of production to ensure consistent results. Basically, large industrial manufacturers have the money to ensure consistent quality control in their ceramic products. Individual potters often find themselves in a situation where a considerable amount of their monthly income is dependent on a whole kiln load of pots coming out perfectly. A single kiln full of pottery can represent many hours of manual labor and artistic talent with none of the quality control benefits that large industry can employ in their production of ceramic products.

How to Avoid the Stress Inherent in Being a Potter

A whole book could be written on the mental health of potters. However, a few basic facts about creating ceramic objects will hopefully prevent many future tribulations when working with this problematic erratic material. If there was one word to describe ceramic materials and related heating processes, it would be "variable." Ceramic materials that compose clay body and glaze formulas can sometimes change immediately or alter slowly and imperceptibly. Kiln firings, even in relatively stable and consistent electric kilns, do not always produce uniform or dependable results. With these key factors in mind, the potter must plan for either initial high failure rates or results in clay and glazes that are sometimes different than what is expected or planned. While some of these "lucky accidents" or irregularities are artistically pleasing, some are simply defects that do not look good or cannot be sold. The potters who understand the materials best are the ones who plan the production of their work carefully. What does this mean in everyday practical advice? If you are thinking about throwing a set of six dinner plates, start by making twelve plates and then matching the best ones to form a complete set of six. If you are commissioned to do a sculpture piece, make two or three to arrive at a successful finished sculpture. In this way, the potter works with the variable quality of the ceramic materials and firing conditions and does not get unnerved by a bad outcome. The end result is less stress and reduced pressure on the potter's workload.

For potters who are interested in selling their functional pots or sculpture, the best advice is often enrolling in several business courses at a local college. Ceramics, as stated, is a labor-intensive, low pay, high-risk, marginal activity at best. When potters get past the point of selling their ware to friends and relatives, the skills and knowledge needed to persevere are not in making good pots but in understanding business practices and knowing the market.

A major fault found in many beginning and even mature pottery producing businesses is underpricing the pots. Careful analyses of all expenses needed to produce the pots are required. The potters then must pay themselves an hourly rate plus a profit margin. Overlooking pricing strategies and market characteristics is one of the major stress related problems faced by potters trying to sell their own work.

Safety Issues in Single Potter Studios, Multi Potter Studios, Craft Centers, and College Ceramics Programs

Single Potter Studios

Potters working by themselves in their own studios do not have to develop and maintain safety procedures for anyone but themselves. The range of safety measures employed by an individual runs from non-existent to almost hospital room cleanliness. Even in today's atmosphere of all things ceramic being toxic, it is open to debate whether either extreme is high risk or superfluous. The results of "The Potter's Health & Safety Questionnaire" (page 141) indicate a majority of potters practice a conservative approach when handling raw materials, kiln firings, and pottery equipment. The real question then becomes what is enough in terms of protection of the individual and others who come in contact with the potter's work. It is only through education from different sources and the development of a safety plan for the individual workspace that a reasonable expectation of safety can be anticipated from the ceramic workplace. Often an individual working alone has a difficult condition to monitor in regard to keeping a safe and clean studio. If a glaze spill is allowed to remain on the floor or a kiln is not vented, who is to notice? It is easy to tell yourself you will get back to clean up later in the day. Self-discipline and a thorough understanding of cleaning procedures are needed when working alone. It is in the potter's self interest to maintain his or her own health if for nothing else than to have the ability to make more pots or ceramic sculpture.

Multi Potter Studios

In private ceramics studios where there are multiple potters working, there should be a common understanding of safety procedures. The safest best-run studios have a group of potters who have a common understanding of how to use ceramic raw materials and equipment. Each potter must be responsible for cleaning up not only his or her own waste but also the debris left by others in the studio. This last situation is often the cause of many misunderstandings and conflicts within multi-potter studios that are not carefully organized. Before such studio groups are formed, there should be a list of safety rules or procedures that everyone can agree to and more importantly adhere to over their participation in the studio. If one potter or several of the potters within the group do not adhere to the studio rules, the whole organization suffers.

Often there are different philosophies among individuals as to what constitutes a clean and safe studio environment. In fact, this is one of the major problems that causes the break up of group studios. Another factor in the dissolution of group studios is the potters' under capitalization with regard to installing safety equipment. While private studios or group studios do not usually have the expertise or monetary resources to purchase sophisticated air monitoring and venting systems, they still can do a lot to protect their work areas. Many ceramics supply companies now sell room ventilation systems at reasonable prices that can fit into a potter's budget.

Craft Centers

A slightly different form of the health and safety problem can exist in schools, craft centers, and organizations where numerous students are taking ceramics courses. Whether there is one student or hundreds, the standards for health and safety procedures within the studio must come from the instructor and the administrators responsible for the teaching institution. Many administrators and teachers are still not thoroughly educated in all of the details concerning health and safety issues as they pertain to ceramics studios. The responsibility of the administrators is to educate themselves on the current protection measures for handling ceramic raw materials. With the help of their instructors, they can then set up procedures that can be uniformly adhered to by faculty and students. It is also the responsibility of the educational institution to set up and maintain a safe working environment in clay mixing rooms, classrooms, and kiln rooms.

Many craft centers and schools with ceramics departments draw up a list of safety procedures for each area in the production of pottery or sculpture. The list is compiled into an informative booklet that explains the correct way to mix up a dry glaze, fire a kiln, dispose of waste clay scraps, and many other individual studio tasks. The students are required to read the book completely and then sign their name signifying their understanding of the safety principles involved in working in the ceramics areas. A "sign off" book on

how to handle raw materials and studio equipment is often used in pottery businesses to help employees maintain a safe working environment. The book also serves a legal function, as it can be used if an employee unfairly involves an employer in litigation based on safety factors in the workplace.

It is the craft center's responsibility to research the best available equipment for the ceramics area and set up supervisory personnel to see that it is maintained and used properly at all times. It is essential that all equipment, such as pug mills, clay-mixing machines, pottery wheels, kilns, slab rollers, and extruders be kept in a safe condition. Signage and education of the students should direct them to safety practices, which must be conformed to when using the equipment and raw materials in the studio. A model institution, which has enacted a safe studio setting for their faculty and students, is Massachusetts College of Art in Boston, Mass. In 1991, the college moved into a new building, which presented the ideal situation for new venting systems and ceramic waste disposal mea-

sures. While many educational institutions and craft centers are not in this fortunate position, they can retrofit their existing structures with many venting and safety system options.

Massachusetts College of Art Ceramics Rooms

Raw Material Safety Signs

Signs play an important role in educating students in the safety procedures of the ceramics studio. It is unrealistic to assume a teacher or supervisor will be present at all times during every clay or glaze operation. Signs can direct the students in the operation of machinery and the safe handling of raw materials and clays.

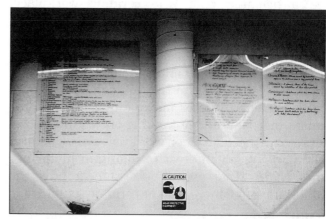

The sign on the glaze mixing room door reads, "CAUTION—Respirators Must Be Worn In This Area."

The white sign on the left lists the chemical hazards of each raw material used in the glaze mixing room. The two white signs on the right are ratings charts of chemical toxicity levels, such as acute and chronic illnesses attributed to each raw material. Major and minor health effects of raw materials are also listed on the charts.

Chapter 3

Studio Furniture and Storage

Studio Sinks

In the studio, one of the most important functional features is also a safety feature. The studio sink is the source of water used for clay forming operations, mixing glazes, mixing clay bodies, and studio clean-up tasks. Ideally, the sink should be located near all of the studio operations to ensure an efficient use of labor and to prevent water from dripping across the studio floor. An absorbent floor mat can be placed in the standing area in front of the sink. While the cost and installation of sinks can vary, it is possible to obtain a common fiberglass laundry sink for under $70.00. The plumbing costs will depend on the location of the sink and local installation rates. Many potters working in basements find this type of sink efficient and easy to use for studio operations.

The sink can be constructed out of stainless steel, fiberglass, or enamel, and any coating can be used for easy cleaning. During the daily studio routine of working with clay and glaze materials, potters wash their hands many times. Some provision must be made for the clay and raw material slurry that develops after cleaning pottery tools or simple hand washing procedures. The slurry or loose clay water has to be captured and carried out of the studio without clogging drains or septic systems. In private septic systems, any clay deposit can slow and then stop household waste from being absorbed into the outside drainage field.

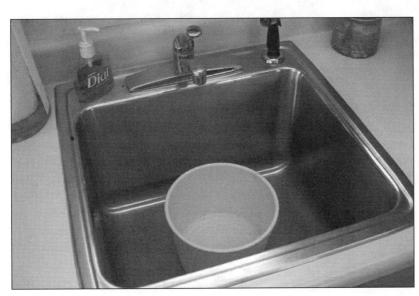

Hand soap and sponges help in any clean-up operation. Sinks that are not adapted for the filtering of clay waste can use a bucket to catch clay, glaze, and raw material debris before they enter the drain and sewage system. The heavier waste raw material sinks to the bottom of the bucket and can be cleaned out periodically. This is a simple easily-adaptable low-cost system that can work in any sink.

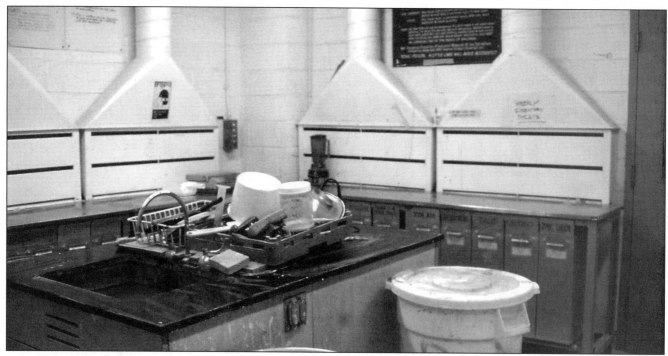

Massachusetts College of Art glaze mixing room

Air is vented out of the glaze mixing room from behind the glaze mixing tables. Raw material bins are conveniently located below the glaze mixing tables to reduce the possibility of spilling raw material in the weighing out process. The sink is centrally located to facilitate glaze mixing. The blue sign between the air filtration units lists the health hazards for each raw material found in the glaze mixing area. Raw materials are listed in relation to their level of toxicity, either being moderate (not severe enough to cause death) or high (may cause death or permanent injury after short exposure rates).

Massachusetts College of Art glaze mixing room

Glaze buckets, tools, sieves, and other glaze mixing equipment are cleaned in the sink. Note the vertical pipe (lower left area of sink), which is attached to the sink drain. Standing water in the sink allows for all solid material to fall to the bottom of the sink where it is periodically cleaned out and removed. This low cost system of drainage can be incorporated into most studio sinks.

Solid material from the bottom of the sink is deposited in the waste container. When full, the container is taken to a landfill for disposal.

Studio Storage Shelves

The production of functional pottery or sculpture requires many types of tools: raw materials, ceramics supplies, and other related production items such as plaster bats and molds. Over time, potters acquire tools and various supplies. Many individual items have to be carefully organized and safely warehoused for their eventual use during the workday.

A clean studio starts with a well-organized workspace. Shelf space is an important part of organizing a ceramics studio. Generally, storing more tools, supplies, and materials on shelves will serve two purposes. First, it will make the tools easier to observe and use. More time spent looking for a misplaced tool means less time spent making pots. The second reason for appropriating greater shelf space to storage is that it should leave more free studio floor space. The ideal or most practical studio set up is an open clean floor area that allows for flexibility in any studio activity. The fewer tools, supplies, and materials on the floor, the less chance of tripping or having to walk around items stored on the floor.

Storage shelves are conveniently stacked near the kiln. The shelves can contain ware to be bisque or glaze fired. The ceramics forming process, which can include bisque firing, glazing, and glaze firing, involves many steps. It is important to keep the distance between steps as close as possible in the studio layout. Ceramics is a labor demanding activity, and reducing the wasted motion of moving pots haphazardly around the studio will diminish the amount of wasted energy and keep the potter more alert. The area around the kiln is kept free of any tools or materials. Kiln shelves, posts, and other kiln firing equipment are stacked on rear shelves (not visible in photo).

Plaster molds, which are heavy, should be kept in an easy-to-reach location. Tools and toolboxes for the storage of trim tools, ribs, sponges, and calipers should be kept in accessible locations next to work areas. Any tool or supply that is used frequently during a work cycle should be kept within easy reach. Glaze buckets are located under workbenches and are positioned on roller wheels so they can be easily moved about the glazing area. They can be moved out onto the floor when the work cycle requires glazing operations and then moved below the storage table when not needed. Glaze containers should be covered and clearly labeled with the glaze name on the bucket and the lid. Workbench areas should be flexible and adjustable for different ceramics operations. The worktables should be designed so they can easily be cleaned.

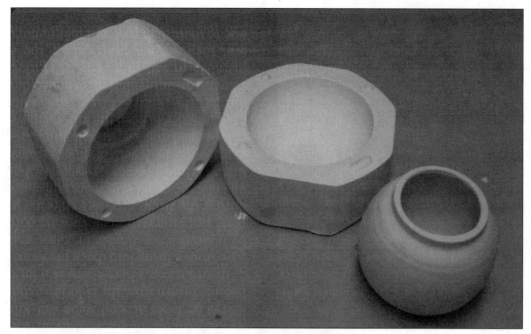

Pouring slips into molds can be a labor-intensive activity. The weight of the liquid clay (casting slip) and the molds can be considerable. Always store molds in a well-ventilated place near the workspace where they will be needed.

The vertical support for storage shelves is constructed from 2" x 4" lumber. Horizontal shelving is constructed from 3/4" plywood. Finished pots, tools, and supplies can be stored on shelves to keep the studio floor and work areas open. The placement of shelves should depend on available space within the studio. However, whenever possible, storage of items on shelves should be in a logical order of use. The sequence of work flow through the studio should follow in the design of shelf placement in the studio. For example, finished pottery or sculpture should be placed on shelves near packing material. Items used most frequently should be placed in easy-access shelving areas.

Glazing Areas

Whether the glaze is sprayed (requiring a dedicated spraying area and equipment), brushed, or dipped, glazing is an essential part of the functional pottery process. When making sculptural forms, glaze application can be optional, depending on the aesthetic goals of the work. In small studio areas, the flexibility of the workshop layout is critical to efficient glazing of ceramic ware. Where space is limited, the potter must plan ahead in the studio design and layout to ensure that there is space available for working with clay and glazes. In larger studios, a separate room for glazing can allow for easier clean up operations and a generally safer workplace. Glaze buckets, brushes, sponges, ware racks, and a water source are all elements that have to be arranged efficiently in the glazing area. All tools and mixing utensils should be laid out on tables or shelves for easy access and effective use during the glazing operation.

During glazing, the floor should be kept free of unnecessary materials and tools. Many potters dip their pots into one or more different colored glaze buckets. Care must be taken to stop or remove wet glaze that can drip on tables or the floor. When glazes are brushed on the ware, a source of water must be available to clean the brushes so they are not left around the studio with dry glaze embedded in the bristles. A source of water is also required for adjusting the water content of glazes and for the eventual clean up of the glazing area. During the focused intensity of glazing, floors can become slippery. When using a spray gun, the spray booth should be designed to capture excess glaze. The spray booth must also exhaust air-containing glaze particles out of the studio. Any excess glaze should be cleaned off all work surfaces to keep it from drying out and becoming airborne.

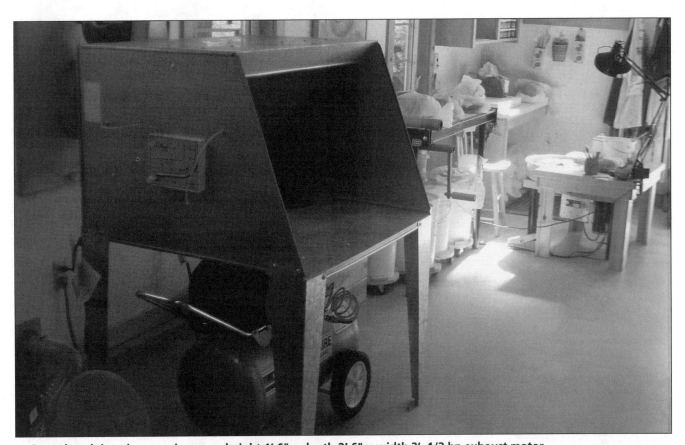

Spray booth interior spraying area, height 1′ 6″ x depth 2′ 6″ x width 3′, 1/3 hp exhaust motor.
A spray gun shoots atomized particles of glaze onto a pot placed in the spray booth. The booth captures the glaze that does not land on the pot. The exhaust motor located in the rear of the booth holds the glaze particles in a filter and then sends the air out of the building. The air compressor that powers the spray gun is conveniently located underneath the spray booth. The air filter in the spray booth has to be changed periodically to protect the exhaust motor from glaze contamination. It is always recommended that potters wear the appropriate respirator when spraying any glaze.

There are many types of spray guns, however, all release a fine atomized particle of glaze. Spray glazes should be used in a spray booth that has an adequate venting system, and a respirator should be used at all times.

The glazing area tabletop is a smooth easy-to-clean metal surface. A wet sponge can wipe away any dry or wet glaze residue. Under the glazing table, raw material containers are conveniently accessible for glaze mixing operations. All of the containers are clearly labeled and can hold 50 lbs. of dry raw material. Smaller batches of glaze raw materials are stored in nearby shelves, from which they can be weighed out and used in glazes. Store raw materials in non-breakable containers. The scale is located near all of the necessary materials needed for an efficient use of the space. Whenever possible, the glazing area should be located next to a source of natural light with full spectrum fluorescent bulbs overhead.

Large raw material bins located under work tables can hold 50 lbs. or more of raw materials. Each bin is labeled with the name of the raw material held within. While wearing a respirator, the raw material is scooped out of the bin and placed on the scale for glaze mixing operations. By keeping all glaze mixing supplies and equipment within close reach, airborne raw material particles are kept at low levels and material spills are less likely to occur.

Raw materials should be stored in low moisture areas near the glaze storage containers. When possible, it is always preferable to order raw materials in their original shipping bags, as this will ensure an accurate replacement material if the potter specifies the raw material name, manufacturer name, and mesh size.

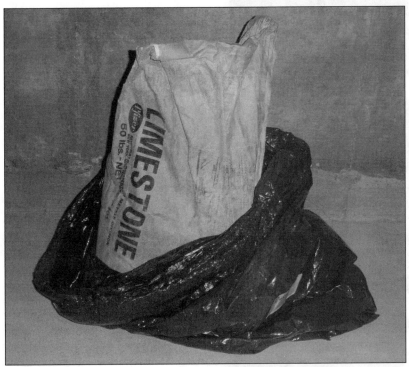

Larger quantities of raw material are frequently packaged in 50 lb. bags from the mine or processing plant. The bags are paper and they can tear and leak raw material. Some bags have a series of perforations to allow excess air to escape during the filling process at the mine. It is not uncommon for a completely sealed bag to puff out airborne raw material when moved about the studio. The raw material bags should be kept in double heavyweight plastic bags to prevent accumulation of excessive moisture and prevent material leakage.

Any raw material spills should be wet mopped up completely when they occur. Plastic bags should have a clear label identifying the raw material. While raw materials will remain useable indefinitely, soluble materials such as Gerstley borate, Colemanite, Borax, Potassium carbonate (Pear Ash), and soda ash should be kept in very low moisture areas and sealed tightly, as they can take on moisture in storage and present future glaze problems.

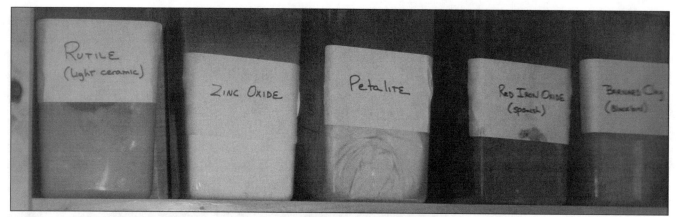

Smaller stocks of raw materials that cannot be stored in large bins can be kept in plastic containers with lids. All containers should be carefully labeled with the material name. If possible, materials used for glaze mixing should be kept close to scales, screens, water, and glaze mixing equipment. The close proximity of supplies and equipment can prevent wasted motion in glaze mixing operations and reduce the possibility of raw material spills.

Glass storage jars are not recommended in the ceramics studio, due to the ease at which they can slip out of the potter's hands and break on the studio floor. Plastic non-breakable jars with secure lids will hold raw materials securely. The lids of storage jars should be wide enough so the raw materials scoop or spoon will fit inside the jar. All raw materials should have a secure label that will not fall off. Permanent printing should identify each raw material and its mesh size. If a label falls off the jar or an ink fades, raw materials all look like white powder. It is not worth the time to test a suspect "mystery" material.

A stainless steel glazing table with raw material storage bins underneath
The scale for weighing glaze materials is located on top of the table.
A folding step stool can be used to reach glaze oxides on higher-level storage shelves. Disposable paper toweling can clean up glaze spills. Extra raw materials are stored in sealed plastic containers with the raw material name on the label. Electric outlets are placed in several areas throughout the studio and can be used for glaze mixing equipment. Whenever electric appliances are used near water, it is always recommended to have an electrician install Ground Fault Circuit Interrupter outlets to prevent electrical shocks.

Massachusetts College of Art glaze mixing room
Raw materials are weighed out and mixed in the glaze room. Even under optimum conditions, removing a dry raw material out of its shipping bag or storage container can send airborne particles into the atmosphere. The micron size particles can remain floating in the air for hours or even days. The glaze table (rear part of room) has a venting system that draws any dry material out of the room before it can land on work surfaces.

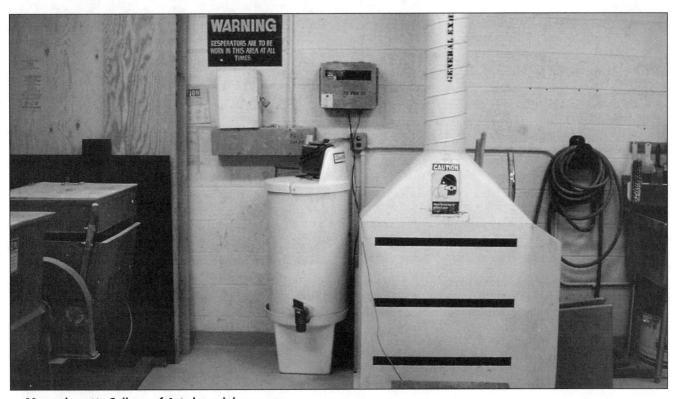

Massachusetts College of Art clay mixing room
Clay mixing machines (left) are located next to the scale (center). The scale weighs out dry materials such as feldspar, flint, various clays, talc, grog, etc. A venting system has been installed behind the scale to capture any airborne raw material that escapes when clay bags are opened and weighed.

Massachusetts College of Art clay mixing room
Located behind each clay mixing machine is an individual exhaust system that will exhaust dry clay particles during the first stages of the clay mixing process.

Five gallon plastic buckets with lids can be used for wet glaze storage. The bucket and top lid should be clearly labeled with the glaze name. A rolling platform has been constructed so the glaze bucket can be moved easily, preventing back strain. The movable glaze storage container offers flexibility in raw material storage, which is essential in small studio spaces.

A full glaze container can be very heavy and difficult to move around the studio. Support stands with wheels can be used under the glaze containers. By making the glaze container mobile, it can be moved with ease to the glazing area of the studio, and then the container can be moved to the glaze storage area. Moving the glaze containers to where they are needed increases the flexibility of studio space.

Wedging Table

Whether using a commercial moist clay or mixing up your own clay, at some point it will have to be wedged on a flat surface and rolled or kneaded into itself. The wedging process further distributes an equal moisture content throughout the clay/water mixture. Even commercially mixed clay requires a wedging procedure after it is removed from its plastic shipping bag.

It is often a good idea to place an absorbent rubber mat on the floor in front of the wedging table to relieve stress on the feet when wedging moist clay. Absorbent floor mats should be used to cushion the feet whenever an operation requires standing for any period of time.

The wedging area should contain all items that are necessary for this stage of the ceramic forming process. Scales, spray bottles, tools, cutting wires, and other supplies should be conveniently located near the table. The table height should fit the individual potter, as the correct elevation will reduce back strain when wedging clay. The wedging surface should be at the level of the potter's hands when they are at rest by his or her side. In this way, the potter does not have to bend down or reach up excessively when wedging the clay. The wedging table can be the source of potential back pain if the potter must strain to move the heavy moist clay. Also, the repetitive motion of the hands in wedging the clay can cause wrist and arm pain, which can evolve into carpal tunnel syndrome. Moist clay should be stored close to the wedging table to reduce the energy needed to move the clay around the studio. Since the moist clay is one of the heaviest and most dense items in the ceramics studio, careful thought should be considered as to its location within the work area. The moist clay should be moved from its point of entry into the studio to the wedging board, forming area, and then on to the firing area in the shortest distance possible between these points. Wasted or repetitive motion in moving moist clay within the studio will reduce the energy level of the potter and increase the possibility of accidents.

The wedging table should be placed near the wheel-working table and next to the clay storage area. By arranging the ceramics studio in the sequence in which the pottery or sculpture will be produced, less effort will be required to move the heavy moist clay around the studio.

Chapter 4

Safety Equipment

Listed are several important pieces of safety equipment. They range from fairly "expensive" vacuums to common household cleaning items, such as sponges and plastic buckets. It is important to remember, in terms of safety to yourself and others working in the ceramics workplace, the actual cost of safety equipment is a small price to protect your health. There is a brief description of each safety device and suggested ceramics supply companies who carry the merchandise. However, many ceramics supply companies throughout the United States and Canada stock the same or equivalent safety devices. If you are interested in a specific safety device, call the ceramics supplier listed for updated product information and current pricing.

Studio Vacuums

The first and most important thing to find out about any vacuum for studio use is whether or not it is rated to capture the sub-micron size particles generated by raw materials. Standard

The CFM Industrial model shown is highly recommended for schools and commercial studios. These units create a high degree of suction and have many practical accessories.

household vacuums are not useable, as they do not have the filter system necessary to remove clay dust from the studio. Using a standard household vacuum might make an air quality situation worse than not vacuuming. Its filter is too coarse, allowing sub-micron particles to be sucked through the filter and then spewed back into the air where they can remain suspended for several days. Slight air currents within the studio can keep the particles constantly moving and create the potential for inhalation. There are many types of studio vacuums, and, as in other pieces of safety equipment, cost is secondary compared to a cleaner workplace. Some studio air-cleaning units are electrostatic in their cleaning process, and they will not remove sub-micron particles from the clay studio. They are designed for removal of smoke and should not be considered for the ceramics area. Listed are vacuums that will meet the requirements for studio use.

Of all the possible methods of entry— inhalation, dermal absorption, and ingestion—the first remains the most efficient way for raw materials to enter the human body. An appropriate vacuum, room air cleaner, and respirator are the potter's first line of defense against unseen ceramic particles. With this fact in mind, the appropriate type of vacuum is an important tool. Ceramic dust vacuums are designed specifically to remove the dangerous sub-micron particles that are potentially harmful to the health. The sophisticated triple filtration systems are designed to contain particles as small as .3 microns (99.97% effective). With proper care, filters can last up to several years. Keep in mind, some standard 4-foot shop vacuums contain cloth and paper filters, and it is important to note that these basic filters are intended for containing standard material such as wood dusts. The standard "shop" vacuum filters will not contain fine ceramic dust and should never be used, as they will only blow particles throughout the studio environment.

It is important to note that multi filtered studio vacuums are designed specifically for the containment of fine dusts. Containing sub-micron dusts requires an extensive filtration system. Naturally, this sophisticated filtration creates extra drag on the airflow and so decreases the suction potential of the vacuums. For this reason, the user should not expect the same suction characteristics as a vacuum that has no filters. The crucial function of theses vacuums is to remove and contain fine ceramic dusts that are hazardous to the potter's health. This is an important function that no "carpet" or "shop" style vacuum can perform.

Commercial Grade CFM Vacuum.

CFM series vacuums are recommended for sweeping dry clay from raw material storage areas. Bags containing clay frequently break or leak raw materials onto the floor, which can then be moved around the storage area or blown into other areas of the ceramics studio. Raw material storage areas should be vacuumed on a daily basis.

Commercial Grade CFM Vacuums Recommended for Colleges and Large Production Potteries

The CFM series are the most practical industrial HEPA filtered vacuums for college, university, and production pottery applications. The CFM models stand 42" tall and are designed specifically to remove sub-micron size particles from the studio.

The CFM units deliver features such as: a large powerful motor with quiet operation (only 68 dB), greatly increased filter area to prevent clogging, greater airflow for maximum suction power, a manometer to indicate when the filters need a shake down, an external shakedown mechanism to free up the filter media for better suction, and a collection chamber that is fast and easy to clean. The floor nozzle accessory is extremely practical for dust control. The HEPA filters can be installed upstream or before the motor with retention efficiency at 1.3 microns. Accessories include: Round Brush Tool, a Double Curved Aluminum Wand, A Wheeled Floor Nozzle, HEPA Filter, Polyester Filters, (25) polyliners and a polyliner adapter, and a 38m PVC hose.

The CFM series of vacuums is highly recommended and can be purchased at Bailey Pottery

Equipment Corporation, PO Box 1577, 62 Ten-Broeck Ave., Kingston, NY 12402, (800) 431-6067. Call for current pricing on all models.

Two models:

C-138-15	CFM 127 (190 cu.ft./minute airflow)
C-138-16	CFM 137 (240 cu.ft./minute airflow)

The GD-1010 HEPA Ceramic Dust Vac

The GD-1010 dust vacuum is designed for the type of ceramic raw material particle sizes found in pottery studios. It holds 2 1/2 gallons of dry bulk and offers a triple filtration system. It also has a disposable collection bag for containing bulk materials. The unit has an 87-cu.ft./minute airflow.

The GD-1010 vacuum has three filters: the HEPA, the cloth, and the paper bag. The HEPA filter is rated at 99.97% at 0.3 microns. As dust enters the vacuum, the bulk materials are contained in a disposable paper bag. The medium and fine dusts will pass through the paper bag and enter the cloth filter. Fine dust will continue through the cloth filter for final containment by the HEPA filters. The HEPA filters are inexpensive to replace.

Features:
- A set of 5 heavy-duty collection bags
- 12" floor nozzle
- 30 feet of power cord
- Basic micro-filter (99.5% at 2 microns)
- 1100 watt motor, 9.2 amp
- HEPA filter
- 6' 6" plastic hose
- 14 lbs. weight of vacuum
- Chrome plated steel wand
- 60 dB sound level at 5 ft.

Model A Vacuum

Tucker's Pottery Supplies Inc., 15 West Pearce St., No. 7 Richmond Hill, ON Canada L4B 1H6, (905) 889-7705. The vacuum has a 3-stage filter system, which stops particles down to 0.33 microns in size. It can hold up to 3 gallons of dry waste and can be used as a wet vacuum in the studio. The Model A has a heavy-duty stainless tank and cover and a 2-horse power motor. Call or write for suggested retail price. (Vacuum not shown.)

GD 1010 HEPA Dust Vacuum.

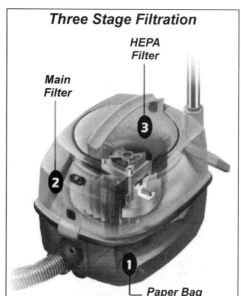

Three Stage Filtration

Main Filter

HEPA Filter

Paper Bag

Three Stage Filtration.

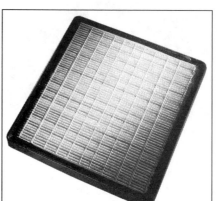

GD 1010 filter HEPA Filter.

Air Cleaning Equipment

Cleaning the air is just one step in an ongoing process to reduce sub-micron particles in the studio environment. The levels of dust and ceramic particles in the studio can be reduced to safe levels when air cleaners, vacuums, and respirators are employed along with consistently practiced housekeeping procedures. Each studio space and budget allowance will require an individual plan, implementing all or a few of the safety devices listed.

The air cleaning system produced by Bailey Ceramic Supply serves a vital function by constantly filtering the air in the studio. Airborne dust is an avoidable part of working with clay and glaze materials. There are two varieties of filtering capabilities: standard Vee-bag filters, which are 95% efficient at .33 microns, and the HEPA filters, which offer increased protection with 99.97% efficiency at .3 microns. The finer particles will pass through the pre-filter and enter the main "Vee-Bag" filter where 95% of all particles .33 microns or larger will be contained. This means the filtered air that is returned to the studio will contain a very small amount of fine particles. The amount is usually within acceptable levels when the pottery studio is small. For large studio operations or for people

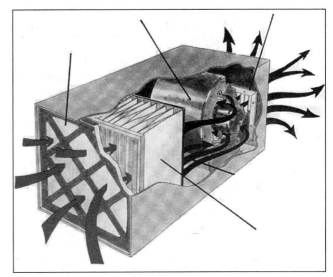

Bailey Air Cleaning System.

who need special protection from dusts, use the HEPA filtered system.

The Bailey Air Cleaning System is known in the industry as an "interception filtration" system. Recent breakthroughs in the use of random fiber media have led to the development of bag filters that are able to strip sub-micron particles from the air and contain them. As the dust enters the cleaner, the larger particles are

Air cleaning system in studio.

trapped in the "pre-filter." The finer particles enter a HEPA-rated main filter. This HEPA filter removes 99.97% of all particles .3 microns or larger; HEPA systems are often required in schools and are recommended where particularly toxic materials are used.

The key factor in obtaining a safe working environment is choosing the proper-sized system for a studio work area. The Air Cleaner should cycle a minimum of 10 complete air exchanges per hour. This means that the equivalent air volume of the room will pass through the machine at least 10 times every hour. The room coverage is figured in cubic feet (not square feet). Multiply the length, width, and height of the studio to determine the cubic footage. Filters should be replaced every one to two years, depending on the amount of dust produced in the studio. Careful selection of the appropriate air cleaner is important, as air cleaner units that are too powerful for the space will actually create air turbulence that will stir up more dust than they can collect. This is one instance where bigger is not necessarily better.

Positioning the Air Cleaner in the Ceramics Studio

Air cleaners either can be hung from the ceiling or mounted on a shelf against the wall at ceiling level. The unit must be positioned to set up a circular flow pattern around the perimeter of the room (Air A). Do not place the unit too close to a corner, as this will allow unfiltered air to bypass the cleaner entirely (Air B).

Larger studios or classrooms may require more than one unit to effectively purify the room. Multiple units must be equally spaced around the perimeter of the room and must draw in the same direction (Air C). Similarly, an air conditioning or heating system must also be considered when determining the *direction of draw* for the Air Cleaner (Air D). They must not work against each other.

An irregular or "L"-shaped room requires specific placement. Mount the air cleaner so that the intake draws from the smaller portion of the room (Air E). The unit *should not* exhaust into the smaller portion, since this will set up a circular pattern within that area alone that will impede the cleaner's effectiveness in the larger area.

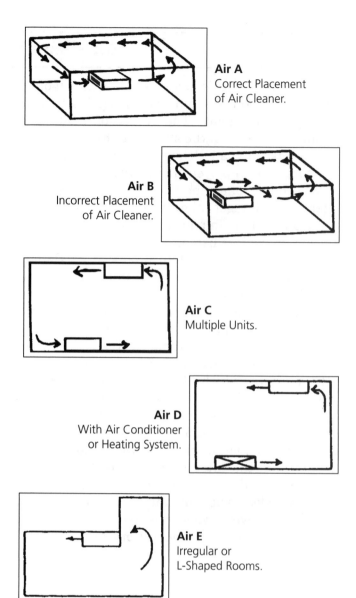

Air A
Correct Placement
of Air Cleaner.

Air B
Incorrect Placement
of Air Cleaner.

Air C
Multiple Units.

Air D
With Air Conditioner
or Heating System.

Air E
Irregular or
L-Shaped Rooms.

Installation: All units either can be hung from a ceiling or mounted on a wall shelf. All models have variable speed controls, a 6 ft. power cord, and will plug into any standard 115v outlet. However, the manufacturer does not recommend using an extension cord with these units. Due to the short power cord on the ceiling-mounted units, it may be necessary to have an outlet installed near the ceiling to accommodate the electrical requirements. As an optional feature, remote speed controls are available for the ceiling-mounted units; wiring by an electrician is required to install the unit.

Specifications

	Model 750	*Model 1800*
CFM:	400 to 800 variable	1400 to 1900
Dimensions:	17" W x 15" H x 38" L	24" W x 26" H x 45" L
Filter Size:	30 sq. ft.	70 sq. ft.
Motor:	1/6 HP	1/2 HP
Input:	115 VAC	115 VAC
	60 Hz, 5.8 amps	60 Hz, 7 amps
Weight:	78 lbs.	125 lbs.
Switch:	Variable	Variable
Max. Room:	20 ft. x 25 ft. x 8 ft. H	20 ft. x 56 ft. x 8 ft. H
Coverage:	(4000 cu. ft.)	(8900 cu. ft.)
Air Exchange/Hour:	11.32	12

Be advised that to properly control ceramic dusts, the potter must incorporate other cleaning practices, including wet mopping the studio, use of a vacuum designed to clean ceramic materials, use of an approved respirator, and providing appropriate ventilation. The air cleaners are intended for general air cleaning and should not be used to control intense dust environments such as clay mixing rooms. The best option for potters is to call the supplier and find out what equipment will be needed for their specific studio situation. Reputable suppliers will take the time to match their air cleaning equipment to fit the potter's studio requirements.

Dust Collection System for Clay Mixing Rooms

Bailey Ceramic Supply Company has developed a custom dust collection system for all brands of clay mixers. It is designed especially for areas that produce high concentrations of clay or raw materials. The source-capture systems are most effective at controlling dust in the clay room and are suitable for school use.

Nilfisk Dust Collection System (Vacuum) Ceramic Supply of NY/NJ, 7 Route 46 West, Lodi, NJ 07644, (973) 340-3005. Catalog description: The vacuum offers an effective and safe system for the collection and disposal of potentially hazardous and toxic dusts in the workplace. These include glaze chemicals, silica-bearing clays and slips, which should be removed regularly from floors, walls, furniture and the other studio surfaces. This system has been specifically designed to pick up and retain ultra fine dust particles in substantial volume. The Nilfisk filtration system, with the HEPA filter, has been tested to be able to capture 99.99% of all particles 0.3 microns or larger. The average clay dust particles are more than twice this size. The dust is collected in self-sealing bags for safe disposal. Its unique design advantages include

Model 750

Model 1800

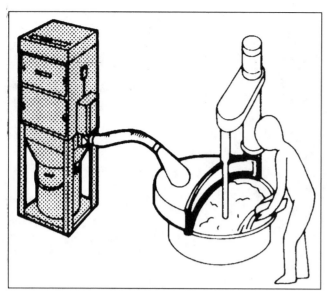

Bailey Dust Collection System.

risk of motor burnout. Accessories include: HEPA filter, micro-filter, 23" straight tube, 3" round brush, 3-in-1 floor nozzle, 6 1/2 foot braided hose, trolley, 20" cord, rubber nozzle, nozzle insert, 5" upholstery nozzle, and one package of 5 two-ply paper bags. 3 1/4 gallon capacity without bag; 2 1/4 gallon capacity with bags. 16" Height x 12" Width, 115V. Ship wt. 28 lbs. Suggested retail price $971.25.

Tibbits Clean Air Machine Tucker's Pottery Supplies Inc., 15 West Pearce St., No. 7 Richmond Hill, ON Canada L4B 1H6, (905) 889-7705. All models remove 200 chemicals from the studio air, including silica dust. They have a special HEPA filter that can remove particles down to 0.3 microns. The units are quiet and the filters can easily be accessed. Models include portable units and built in units to fit existing studio heating or venting systems. Model T101, T102, T30, PC-260-45. Call or write for suggested retail prices.

Orton Downdraft Venting System Orton Ceramic Foundation, 6991 Old 3C Highway, Westerville, OH 43082, (614) 895-2663, fax (614) 895-5610. The venting system is designed to actively remove fumes from electric kilns during the firing process. It is produced in several different models and installs easily on all electric kilns. The system comes with a two-year warranty, and the company offers excellent technical support. Call for current prices.

clog resistance, absolute filtering, dust-free disposal, powerful suction, large recovery capacity, low noise level, and easy handling. This unique absolute filtering system meets or exceeds OSHA safety standards for control of such toxic materials as lead, asbestos, mercury, insecticides, cotton dusts, and any ceramic raw material used by potters. The vacuum uses a primary cooled motor and is equipped with a thermo-valve, which opens when the motor overheats. This system delivers absolute filtration with minimal loss of suction, without the

Spray Booths

In many studio operations, the glaze is sprayed on the pottery or sculpture. A spray gun is designed to discharge under pressure an aerosol mixture of water and glaze materials onto a ceramic surface. By its very nature, this mixture becomes airborne and should be properly trapped before it migrates throughout the studio. Spray booths operate by capturing the sprayed glaze that does not land on the ceramic surfaces and then exhausting it out of the room.

Amaco Spray Booth Model SP1 Ceramic Supply of NY/NJ, 7 Route 46 West, Lodi, NJ 07644, (973) 340-3005. The booth is constructed of steel with a 3/4 hp motor and an exhaust delivery of 1361 CFM. There is a 12" fan that moves air out through a back opening where a standard 10" duct can be attached to vent the exhaust outside. The exhaust motor operates on 110 V AC current. The booth comes with an optional stand or can be mounted on any table. Spraying area: 24" W x 24" D x 26" H. Outside dimensions: 24" W x 44" D x 26" H. Suggested retail price $1,460.00.

Paasche Hobby Shop Spray Booth Model HSSB Ceramic Supply of NY/NJ, 7 Route 46 West, Lodi, NJ 07644, (973) 340-3005. This spray booth is compact in size and easy to assemble. It is a portable booth constructed of galvanized steel for easy cleaning. It can be used without venting to the outside, but, for more efficient results, outside venting should be employed. Dimensions: 24" x 18" H. Suggested retail price $279.00.

Alpine Model SB1 Ceramic Supply of NY/NJ, 7 Route 46 West, Lodi, NJ 07644, (973) 340-3005. The spray booth draws excess spray down through a bottom blower to the rear of the unit for connection to any outside venting system. The unit is easy to clean, having removable wooden slats to prevent chipping or contamination of sprayed ware. The spray booth has a 1/4 hp motor, 900-CFM blower, and all the moving parts are enclosed to provide a safe and compact spraying area using a minimum of floor space. Spraying area: 28" W x 22" D x 33" H. Outside dimensions: 28" W x 22" D x 69" H. Suggested retail price $1,095.00.

Bench Type Filter Spray Booth Model BBF Great Lakes Clay & Supply Company, 120 S. Lincoln Ave., Carpentersville, IL 60110, (847) 551-1070. The spray booth is made to accommodate the spraying of small parts and permits the operator to sit while working. Bench booths offer the convenience of throwaway fiberglass filters. This booth is constructed of 20 gauge galvanized sheet steel and can accommodate top and back exhaust. Optional legs may be added to provide a freestanding booth.

STQPBBF-2 size 2' x 1' 6" x 1' 6" $790.00,
STQPBBF-3 size 3' x 2' 6" x 1' 6" $850.00,
STQPBBF-4 size 4' x 2' 6" x 1' 6" $880.00.

Laguna Pro-V Seamless Spray Booth Model NL-352 Laguna Clay Company, 14400 Lomitas Avenue, City of Industry, CA 91746, (626) 330-0631. Created for Laguna, this modular, polyethylene unit is easy to clean and captures all spray in a funneled recovery tank. The

spray booth is rust proof and has a stainless steel leg assembly. It has a large (42" x 39") opening and 34" depth, which provides a large workspace for spraying. The unit has a molded filter bracket and many additional available options. The outside dimensions are: 55 1/2" H x 48 1/4" W x 50 1/4" D. Suggested retail price $989.00.

Pro V Seamless Spray Booth Tucker's Pottery Supplies Inc., 15 West Pearce St., No. 7 Richmond Hill, ON Canada L4B 1H6, (905) 889-7705. The spray booth is constructed for the studio potter spraying large pieces. The polyethylene surface cleans easily and will not rust. The booth is shaped to collect the glaze run-off. It comes with reusable filters. The inside dimensions are: 42" W x 39" D. The outside dimensions with the legs are 48 1/4" W x 50 1/4" D x 74 1/4" H. Call or write for current retail pricing.

Spray Booth—Medium Duty Tucker's Pottery Supplies Inc., 15 West Pearce St., No. 7 Richmond Hill, ON Canada L4B 1H6, (905) 889-7705. The spray booth is designed for medium duty spraying or airbrushing. It can be mounted on a table or can be purchased with an optional stand. A 980-CFM fan draws out the exhaust air. Standard furnace filters and ventilation to the outside are required. Dimensions: inside 42" W x 39" H x 34" D. Outside with legs 48 1/4" W x 50 1/4" D x 74 1/4" H. Call or write for current retail pricing.

Respirators

North brand Respirator #5500 with P-100 cartridges Tucker's Pottery Supplies Inc., 15 West Pearce St., No. 7 Richmond Hill, ON Canada L4B 1H6, (905) 889-7705. Offers protection from clay dust. Can be used for studio cleaning and in any situation where dry raw materials are mixed. Call or write for current retail pricing.

MSA Affinity Pro Disposable Respirator Kickwheel Pottery Supply, Inc., 6477 Peachtree Ind. Blvd., Atlanta, GA 30360, (770) 986-9011. The respirator is approved by NIOSH (National Institute of Occupational Safety & Health) and has two fixed straps for breathable comfort and safety. Rated 42 CRF Part 84. Dust & Mist. Price $4.00.

MSA Advantage 200 Respirator Kickwheel Pottery Supply, Inc., 6477 Peachtree Ind. Blvd., Atlanta, GA 30360, (770) 986-9011. Approved by NIOSH and MSHA (Mine Safety & Health Administration). Black Hycar face piece protects against dust, mist, and vapors. Mask

Complete: w/GMA filters & Prefilters $48.00, Type F Prefilter set (2) $4.00, Type F Dust Canister (2) $11.00, GMA Canister filter (2) $36.00.

Dustfoe 88 Model SFQDF88 Great Lakes Clay & Supply Company, 120 S. Lincoln Ave., Carpentersville, IL 60110, (847) 551-1070. NIOSH and MSHA approved lightweight respirator with rubber face cushion and adjustable head straps. Price Dustfoe 88 Mask $25.00, Filters Model SFQDF88RF (pack of five) $12.50.

Dust Respirator Model TM-3010 Laguna Clay Company, 14400 Lomitas Avenue, City of Industry, CA 91746, (626) 330-0631. The new style respirator is approved by NIOSH/MSHA for dust. Provides protection for three eight-hour workdays. Price $1.35 ea., Box of 20 $18.00.

Dust and Mist Respirator Model TM-3018 Laguna Clay Company, 14400 Lomitas Avenue, City of Industry, CA 91746, (626) 330-0631. The respirator has an exhale valve that offers protection against both dust and mist for three eight-hour workdays. Approved by NIOSH/MSHA. Molded mesh shell resists collapsing. This model also has smooth rubber head straps for extra comfort. Price $3.75 ea., Box of 10 $29.50.

3M Series 6000 Respirators Model TM-3015 Laguna Clay Company, 14400 Lomitas Avenue, City of Industry, CA 91746, (626) 330-0631. This model of respirator needs no retainers to attach filters to the unit. It has a low profile fit, allowing for improved visibility, and eyeglasses can be worn with the respirator. Approved by NIOSH/MSHA. Small, Medium, Large sizes. Price $24.95.

Survivor Air Purifying Respirators Model TM-3025 Laguna Clay Company, 14400 Lomitas Avenue, City of Industry, CA 91746, (626) 330-0631. This model of respirator has a replaceable filter unit and a four-point elastic head strap for a comfortable fit on the face. The respirator is washable and hypoallergenic. Approved NIOSH/MSHA. Masks are guaranteed for five years. Small, Medium, Large sizes. Price $35.95.

Gloves

Heat Protective Kevlar Gloves (non asbestos) Ceramic Supply of NY/NJ, 7 Route 46 West, Lodi, NJ 07644, (973) 340-3005. Catalog description: These heavy-duty gloves are made from Dupont Kevlar and are inherently flame resistant. They will withstand 900°F temperatures and are lightweight, flexible, and comfortable. They are most useful in unloading hot kilns, protecting the hands and lower arms from being burnt by hot pots and shelves. Heavy-duty gloves also protect the hands when reaching into a kiln. Some fired glazes can have very sharp edges, which can cut unprotected hands. G14 Model 14" long, suggested retail price $29.75. G23 Model 23" long, $44.00.

Kevlar Gloves/Mittens (non asbestos) Tucker's Pottery Supplies Inc., 15 West Pearce St., No. 7 Richmond Hill, ON Canada L4B 1H6, (905) 889-7705. Gloves and Mittens can be used for unloading hot kilns. They protect the hands and arms from burns. Call or write for current retail pricing.

Blue Beast Kiln Gloves Model GLV1 Southern Pottery Equipment & Supplies, 2721 West Perdue, Baton Rouge, LA 70814, (225) 932-9457. Heavy-duty gloves, leather with "Kevlar" lining. Price $12.65.

Kiln Gloves Model GLV3 GLV1 Southern Pottery Equipment & Supplies, 2721 West Perdue, Baton Rouge, LA 70814, (225) 932-9457. Fiberglass 14" Raku gloves. Price $38.00.

Leather Welders Gloves Model SFQLWG Great Lakes Clay & Supply Company, 120 S. Lincoln Ave., Carpentersville, IL 60110, (847) 551-1070. Made from special heat resistant leathers, these gloves outwear asbestos gloves and are safer. Fleece lined for comfort with gauntlet cuffs for added protection 11" long. Price $19.00.

Safety Glasses

Safety Spectacles Model MY-107 Laguna Clay Company, 14400 Lomitas Avenue, City of Industry, CA 91746, (626) 330-0631. The green tinted glasses are designed to meet A.N.S.I. standards. The glasses are comfortable to wear and offer strength and durability. The also have distortion-free semi-windshields. Price $17.50.

Safety Goggles Model SFQGLE Great Lakes Clay & Supply Company, 120 S. Lincoln Ave., Carpentersville, IL 60110, (847) 551-1070. Clear plastic goggles with a soft frame and vented sides for optimum protection $4.50.

Safety Glasses Model S-5685 Uline, 2200 S. Lakeside Drive, Waukegan, IL 60086, (800) 295-5510. Wrap around frame for viewing at all angles, impact resistant, adjustable for a comfortable fit. Price $7.00.

Lift-Front Goggles Tucker's Pottery Supplies Inc., 15 West Pearce St., No. 7 Richmond Hill, ON Canada L4B 1H6, (905) 889-7705. The goggles have a hinged section that allows for the shaded visor or clear view use when looking into the kiln. Call or write for current retail pricing.

Infrared Goggles Ceramic Supply of NY/NJ, 7 Route 46 West, Lodi, NJ 07644, (973) 340-3005. The glasses have a green polycarbonate lens capable of filtering ultraviolet and infrared radiation. They should be used whenever looking into a firing kiln. Model INFRA-GOG suggested retail price $15.00.

Impact Goggles Ceramic Supply of NY/NJ, 7 Route 46 West, Lodi, NJ 07644, (973) 340-3005. Clear plastic high impact glasses designed to protect the eyes from flying particles. Goggles mold to the face comfortably and may be worn over glasses. Frame is perforated for full ventilation. Impact goggles are designed to be worn when chipping fired glaze off of kiln shelves or when using a grinding wheel to remove glaze from the bottom of pots. They can also be used to protect the eyes from glaze mixing or clay mixing operations where wet or dry particles can be released. Model IMGOG $3.55.

"Cup-style" Welders Goggles Tucker's Pottery Supplies Inc., 15 West Pearce St., No. 7 Richmond Hill, ON Canada L4B 1H6, (905) 889-7705. The goggles offer a tight-fitting eye protection for looking into kilns. Call or write for current retail pricing.

Miscellaneous Equipment

Sweeping Compound Model SWEEP Ceramic Supply of NY/NJ, 7 Route 46 West, Lodi, NJ 07644, (973) 340-3005. Before sweeping the ceramics area, wear the appropriate respirator and spread the oil-based compound over the floor in order to keep the dust to a minimum. The sweeping compound can be reused until it reaches its capacity. 25 lb. $30.00, 100 lb. $100.00.

Sweeping Compound Model S-6633 Uline, 2200 S. Lakeside Drive, Waukegan, IL 60086, (800) 295-5510. No grit oil and sawdust compound for sweeping the studio. Price $18.00 for 50 lbs.

Aprons Model APDEN Ceramic Supply of NY/NJ, 7 Route 46 West, Lodi, NJ 07644, (973) 340-3005. Aprons protect the clothes from clay and raw material dust. They also capture any wet clay or glaze that might be splashed onto the potter during clay mixing or glazing operations. Price $6.50.

The simplest and most commonly available cleaning items, such as paper towels, sponges, and plastic buckets are often the most effective items to use when cleaning the pottery studio. Discount hardware stores carry a full line of low cost cleaning supplies.

First Aid Kits Model H-860 Uline, 2200 S. Lakeside Drive, Waukegan, IL 60086, (800) 295-5510. Price $29.00.

Weight Belt Model MY-106A Laguna Clay Company, 14400 Lomitas Avenue, City of Industry, CA 91746, (626) 330-0631. This unique safety product is designed to support the lower back when lifting heavy objects. The belt is strong and pliable with a nylon covering for strength. Sizes include: XS (24-28), S (28-32), M (32-36), L (36-40), XL (40-44), XXL (44-48), larger sizes available. Price $28.90.

Back Support Belt Model H-855 Uline, 2200 S. Lakeside Drive, Waukegan, IL 60086, (800) 295-5510. Flexible, ventilated elastic belt, adjustable and machine washable support belt. Price $29.00.

Soft Cushioning Mats Model H-899 Uline, 2200 S. Lakeside Drive, Waukegan, IL 60086, (800) 295-5510. Soft mats to cushion feet, appropriate for many studio applications. This product is ideal for placing on the floor in front of wedging tables or any area where prolonged standing takes place. Price $52.00.

Professional Potter's Stool Creative Industry Model St-1 P Tucker's Pottery Supplies Inc., 15 West Pearce St., No. 7 Richmond Hill, ON Canada L4B 1H6, (905) 889-7705. Specially designed padded stool for increased comfort and leg circulation. Unique ergonomic design. Adjustable height and swivel motion for versatility. The seat tilts in three positions. Five-leg base with glides for stability. Price $350.00.

Plastic Buckets/Sponges/Towels (various sizes) available at all hardware stores. Plastic non-breakable buckets, sponges, and towels are an essential part of any studio clean up operation. The buckets can be filled with water and the sponges/towels can be used to wipe down any work surface. Simply wiping surfaces with a dry cloth only moves clay and glaze particles to other surfaces, or sends them into the air.

Chapter 5

Kiln Venting Systems

Having adequate ventilation for electric kilns will promote a safe work environment. Over the past few years, manufacturers have devised different methods of removing kiln exhaust from the ceramics studio. Listed are several systems that should aid potters in venting their own pottery kilns. Why is this important? Apart from the sometimes objectionable smell encountered in the first stages of a kiln firing, there can be several potentially harmful emissions released when clay and glaze materials are heated. There has been increased concern over limiting or eliminating any health or safety hazards in the workplace or home. Almost every day, we hear of risk factors and potential dangers to our well being. With such a high degree of kiln venting information and awareness now available to potters, it is conservative planning to investigate our workplaces and recreational activities. The goal should be to incorporate any safety measures to ensure low risk ceramics studios for ourselves and others who use the workspaces.

When working in ceramics, we all come into direct and indirect contact with clay and glaze materials. Specifically, clay goes through several transformations when heated to progressively higher temperatures. Mechanical water is driven off at 212°F, followed by the release of chemically combined water in the 1000°F to 1100°F regions. While these "hidden" effects are not noticed by the potter, other changes in the clay are more apparent, namely the oxidation or burning off of organic matter present to some degree in all clays. Organic matter that travels along in clay can take the form of pieces of wood, leaves, coal, sulfur, or any other combustible material that is mined with the clay. When exposed to enough heat, organic material burns, releasing particles and gases. Kiln exhaust fumes can release volatile metals and fluorides from clay and glaze raw materials. During the firing, carbon monoxide is also produced and may be generated at higher levels than recommended government Occupational Safety & Health Administration (OSHA) standards, which are 35 p.p.m. (0.0035%) for continual exposure or 200 p.p.m. for short-term exposure rates. Carbon monoxide is oxygen hungry in the

Massachusetts College of Art kiln room.
A system of booths has been constructed that captures and removes electric kiln exhaust fumes. During bisque firing, organic materials are released from the clay. In the glaze firing, organic gums and binders are volatized and removed by the venting system. Both types of firing require adequate kiln venting to remove any fumes and vapors from the studio area.

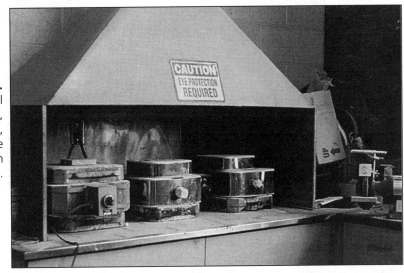

Massachusetts College of Art kiln room.
A central exhaust hood vents three small electric test kilns. When the kilns are firing, the exhaust venting system is turned on, removing volatized particles from the studio atmosphere. The venting system actively draws vapors out of the kiln room.

blood stream, and high levels in the studio environment can produce fatigue, headaches, nausea, sore throats, and many other ailments.[1]

The "rotten eggs" smell often encountered in bisque firing is the result in part of small quantities of sulfur found in the clay being decomposed or oxidized. The actual amounts of sulfur can vary from one type of clay to another. Sulfur combined with water can be very corrosive to metal kiln parts as well as the linings of the lungs. Some studio potters also report that the window glass in the kiln room has been etched by repeated exposure to non-vented kiln emissions. The amount of sulfur can vary. For example, stoneware clays might have significant amounts of sulfur, while kaolins may have very little or none. The amounts of sulfur or any organic material found in clays can also increase or decrease within a specific type of clay from year to year or even from bag to bag. Other gases that can be released from ceramic materials are chlorine and fluorine, a by-product from fluorspar and cryolite, two common glaze materials. Both gases can cause lung irritation and respiratory tract discomfort. In a sense, the volatilization or

burning out and cleaning of the clay is a good outcome because if organics are left in the clay they can cause future defects in the fired clay body or glaze. However, the goal of any kiln venting system is to capture and remove the unwanted carbonaceous materials and other contaminants from the studio area.

Massachusetts College of Art (621 Huntington Avenue, Boston, MA 02115-5885) is one of the leading educational institutions in enacting health and safety measures for their ceramics studios, kiln rooms, and raw material storage areas. There are five gas kilns, five electric kilns, and a Raku kiln in the ceramics department. Undergraduate and graduate students are taught how to mix glazes and fire kilns in accordance with safety procedures. The ceramics areas are equipped with room venting systems and specific area venting systems to remove raw material particles from the kiln room, glaze mixing room, clay mixing areas, and student ceramics studios. Each kiln in the ceramics department is vented to an outside air source to remove organic materials from clay and glazes during the firing process.

Vent-A-Kiln, EnviroVent, and Orton KilnVent Systems

Electric kiln venting systems are very effective devices for removing unwanted fumes and particles from the studio. With this fact in mind, let's review some popular kiln venting systems that are available at many ceramics suppliers throughout the Unites States and Canada.

Solutions to Clean Studio Air

Vent-A-Kiln System—manufactured by Vent-A-Kiln Corporation, 62 Hertel Ave., Buffalo, NY 14207, (716) 876-2023, fax (716) 876-383, www.ventakiln.com. Suggested Retail pricing 265-CFM models $340.00 to $416.00, depending

---

[1]Information obtained from "Venting Solutions, A Resource Guide," The Edward Orton Jr. Ceramic Foundation.

on the vent size required for an electric kiln. Suggested Retail pricing 500-CFM models $474.00 to $755.00, depending on the vent size required for an electric kiln.

Vent-A-Kiln Systems consist of either a round, rectangular, or square hood design, fitted with an electric exhaust motor (115V with two speed CRM air flow control) to capture and exhaust kiln fumes. Vent-A-Kiln is produced in models with 265 CFM or 500 CFM exhaust capacities. The unit comes in various sizes to fit every make and model of electric kiln. The vent system is mounted over the top of the kiln and can be raised to simplify loading and unloading of the kiln. Heat generated from firing the kiln, along with any combustible emissions, is passively collected in the conical-shaped exhaust vent. The kiln exhaust then exits the studio via a 10-foot hose, supplied with the system. The flexible aluminum ducting comes with clamps and mounting plates for easy installation. The Vent-A-Kiln design does not require kiln modification, and the unit can be moved to vent more than one kiln within the studio. However, it can only vent one kiln at a time. The cost to operate the Vent-A-Kiln averages one cent per hour. In any safety situation, the cost for adequate protection should not be a deciding factor. The unit meets applicable OSHA standards, is covered with a full three-year warranty, and runs on 115V household current.

The EnviroVent—manufactured by Skutt Ceramics Products, Inc., 2618 SE Steele St., Portland, OR 97202 (503) 231-7726. www.skutt.com. Suggested Retail price $380.00.

The EnviroVent is constructed from stainless steel and cast aluminum. It is an active downdraft venting system mounted on the outside bottom of the kiln. The system actively draws fresh air from several holes drilled into the top of the soft brick kiln. Twist drills are provided to make the top air entry holes in the kiln. Detailed instructions make installation very easy for even the beginning potter. The exhaust is then drawn into flexible 4" aluminum ducting, supplied with the unit. If required, additional ducting can be purchased and extended to an outside air source. In the EnviroVent system, fumes are directly extracted from the kiln, causing cleaner bisque firings, sharper glaze colors, and improved heat distribution within the kiln. The unit runs on 115V household current with the fan motor located under the kiln away from rising heat. The cost to operate the

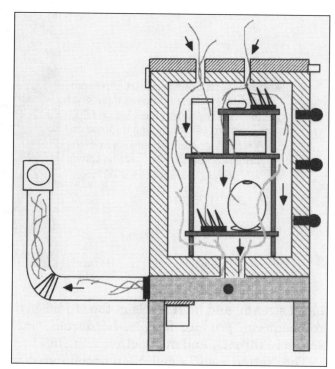

The Orton KilnVent system draws outside oxygen-rich air down through the top of the kiln and exhausts it through the bottom of the kiln. Due to the active venting system, carbon monoxide, organics, volatile metals, fluorides, and sulphur oxides are removed from the kiln and kiln room area. The Orton KilnVent system is manufactured in several different models to fit each type of electric kiln installation:

unit averages one cent per hour. The EnviroVent has a two-year limited warranty.

The Orton Kiln-Vent System— The Orton Kiln-Vent system can be purchased through the Edward Orton Jr. Ceramic Foundation, 6991 Old 3C Highway, Westerville, Ohio 43082-9026. Ask for current pricing on available models.

The Orton downdraft Kiln-Vent system pulls fumes out through the bottom of the kiln, while allowing air to enter through the top of the kiln. Electric kilns are normally hotter at the top. With the Kiln-Vent, hot gases near the top of the kiln are drawn down, providing better temperature uniformity. The downdraft system is a patented system, which removes fumes and odors from the kiln while bringing in outside air to improve firing conditions in the kiln. Downdraft venting does not significantly increase firing time or affect the ability of the kiln to reach temperature. It also removes fumes from the kiln room, which can impact the working environment.

During the firing, hot air expands in the kiln just like air in a hot air balloon. The hot air and gases are forced out through cracks in the

Suspended

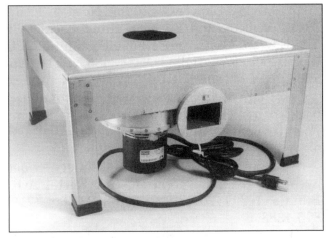

Stand

Plate Mount

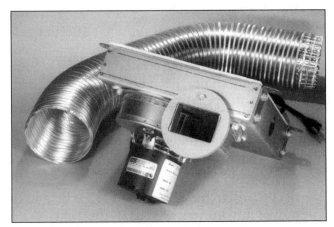

Kiln Mount

kiln, making it difficult for new air to enter the kiln. Many glaze and clay body defects are caused by insufficient oxygen circulation within the kiln. For example, metallic lusters are suspended in oil and many glazes contain gums, all of which have to be removed during the firing. Outside air drawn into the kiln replaces carbon monoxide and adds oxygen, which is needed for the combustion of organic material found in clays and glazes. Fumes from kilns may also contain organics, volatile metals, fluorides, and sulphur oxides, which should be removed from the work area. The increase in oxygen also reduces corrosion of metal heating elements, outside metal kiln surfaces, and Kiln Sitter parts, increasing their useful service life.

Kiln-Vent costs less than 1 cent per hour to operate, and does not require manual venting (accomplished on many models by slightly opening the kiln lid and removing cone viewing hole plugs).

Junior

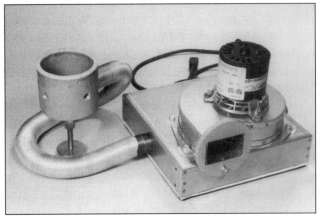

Floor

Alternative Venting

In the past, before the popular venting systems came into the marketplace, a common method of curtailing electric kiln fumes was to open the windows of the studio to create a cross draft. Many potters still use this "low tech" method together with a house fan to circulate air within the kiln room. Is this old method safe? Increasing your safety margin is always a good practice. It has been proven that the newer venting systems do remove greater volumes of unwanted kiln exhaust than just opening the studio windows. Winter months and the variable factors of airflow within any given kiln room dictate mechanical approaches to clean air. Consequently, the best course of action is to take advantage of the new highly efficient venting systems currently available to potters. As with the purchase of any studio equipment, it is always a good idea to research all the available products and manufacturers. A very useful tool in making a decision is to call the kiln vent manufacturer or the ceramics supplier who sells the product and ask for the phone numbers for customers who have purchased a kiln venting system in your area. Most potters will gladly tell you the good and any deficient points of the venting system they purchased. Ask to visit their studios to see the kiln vent in operation. Several electric kiln-venting companies have booklets and videos, which are very informative.

Suggested Readings & Videos

"What Contemporary Studios Need to Know About Venting and Firing a Kiln," booklet by The Edward Orton Fr. Ceramic Foundation, PO Box 2760, Westerville, OH 43086, (614) 895-2663 fax (614) 895-5610.

"Venting Solutions—A Resource Guide," booklet by The Edward Orton Fr. Ceramic Foundation, PO Box 2760, Westerville, OH 43086, (614) 895-2663 fax (614) 895 5610.

"An Educational Guide to Kiln Safety," video by Vent-A-Kiln Corporation, 621 Hertel Ave., Buffalo, NY 14207, (716) 876-2023, fax (716) 876-4383.

"Designing a Kiln Room," booklet by Skutt Ceramics Products, Inc., 2618 SE Steele St., Portland, OR 97202, (503) 231-7726.

Safety Tips for Electric Kiln Venting

- Place the kiln away from regular pottery shop activities in an area that can be adequately vented. The optimum place for electric kilns, or any type of kiln, is a separate kiln room that can be adequately vented to an outside air source.

- The kiln should stand on a non-combustible surface and away from any studio walls.

  Always follow manufacturers' recommendations on kiln placement. While all electric kilns produced in the United States meet minimum safety requirements, a firing kiln does give off a lot of heat. Keep all combustible materials away from the kiln. As an added safety consideration, do not place anything that might cause falls or accidents around the kiln. There should be a three-foot space around the kiln with a one-foot air space beneath the kiln. The potter should be able to walk around the kiln during the firing to ensure that it is firing properly.

- In studios with wood floors, refractory brick or refractory ceramic board should be placed on the floor beneath the kiln.

- If the kiln does not have a venting system, open the windows and use a fan to create a cross draft in the kiln room. This procedure will reduce the concentration of particles suspended in every cubic foot of air space in the studio.

- Each kiln venting system has different set-up and operating requirements. Before using a kiln venting system, carefully read and understand the manufacturer's installation and operating instructions.

- In any kiln venting system, always have the exhaust exit to an outside air source. Do not vent the exhaust into another room, as it will contaminate the entire work area.

- Periodically check and maintain the condition of any kiln venting system.

- With any venting system, keep the electric power cord away from the kiln. Do not use an extension cord to power the kiln venting system, as this can create a fire hazard or cause falls in the studio.
- Electric kilns are not designed for burnout firings. Do not place large amounts of combustible material in the kiln. Electric kilns can accept wax resists on pots, organic material found in clays, and organic binders used in glazes, as these relatively small amounts can be effectively volatized and removed by a venting system.
- While heavy smoke or smell from the firing electric kiln indicates insufficient venting, keep in mind that one of the byproducts of burning organic materials found in clay and glaze material is carbon monoxide, which is colorless, odorless, and dangerous. Always create a kiln room environment where there is air circulation and adequate ventilation.

Hydrocarbon Fuel Kiln Venting Systems

A clay body's organic material content is volatized or burned off when heated in an electric kiln. It is also volatized in kilns fueled by hydrocarbons such as gas (natural, propane), coal, oil, or wood. However, hydrocarbon based fuels do need different types of venting requirements as compared with electric kiln venting systems. When a hydrocarbon kiln is heated, the kiln atmosphere can contain oxygen, nitrogen, carbon dioxide, water vapor, carbon monoxide, sul-

Soot or carbon can be deposited on the outside surfaces of hydrocarbon fueled (natural gas, propane gas, wood, coal, oil) kilns. When the amount of gas exceeds the amount of air at the burners, a reduction (carbon monoxide) kiln atmosphere is created within the kiln. Carbon is a byproduct of incomplete combustion. While some carbon is normal during a kiln firing, excessive carbon can be deposited on floors, walls, storage racks, and other kiln room surfaces. Carbon can cause air quality problems, due to the small lightweight particle size of the material that can be blown around the kiln room.

A well-ventilated kiln room is important, as it reduces the amount of volatized organic material that can be released during a kiln firing. A household fan placed near the electric kiln and an open window is a low cost method for removing unwanted kiln emissions.

In the Massachusetts College of Art kiln room, the gas kiln is vented to actively remove kiln gases (top left of venting system) and also capture passive gases that escape from the kiln door or cone viewing holes (top right of venting system) by an overhead hood system. The entire kiln room also has fans and an exhaust system to constantly exchange the kiln room air (Bailey Pottery Equipment Corp. gas kilns).

fur dioxide, and sulfur trioxide.[2] The amount and ratios of burning fuel gases are controlled by the potter knowingly or unknowingly adjusting the burners, damper, and secondary air ports on the firing kiln. Oxygen and nitrogen are pulled into the burner by room air. Water vapor and carbon dioxide result from burning hydrocarbons (fuel). When more fuel than air is introduced into the burner, carbon monoxide or a reducing kiln atmosphere is created.

Carbon monoxide is an odorless, colorless, heavier-than-air, toxic gas that is a by-product of incomplete combustion. The effect of exposure to carbon monoxide depends on the individual's physical health, age, sex, weight, use of cigarettes, and other factors. As little as 40 p.p.m. can cause mental fatigue or partial loss of vision. Higher concentrations, above 1000 p.p.m., are lethal. With this potentially deadly gas, adequate ventilation in the kiln room is essential to prevent accidents.

Sulfur trioxide and sulfur dioxide can also form in the kiln exhaust gases if sulfur is present in the fuel, or from byproducts in the clay and glazes fired within the kiln. Some clays have naturally occurring high levels of sulfur, while other clays can have less sulfur content. Depending on the source of the clay, any organic material can still cause potentially harmful

Vertical stack (left side of photo) exhausts passive kiln gasses leaking from the door and bricks. Vertical stack (right side of photo) exhausts kiln atmosphere generated by natural gas burners.

---

[2]*Ceramic Science for the Potter* by W.G. Lawrence, published by Chilton/Haynes, 1972.

vapors during the first stages of the firing. The "rotten eggs" acrid smell of sulfur is often the first indication potters have of poor kiln room ventilation. Incomplete combustion can also cause carbon particles to form, which can be seen as deposits of black soot or powder. The carbon is usually deposited on the outside surfaces of the kiln and can also be released into the kiln exhaust, causing black smoke to exit the stack. Soot can land on kiln bricks, tools, equipment, and the kiln room floor. Each type of kiln and kiln site will require a specific venting system for the efficient exhausting of the kiln gases. Whatever the method of kiln venting, in electric fired or hydrocarbon fired kilns, it is important to remember all of the gases and particles have to be safely taken out of the kiln and then removed from the kiln room.

Salt Kiln Venting

In the twelfth century, Germany was the first country to develop traditional salt-glazed functional pottery. The process starts when salt (sodium chloride) is thrown into the kiln at high temperature (2300°F) where it reacts in the presence of moisture to form a sodium-alumina-silicate glaze on a mature vitreous clay body. The reaction is most evident on exposed non-glazed clay surfaces, forming a distinctive "orange peel" texture. Salt vapors landing on glazed areas of the ware can also have a fluxing effect on the glaze.

The salt glaze can be expressed as:
$$2NaCl + H_2O \text{ --- } 2HCl \text{ --- } + Na_2O$$
$$Na_2O + XSiO_2 \text{ ---- } Na_2O \cdot SiO_2$$

Along with the byproducts generated by hydrocarbon based fuels, salt kilns release varying amounts of chlorine gas and hydrochloric acid; in a confined area, both can cause corrosion of lung tissue. When salt (sodium chloride) deposited into the kiln breaks down or releases chlorine gas within the kiln, most of the gas is vented out through the kiln stack. As the gas comes in contact with moisture in the atmosphere, hydrochloric acid is formed. The corrosive effects of this reaction can sometimes be observed on metal supports associated with the salt kiln and, in a more subtle fashion, in the ecology of the locale. The leaves on trees around some salt kiln stacks can become brown from the chlorine exhaust vapors.

In situations where there is a lot of back pressure from a firing kiln (back pressure in a kiln can be noticed when flames or gases exit the burner ports or pyrometric cone viewing ports of the kiln during the firing process), chlorine gas can enter an enclosed small kiln room and cause lung irritation. While recent research has indicated extremely low levels of chlorine gas and hydrochloric acid release in salt kilns, it is always a good practice to keep the kiln room well ventilated during the entire firing and salting process. Expensive antipollution exhaust devices can be installed in salt kiln exhaust stacks, but in general they are not practical for the studio potter due to their high cost and maintenance.

Soda Kiln Venting

In 1972, the New York State College of Ceramics at Alfred University was one of the first ceramics departments to commit itself fully to the testing and development of a substitute salt firing system. In the evaluation of approximately 240 different sodium compounds, two sodium based compounds (sodium carbonate and sodium bicarbonate) met the required conditions of duplicating salt glazed effects on exposed clay body surfaces while also offering an environmentally cleaner and safer alternative to salt firing. When heated, sodium carbonate or sodium bicarbonate (sodium bicarbonate changes to sodium carbonate when heated to 850°C) breaks down into a vapor containing carbon dioxide, water, and sodium. In a firing kiln, the sodium vapor reacts with the alumina and silica present in exposed clay body surfaces to form a sodium-alumina-silicate orange peel glaze texture. Chlorine gas and hydrochloric acid are not present in soda-fired kilns. Soda kiln exhaust emissions are considerably diminished compared to traditional sodium chloride salt kilns. As with other types of kilns, proper venting of the kiln exhaust must also be enacted during a soda kiln firing.[3]

[3.]*What Every Potter Should Know* by Jeff Zamek, published by Krause Publications, 1999. Sodium Vapor Firing Part 1, 2. New York State College of Ceramics at Alfred University, research thesis.

Raku Firing

A fiber Raku kiln is being unloaded after a firing. Temperatures within the kiln can reach 1800°F to 1900°F. The area around the kiln should be kept clear of obstacles to prevent accidents during the fast-paced Raku firing process.

With any kiln firing, there are risks involved, including minor burns from touching a hot kiln or major accidents such as the kiln stack igniting the roof structure and burning the studio down. Inherent in the Raku process is an increased exposure to many potential safety and health risk situations. The Raku procedure involves firing a kiln up to approximately 1860°F and then removing the pots from the still red-hot kiln. As the pots are taken out of the kiln, they are transported to either a container where combustible materials produce a carbon monoxide atmosphere or the pot is allowed to fast cool in a water bath. In a variation on the cooling procedure, the pot is set aside to cool down in the air. All of this activity takes place at a fairly fast pace, as there is a time limitation from when the pot is taken out of the kiln until it reaches the combustible material, which is usually housed in a non-flammable container such as a galvanized garbage can. Once the hot pot is placed in the container and touches the combustible material, which could be straw, paper, seaweed, or anything that can burn, smoke and carbon are sent into the air along with flames. At some point, the still hot pot is withdrawn and allowed to cool.

Glaze tongs removing a Raku pot from the hot kiln.

The Raku Kiln has been constructed using chicken wire external bracing, which suports an eight pound density refractory fiber blanket. The people shown here are unloading the Raku kiln with glaze tongs. Everyone participating in the firing should have a clear understanding of his or her job. Only the people involved in the Raku process should be around the kiln. A firing kiln is not the place for aimless bystanders.

From this brief description there lie many potential dangers and health risks to the unwary potter and anyone standing around during the Raku process. Before beginning the Raku firing, inspect the kiln, safety equipment, gloves, kiln goggles, high impact face shield, clothing, glaze tongs, and respirator. The Raku process is exciting and quick when compared with other forms of firing ceramic ware, and it is easy to lose track of objects and people standing around the kiln during the removal of the pottery. Instruct all bystanders and helpers on exactly what is going to take place during the kiln firing and cooling process, stressing that they should keep a safe distance from hot pots and kilns. If helpers are needed, everyone should be familiar with their responsibilities during the whole firing process. It is a good idea to have a non-firing "run through" of all the procedures so everyone can physically see every step of the procedure. Special attention should be placed on the areas around the kiln, as they should be clear of any tools or obstacles to prevent trips and falls. When the Raku firing does take place, a potter's attention is focused narrowly on the red hot pot, and he or she can fall over any object left on the ground.

Once the Raku glaze is mixed by following the principles of safe glaze mixing (respirator use and raw material clean up procedures), it is then applied to the pot. At any point that the glaze is in the dry form or is sprayed in the wet form, a respirator should be worn. The Raku kiln is most often fueled by propane (liquid gas)

The correct clothing is essential for a safe Raku firing. Always wear long-sleeved shirts, head protection, long Raku gloves, a respirator, looking into a firing kiln, use the approved shaded goggles to protect your eyes from infrared and ultraviolet light. When unloading the kiln, always wear impact-resistant goggles or shielded head gear to protect the eyes and neck from a potential pot exploding.

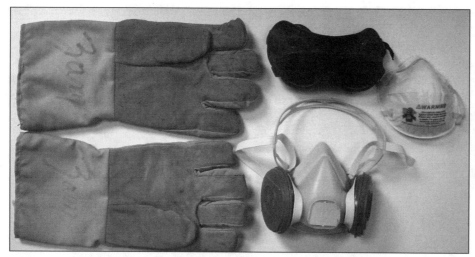

The high temperature insulated leather lined gloves stop burns from hot kilns and pots. The kiln goggles prevent eye damage when looking into kilns. A "paper type" respirator is used when mixing dry glazes. A cartridge type approved respirator is designed for use when taking pots out of the reduction medium, which can cause heavy black smoke.

with the kiln located outdoors; in some instances an electric kiln can be used to fire the ware. When using any gas-fueled kiln, proper venting of exhaust is a critical factor in preventing escaping gases from introducing carbon monoxide into the kiln firing room. With propane-fired kilns, which always should be fired outside (due to the danger of propane being heavier than air and sinking to the floor of an enclosed space and causing an explosion or fire hazard), exhaust gas simply rises into the atmosphere. When an electric kiln is used, it should be turned off and the circuit breaker pulled at the electrical box to ensure the potter does not touch a live heating element in the kiln with the metal Raku tongs. The kiln firing chamber itself should be designed for easy entry and exit of pottery placed within the kiln.

During the firing process, the eyes should be protected from ultraviolet and infrared light by the proper shade of protective goggles. All objects must be removed from the area around the kiln to prevent any accidental ignition of combustion materials. The kiln should be placed near the container that will hold the combustible materials that will cause reduction and carbon to react with the pots upon cooling. When hot pots are removed from the kiln, the potter should wear a high impact face shield to protect him or herself from any shards of clay and glaze blowing off the pot, which can happen at any time during the Raku process. Long Raku tongs, which are used to grip the pot from the hot kiln, will also protect the potter from excessive heat. Heavy-duty Kevlar kiln gloves, a protective facemask or safety impact goggle, and a complete covering of clothing are essential to prevent excessive heat exposure and

burns. In the summer months, when many Raku firings take place, short pants and open shoes along with short-sleeved shirts are not recommended. The use of a respirator is a recommended safety precaution when the pots are placed into the reduction medium, as the immediate combustion creates dense smoke and fumes, which are released into the surrounding area. In many cases, standing upwind from the smoke is not enough to protect the eyes and lungs from irritation.

Raku fired pottery serves a predominately decorative purpose and should only occasionally be considered for functional use. There are two primary reasons for its non-functional status: the absorption rate of the clay body and the sometimes-permeable quality of its fired glaze. The Raku clay body has a high absorption rate, which causes it to take on moisture when washed or stored even at room atmospheric conditions. The high absorption rate and open quality of the fired Raku clay serves to reduce thermal shock and

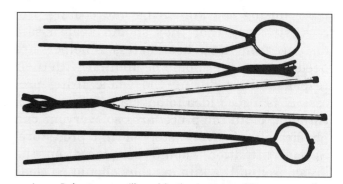

Long Raku tongs will enable the potter to lift pots out of the hot kiln. In the Raku process, once the pots reach temperature the burner is usually turned off and the pots are lifted out of the kiln with tongs. There is still residual heat from the pots, kiln shelves, and posts that can cause burns. The tongs keep the hot pots at a safe distance.

cracking as it is taken immediately out of a hot kiln and cooled quickly. The absorption rate of a clay determines how much or how little water will be absorbed into a fired clay object. Raku pots, because of their open absorbent quality, are not as durable as higher temperature wares, which have lower absorption rates and are more vitreous. High temperature porcelain fired pottery typically has a very low absorption rate, which means a vessel formed from porcelain and fired to its correct temperature can hold water without the benefit of a glaze. A Raku glaze, or any glaze for that matter, should never be considered as a sealant or a barrier to keep water contained. The glaze only serves an aesthetic purpose and creates a smooth surface for easy cleaning. Raku glazes tend to be "soft" or easily scratched and can be soluble, leaching their oxide content into food or drink. If the potter is insistent on producing functional Raku pots, a careful consideration of the function should be considered. For example, making a vessel to hold a drink would not be as practical as a penholder.

After watching and participating in many Raku firings at schools, craft centers, and with my own students, the most common mistakes happen when the area around the kiln is not kept clear of all unnecessary items. Potters frequently concentrate exclusively on pulling the hot pot out of the kiln and placing it in the reduction medium. Many times I have seen people trip or lose their balance as their attention is fixed upon the pot, and they do not realize how close they came to getting a severe burn. Raku firing can be fun and exciting as it speeds

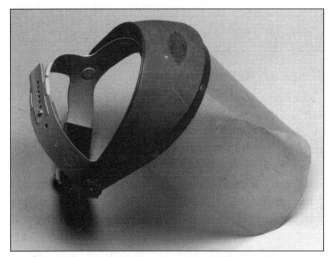

The full-face shield can protect the potter, as sparks and pottery shards can fly off the pot at any time in the Raku firing and cooling process.

up the whole process of glaze maturation and obtaining a finished product, but always plan ahead. Potters should attend a Raku workshop, read a good Raku book, or look at Raku videos before attempting this method of firing. I recommend Steve Branfman's book, *Raku—A Practical Approach* (Krause Publications, 2001). Branfman covers all aspects of Raku firing and is one of the leading experts in this exciting way to fire pots.

With the widespread use of ceramic refractory fiber that can be formed into a lightweight blanket, Raku kilns can be built with a chicken wire exterior skeleton to hold the one inch 8 lb. density ceramic fiber blanket in place.

Kiln Emissions in the Pottery Studio

One of the central questions that comes up when discussing either electric kilns or hydrocarbon-fueled (natural gas, propane gas, oil, coal, wood, sawdust) kilns is whether their airborne emissions are causing harm. Potters often work in home studio situations where children are present, who, along with people with chronic illnesses, are the most sensitive to toxicity issues. Many potters take lessons at educational institutions where other students and non-potters are located in or near the ceramics room. Overwhelmingly the craft of ceramics is practiced by small groups of potters where there has been limited direct on-site research into potential health hazards associated with making pots. While large dinnerware or sanitary ware industries have the financial capacity

of the industry and government regulations determine safety monitoring in the workplace, most potters do not have the physical numbers or economic resources to investigate and report any potential health and safety concerns. The lack of hard statistical data has led to many erroneous and confusing statements concerning the level of toxicity in ceramics studios. It has also caused a great level of anxiety from potters who do not have enough relevant information to act upon. In some instances, industry related exposure rates and durations of exposure to ceramic materials such as feldspars, clays, flint, etc., have been extrapolated to include potters. The projection of such industry related statistical information as it relates to the pottery making community is at best questionable.

Kiln Emissions and Potters Exposures

Research Report Summary

When specific research into the field of ceramics as practiced by potters is accomplished, some surprising conclusions can be drawn from the findings. Namely, as in the study of "Eye Injury Due to Radiation" by Edouard Bastarache M.D. (page 76), the results indicate lower levels of potential health dangers for potters. Whether these initial findings will prove themselves consistent over greater numbers of medical studies in the field of ceramics is open to question. One other study has been completed in the past few years that addresses the issue of potters' exposure to kiln emissions. A Canadian study titled "Kiln Emissions and Potters' Exposures" supplies information directly related to studio potters.[4]

In Canada, over ten thousand potters operate their own studios or work in other potters' small ceramics studios. Ceramics workplaces comprise private individual studios, recreation centers, elementary schools, secondary schools, and ceramics departments at colleges and universities. The research monitored fifty studios in recreation centers, professional studios, elementary schools, secondary schools, and ceramics departments at colleges. Air samples were taken at different locations within the ceramics areas to assess concentrations of nitrogen dioxide, sulfur dioxide, carbon monoxide, fluorides, aluminum, antimony, barium, beryllium, arsenic, cadmium, chromium, cobalt, copper, gold, iron, lead, lithium, magnesium, manganese, mercury, nickel, selenium, silver, vanadium, and zinc.

The results of that research revealed several interesting points concerning kiln emissions in various types of pottery studios. Almost all measured values were below permissible concentration thresholds set by the American Conference of Governmental Industrial Hygienists (ACGIH). There were two exceptions that exceeded individual threshold limits: one firing in a gas kiln (sulfur dioxide levels exceeded short-term exposure limits) and one in an electric kiln (acrolein

exceeded ACGIH guidelines). Both high levels were reported in small kiln rooms without venting systems. However, the overwhelming majority of kilns surveyed showed low concentrations of all tested emissions, where custom venting hoods and active venting of the kiln took place. Conversely, the least effective ventilation systems relied on passive diffusion of kiln exhaust and window fans.

During the research, it was discovered that there was a great diversity of kiln room sizes, kiln types, kiln sizes, and density of ware stacked within the kilns. There was also diversification in kiln venting systems' different flow rates of exhaust venting. Kilns were fired outside, indoors, and in enclosed sheds to various temperature ranges and firing cycle lengths. Bisque and glaze firing were monitored. The potters surveyed used 48 different clay bodies with glazes containing a wide range of metallic coloring oxides. In the report's conclusion, air contamination due to kiln emissions was not found to be a major problem among potters. The report did not investigate other pottery related health hazards such as silica found in clay and glaze materials.

I cite this report as being the type of information needed by potters to examine other ceramics related activities in their studios. In the case of pottery kiln emissions, the exhaust gases have been well documented as to the specific type of gas or heavy metal released and the potential danger to potters. However, when a relevant study is completed on the rate of kiln emissions potters actually experience in their studios, the levels are well within the safe range. The range of kilns, clay bodies, studios, type of kiln firings, location of the kiln firings, and venting systems used by Canadian potters certainly is a closer representation of potters' circumstances in the United States than comparing large scale industrial emissions.

[4.]*Kiln Emissions and Potters Exposures* by Bob Hirtle, Kay Teschke, Chris van Netten, and Michael Brauerthe in conjunction with the University of British Columbia, Department of Health Care and Epidemiology, Vancouver, B.C., Canada and the University of British Columbia, Occupational Hygiene Program, Vancouver, B.C., Canada. Published in the American Industrial Hygiene Association Journal 59:706-714 (1998) supplies information that pertains directly to potters.

Chapter 6

Safety Procedures & Clothing in the Ceramics Studio

Learning from one's personal experience can be a painful and costly endeavor. However, we usually don't forget such lessons. One day in the ceramics studio, I saw my friend Pat unloading a kiln. One of the glazes had run off of her pots causing a sharp edge. Pat, who had long blond hair, decided to remove part of the glaze by using a grinding wheel. Suddenly from the other side of the studio I heard her scream. A section of her hair got caught in the spinning grinding wheel and was forcibly removed from her head. As the class gathered around her, she was holding an eighteen-inch length of hair in her hands. I later used this hair in a sculpture piece but that's another story.

Safety in the ceramics studio hits home hardest when there is a price to pay for inattention. At one time or another, most of us have heard cautionary tales, some of which are similar, namely potters who got burns from hot kiln shelves, cut their hands on fired glaze shards, or dropped hard bricks on their feet. All of these accidents could have been prevented by thinking through each process with the goal of self-protection. Once the risks are understood, taking adequate measures to protect yourself will ensure a safe workplace.

While not the first consideration upon entering a pottery studio, the choice of what to wear can add to the safety factor when working with clay. The commonly held belief that anything is good enough to wear is often true. In part the "comfortable clothing" approach is based on the low incidence of accidents caused by a wrong choice of clothing. However, a good safety record can be further improved by considering exactly what activities are involved in the entire process of forming, glazing, and firing clay, and then adjusting the clothing to fit the specific activity. Situational awareness (knowing where your body parts are in relation to moving objects or activities) also plays a large role in maintaining a safe studio. The idea behind the analysis of activity and appropriate clothing is to arrive at a "uniform" that will allow maximum safety while maintaining comfort for all ceramics studio operations.

Clay Mixing

The choice of correctly fitting clothing for working around clay mixing machines or pug mills will help prevent accidents. Loose or untied clothing could potentially become caught in the moving parts of equipment. Cotton clothing is comfortable but can catch clay dust and should be cleaned every day. Long hair should be pulled back or placed under a hat. Long sleeve shirts can get caught in the moving blades or gears of pug mills or clay mixers. Long pants, a tee shirt, socks, and sneakers for non-slip movement are a good choice for clay mixing operations. Do not wear watches, neckties, jewelry, or rings around clay mixing equipment. The need for non-skid shoes cannot be emphasized too much anytime clay mixing or clay pugging operations are taking place.

Glaze Mixing

When mixing any dry or wet glaze material, always wear the correct type of respirator. Contact lenses are not recommended, as dry materials can get trapped behind the lenses and cause irritation to the eyes. Eyeglasses should be cleaned daily. Clothing should be comfortable and easy to clean after a day's use in the studio. Pockets on shirts or decorative elements attract and hold clay and raw material powders. Simple, unencumbered, easy-to-clean clothing is best when mixing any glaze raw materials. Aprons can be used, as they can be cleaned on a regular basis, but keep in mind small particles of raw materials can and do cling to shirts, socks, shoes, and pants.

The scale is an important tool for weighing out dry glaze materials. It should be placed on a smooth level surface near the storage of glaze raw materials. A note pad should be available to indicate the amounts of material weighed when making a glaze.

Clay Forming Operations

Several pieces of equipment such as pottery wheels, clay extruders, slab rollers, jiggering wheels, and ram presses all present the possibility of catching a potter's clothing due to their moving parts. Care should be taken to remove any jewelry and to pull back loose hair to keep such things from being caught in any clay forming equipment. Another reason for removing any rings or watches is the slow but steady abrasion caused when moist clay contacts any jewelry. Clay can have hard grog particles or coarse materials that can wear down metals.

Open toe sandals or bare feet are comfortable on a cool studio floor but can easily cause a safety hazard, as the feet are not protected from moving flywheels and heavy equipment. Sneakers or non-skid shoes offer protection and traction in the potentially slippery ceramics studio. Some boots or shoes have cleats or deeply recessed ridges on the soles. Before leaving the studio, inspect the soles of your shoes to make sure that all moist clay has been removed. Frequently, potters walk out of their studios with clay stuck to their shoes and as the clay dries it shrinks, causing clumps of dry clay to be deposited in their cars and houses.

Kiln Loading & Firing Operations

Before loading a kiln, it is important to make sure the kiln shelves are free of fired glaze drips from previous firings. Glaze falling onto kiln shelves, or pots that have dripped glaze onto kiln shelves, often leave jagged sharp edges that can easily cut the hands. This task of removing such drips can be accomplished in part with safety glasses for eye protection and gloves for hand protection. Always wear protective eyeglasses or a face shield, as they will prevent sharp shards of glaze from hitting the face. For this particular task, it is also a good practice to wear a long sleeve shirt and a hat, as slivers of glaze can fly in any direction. After chipping the glaze drips off the shelves, all debris must be brushed or vacuumed from the floor.

Once the shelves are clean, another safety factor is the weight of kiln shelves and posts. Feet should be shielded by wearing heavy shoes or boots. Foot protection can prevent injury from dropped shelves or hard brick posts during the loading and unloading of the kiln. Potters who have had years of experience loading kilns are aware of how many times a post or shelf has slipped from their hands. In loading many types of electric kilns, the potter has to reach over the lid of the kiln to load kiln shelves or ware. It is sometimes necessary to build a sturdy step near the kiln to reduce back strain caused by bending over the kiln with heavy shelves.

Clothing should allow for unencumbered access to the interior of the kiln for loading and unloading pots, posts, and shelves. When unloading a kiln, the use of heat-resistant gloves should be considered, primarily to protect the hands and arms from the possibility of sharp fired glaze edges on pots and shelves. Potters have noticed blood on kiln shelves caused by a fired glaze surface that was so razor sharp, they didn't realize

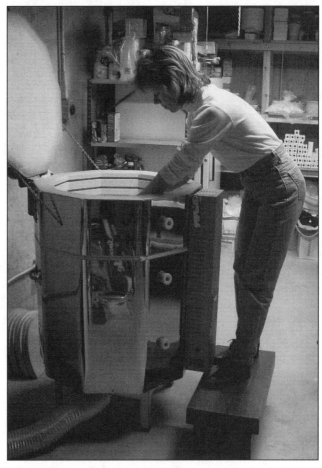

The motion of lifting a kiln shelf can cause back injury. To prevent back strain when stacking heavy shelves into an electric kiln, place a sturdy step near the kiln. This will allow the potter to life the shelves without twisting the body.

they had been cut. Unloading the kiln when it has cooled down is always safer for the potter and the pots. If the pots are too hot to touch with the bare hands, the kiln shelves will be hotter due to their increased mass. It is always a good practice to wait awhile; rushing the unloading process is not worth a painful burn on the hand or a dropped kiln shelf.

Studio Cleaning Procedures

Studio housecleaning is not as exciting as making pots or ceramic sculpture, but it contributes to a healthy and safe work environment. The choice of clothes should be based on shirts, pants, socks, shoes, etc. that can easily be cleaned daily. Shoes can be cleaned with a damp sponge after working in the studio. Synthetic clothing and blends of cotton, nylon, or rayon can melt when exposed to the high heat conditions found close to firing kilns. Furthermore, any item that has to be dry-cleaned is not the best choice, due to the expense of almost daily cleaning.

The processes of mixing clay, weighing out dry raw materials, and forming pots often

All raw materials should be stored in non-breakable containers with secure covers. Raw materials should be kept near the area where they will be used. Each container should be labeled with the name of the raw material. It can be frustrating and time consuming to search for a misplaced raw material. It can also be exasperating to identify a raw material that is not clearly labeled.

result in powdered raw materials and moist clay deposits on clothing, hair, shoes, and eyeglasses. The idea behind frequent clothing changes is to reduce the possibility of depositing ceramic material outside the studio and into eating and living areas. An effective safety plan is to shower and have a change of clothing ready after a day's work in the studio. Any clean up should be accompanied by the proper respirator to prevent inhalation of airborne ceramic materials and a review of potential studio risk factors.

Other Studio Equipment

The pottery shop can be equipped with high speed grinding wheels, drills, clay extruders, or heavy objects such as storage shelves filled with pots, wedging tables, bats, and raw material bags. Again, as stated, it is a good idea to remove any loose clothing or jewelry that can be caught in a pottery-related activity. Before using handheld power drills and mixing attachments, wear protective glasses to prevent any spraying when mixing glazes. Hands should be kept away from sharp moving blades during mixing and when cleaning the equipment.

Thinking through each step in the process of making pots with the goal of protecting yourself is a wise safety plan. Each activity—wheel throwing, slab building, clay mixing, kiln stacking, and kiln firing—can be broken down into segments and examined for its hazard potential to the potter. For example, ask yourself what specific steps are involved in mixing a batch of glaze.

- Wear clothes that can be easily cleaned, as dry raw materials float in the air and may land on any surface.

- Wear a respirator to protect yourself from airborne particles.

- Assemble and open dry raw material bags (each bag or container should be labeled with the material name, mesh size when available, and the manufacturer). An organized workspace prevents spills and raw material contamination. An exact label description of a raw material ensures the same material and mesh size when it's time to reorder.

- Lift raw material containers or bags correctly to prevent arm or back injury. Materials are often sold in 50 lb. bags. Do not try to lift the whole bag, but scoop out some of the material needed to mix the glaze batch.

- Weigh out raw materials in a clean well-lit workspace. Keep a paper and pencil ready to record the exact amounts of each material used in the glaze formula. Write down each raw material as it is placed into the glaze bucket, as this will prevent weigh-out mistakes.

- Consider the weight of the glaze containers (calculate the water weight of the glaze [1 gallon of water = 8.336 lbs.], the dry glaze material weight, and the weight of the glaze container). Liquid glazes in large containers can be difficult to lift, causing back pain or spillage.

- Once the wet glaze is in the container, plan how it will be mixed and sieved (any spills should be wet mopped up immediately to prevent slipping and the possibility of tracking glaze through the entire studio).

- After all the glazes are mixed, they should be covered, labeled, and stored near the glaze application area in the studio.

- Seal all raw material bags or containers, and return them to their assigned storage areas.

- Clean all clothing and shoes daily.

Have a Clothing Plan

Just as you would plan for the purchase of a potter's wheel or kiln, the suitable choices of clothing will be a critical part in any ceramics studio operation. Advancing in any craft or activity involves a deeper understanding of its sometimes-hidden parts. The idea behind making good pots or sculpture is not to have the materials, tools, equipment, or clothes get in the way of the creative process. It's hard enough making clay objects without imposing preventable barriers to the work cycle. We have all been wedging a ball of clay or throwing a pot on the wheel while trying to avert a shirtsleeve from falling down into the moist clay. It's a slight annoyance but the same situation around a clay mixing machine or a pug mill can turn into a serious accident. Note each time your clothing gets in the way of making pots or might create an unsafe situation in the ceramics studio, and then take steps to change or adjust the situation when it occurs. Do not put this off until the next day. The technique of identifying problems and making corrections will improve the overall quality of life in the studio and make it a safer place to work.

Making it Look Easy

There is great joy and wonder in seeing any expert perform his or her craft. One of the first observations is how easy it looks. What the casual observer does not see are the many hours of planning and care that precede every motion the craftsperson performs. Extra planning and thought behind each action can be accomplished at any level in ceramics. Whether it's the beginning student or the advanced professional, elimination of wasted effort allows the potter to make more pots. Cleaning up glaze spills resulting from a disorganized studio or healing from burns caused by unloading hot kiln shelves both take time and energy away from creating pots and sculpture. Ceramics activity involves many small bits and pieces—raw materials, moist clay, tools, equipment, kilns, etc.—to complete a finished object. It's the potter's responsibility, often unseen by others, to keep all parts of the process in safe useable order. The choices of suitable clothing and safety practices are important aspects in making it look easy. From a purely economic viewpoint, any accident can stop or limit the production of pots or sculpture.

Chapter 7

Respirators for the Studio Potter

Airborne Transmission

Before Choosing a Respirator – Keep the Studio Clean

Keep in mind that no individual respirator can filter 100% of the particles in the air, although the best can be 99.97% efficient. After reading such numbers you might think, "that's good enough for me." Well it is, but unless you plan to wear a respirator all the time you're in the studio, consider the importance of also keeping a clean studio. Several simple steps can be taken to lower the levels of micron size particles floating around the workplace. Remember particles on this scale cannot be seen by the naked eye, making them even more problematic, as the potter can often forget their potential hazard. Inhalation is the primary method of entry into the human body for ceramic raw materials. The overall goal should be to reduce your exposure per unit of time to any potential respiratory hazard. Potters should routinely carry out studio clean-up procedures. Obviously, if the studio has less clay or dry material dust in the environment, any respirator can be more effective. The major safety issue occurs after taking off the respirator while working in the studio. Simply stated, it is essential to keep the studio clean at all times.

Permissible Exposure Limits

Respirators or dust masks, as they are commonly called, are designed to filter out solids or vapors. Before choosing a respirator, make sure its filter is designed for your intended purpose. A respirator that filters out vapors will not be suitable for protection against solid particles. A Permissible Exposure Limit (PEL) is the level of airborne exposure where some means of protection is required to decrease the exposure of the potter. The level is set by OSHA. The PEL rating can be found on the Material Safety Data Sheet (MSDS), which can be obtained from the ceramic supplier or manufacturer. While this system of airborne exposure does quantify a level of contamination in the air, it is geared for industrial use in that air monitoring has to be employed to determine the exposure concentration in any given studio.

The air quality test is often out of the monetary reach of potters. In fact, there have been no reported cases of potters who have tested the PEL air quality limit in their studios. If potters had a permissible exposure limit for their studios as a reference point, they would be able to better utilize the MSDS. With this economic fact in mind, it is always best to use the highest rated respirator for the type of filtering needed anytime there is a doubt about the air quality in the workplace.

Permissible Exposure Limits for Potters

The air quality inside potters' studios would be an excellent area for a nationwide study. A professional potters organization or a nationally known college of ceramics could conduct such a research project. The monitoring and resources available would be within the reach of such institutions, and the results could be published for everyone's benefit. While each studio would offer different concentrations of particles, depending on the individual potter's housekeeping procedures, studio size, raw materials in use, studio air venting, kiln venting, and other variable factors, a baseline exposure level could be calculated. Potters would then have a better quantitative number to judge what is considered the national norm. At the very least, it would offer a starting point, which could be used to determine the average airborne exposure rate for potters' studios.

When to use a Respirator

The ceramics studio produces several situations where dry materials or vapors are deposited in the air or come in contact with studio equipment and furniture. Every individual situation requires the use of an approved respirator or venting system.

Dry Material Storage Areas—The use of an approved respirator is required.

All dry materials, clays, metallic coloring oxides, feldspars, stains, and other ceramic raw materials should be stored in clearly labeled non-leaking containers or plastic bags. The most efficient place for storage of dry materials is where they will not have to be moved far from their original location. For example, reaching into a bag of feldspar and carrying it across the room to use it in a glaze formula presents several potential safety issues. Carrying any dry material always increases the risk of loose material dropping to the floor and then being dispersed throughout the studio. It also brings up the issue of wasted motion when walking back and forth to gather raw materials, which can cause fatigue and mistakes.

One potter stored 50 lb. bags of glaze materials on the other side of their studio from the glaze mixing and weigh out area. He had to walk the entire length of the studio each time a raw material was needed for a glaze formula. As he was carrying the material, small amounts were dropped to the floor. This inappropriate placement of materials often caused him to forget the amount of raw material he weighed out for a glaze formula. When the glaze mixing area was moved next to the raw materials, the operation went faster, cleaner, and raw material weigh outs were accurate. In a well planned studio, the raw materials will be located near the glaze mixing area, with scales, sieves, and glaze buckets nearby.

Clay Mixing Area—The use of an approved respirator is required.

During clay mixing operations, dry clay, flint, feldspar, and other materials are emptied out into a central container and are then mixed with water. During the initial part of the procedure, powder is thrown into the surrounding air and eventually is carried by air currents throughout the studio in different concentrations. When water is added to the mix, more dry particles are released with the same result in dispersion. It is only when most of the dry materials are saturated with water, forming a plastic clay mass that the amount of dry materials released into the air is decreased. Clay mixing areas should be vented and cleaned of waste dry materials after using the clay mixer. The clay-mixing machine should be thoroughly cleaned, as dry clay in the machine can become airborne and release into the studio.

Reprocessing of Moist Clay—The use of an approved respirator is required.

Many potters reprocess scrap clay or dry clay trimmings. Both situations can lead to dry clay particles being deposited on the studio floor and other areas where they can then be moved about the room and inhaled. It is always safer to place dry trimmings and dry scrap clay into a water-filled container until they are needed for reprocessing. The central goal is to keep dry clay or dry raw materials from becoming airborne and inhaled. This can be accomplished by using a respirator when dust conditions are encountered and by proper studio ventilation. Ideally, the most effective situation occurs when both measures are used. Both the respirator (barrier system) and the air venting system (barrier and removal system) will reduce the airborne particles in the studio.

Glaze Mixing Area—The use of an approved respirator is required.

As in mixing dry clays to form a moist clay body, dry glaze materials have to be taken out of their package or storage containers, weighed out, and placed in a glaze container, after which water is added to the container. During the whole operation, dry glaze particles are released into the studio environment. After mixing several glazes, the surface of the glaze table can contain small particles of raw materials. A thorough wipe down of all surfaces and equipment has to be enacted after the glaze mixing operation to prevent airborne raw materials from being moved about the studio.

Glaze Application Area—The use of an approved respirator is optional, depending on the glazing operation.

Whether the glaze application method is brushing, spraying, or dipping, the primary concern for protection is reducing the amount of dry glaze particles in the air. It is recommended that a respirator be used when handling any dry glaze surface. Glaze spraying operations require an adequately vented spray booth and the use of a respirator to block any atomized particles of glaze from entering the lungs. Often potters will apply glaze to a bisque surface, and upon drying they will rub out any air bubbles or imperfections in the glaze. Rubbing the glaze can cause dry glaze flakes to be sent into the immediate glaze application area. A respirator should be worn when smoothing any dry glaze surface down with the fingers or rubbing tools.

Pottery Trimming Area—The use of an approved respirator is optional.

In terms of studio air quality, the best time to trim excess clay from pots or sculpture is when the clay is still in the moist "leather hard" condition. The clay particles are contained in the moisture content of the clay. Some potters will trim pots or sand the surfaces of "bone dry" pots to achieve a specific effect. This practice is not recommended, as it releases fine particles of dry clay, feldspar, flint, or any other ceramic material into the air and onto surrounding surfaces. Aside from the health and safety aspects of working on dry clay structures, this practice also has the potential to crack or chip the fragile clay body. However, in actual studio experience, some potters will work with bone dry clay, and under these conditions a respirator should be worn at all times and a thorough cleaning of the work area should follow.

Cleaning Kiln Shelves—The use of an approved respirator is required.

Periodically, kiln shelves and support posts have to be cleaned, due to the buildup of kiln wash. The kiln wash offers a refractory or heat resistant coating on the kiln shelf surface to protect it from possible glaze drips or a clay body fusing to the shelf during the firing. Kiln washes or coatings can be composed of various high temperature heat resistant raw materials, but many contain equal parts of kaolin clay (alumina and silica) and flint (silica). Removing excess kiln wash or glaze drips from shelves can involve the use of a chisel or portable grinding wheel. Both methods can release large amounts of kiln wash dust into the air. Alumina and silica found in kiln wash formulas should not be allowed to become airborne without the potter using a respirator. Scraping or grinding kiln shelves is an activity best done outdoors, with a respirator, or in a well-ventilated studio. Excess kiln wash dust should be cleaned from studio floors or worktables immediately upon completing the shelf grinding operation.

Studio Clean Up Procedures—The use of an approved respirator is required.

Every potter should devise a daily procedure for cleaning his or her workspace and studio. In situations such as schools or craft centers, the ceramics teacher should be responsible for setting up and maintaining the students' clean-up schedules. While it is unreasonable for the teacher to do all of the actual work of cleaning the studio, one person should be responsible for delegating the responsibility for this activity. Each studio workspace will require different clean-up procedures, depending on its size, amount of potters using the space, equipment, kilns, and physical layout of the studio. It is important to realize that areas under work tables and storage shelves can collect a fine layer of dry particles, which can get swept into the studio atmosphere by drafts of air. When cleaning the studio, use an oil-based sweeping compound to capture dry raw materials on the floor. Then a wet mop should be used on all floor surfaces in every work area. This double cleaning method will lower the percentages of dry particles thrown into the air during cleaning.

It is a safe practice to use a respirator anytime there is a raw material dust or vapor-producing technique used in the studio.

Dry Raw Materials—What Sizes Are We Talking About

At some point when sweeping out the studio, every potter asks himself or herself, "what should I do to protect myself from the clay dust?" Clay is a very small (hexagonal plate) particle size material, which can range from 100 microns to 0.1 microns, depending on the specific type of clay. A micron is 1/1000th of an inch. By comparison, human hair has a diameter of 5 to 60 microns, which is determined partly by the genetic characteristics of the individual. Potentially, the most hazardous particle sizes are below 10 microns. However, particles in the .3-micron range can zigzag through the filter, with some getting trapped and a percentage passing through the respirator. Larger size particles travel in a straight line and get trapped in the filter. The particles that are most respirable are less than 10 micrometers in diameter and can possibly be trapped in the lungs. Respirators are very effective at blocking particles but no respirator is 100% efficient at blocking 100% of particle sizes. The potter's goal should be to cut down inhalation of particles to safe levels.

To say that clay is composed of small particles doesn't completely illustrate the scale of this unique substance. For example, as stated earlier, 2.61 grams of kaolinite (clay) having a particle size of 0.01 microns could cover more than six thousand square feet of surface area if each clay platelet was placed end to end.[1] Imagine what's floating around in your studio when you're walking or sweeping up at the end of the day. On days when direct sunlight enters the studio, it's possible to see raw material or clay dust floating in the air. The stuff you can't see is of the micron or less particle size and can cause respiratory problems. A safe and conservative approach will go a long way in protecting you from airborne particles, visible and invisible. Luckily, this area of studio safety has been thoroughly researched by industry, and potters can take advantage of the latest array of respirators.

Respirator Filters

Every respirator has some type of filter to trap particles. In the past, some of the most effective filters have been HEPA (High Efficiency Particulate Air) filters. The HEPA Corporation developed them more than thirty years ago. The name has become generic, with many other companies producing this classification of filters. For many years, they have been the standard for the industry. The HEPA filter has a 99.97% efficiency rating, which means it filters 99.97% of solid particles down to a .3-micron size. Some particles at .3 microns do not have enough weight to go through the filter, while particles bigger than .3 microns have a larger mass, causing them to travel with greater velocity to the filter. HEPA type filters had been recommended whenever heavy metals, such as chrome, cadmium, vanadium, and cobalt were in the work environment. Such materials are typically found in glazes, as they contribute to glaze colors. Metallic oxides can also be found in clay bodies as a natural part of the clays or as an added coloring oxide. For example, iron oxide is added to clay bodies for a dark brown fired color. Metallic coloring oxides and their carbonate forms are also used for various colors in glazes and engobes or colored clay slips.

New Standards for Respirators

As of July 1998, NIOSH has instituted new standards for all respirators (Title 42 code of federal regulations parts 84 or 42 CFR 84). The new specifications for respirators are designed for higher levels of protection against particulate hazards in the workplace. All new respirator packaging will have a product code of 42 CFR 84 that will be conspicuous on the respirator box. Also listed will be a selection guide code of N = no oil in environment, R = oil resistant, or P = oil proof. Potters will need respirators labeled N95 (no oil and 95% efficient) or N100 (no oil and 99.97% efficient). When purchasing any respirator, look for the new NIOSH codes on the box and the instruction sheets.

---

[1] Cited in *Ceramic Science for the Potter* by W.G. Lawrence, Chilton/Haynes, 1972, p 39.

The National Institute of Occupational Safety and Health publishes a pocket guide that lists all raw materials and their permissible exposure levels. The 3M company also publishes a similar listing on raw materials, which is updated annually. Potters can use either guide to decide the safe levels of specific raw materials in their studios. If needed, the guides can be used to determine the type and efficiency level of respirator needed in the studio. However, if the potter wanted to pursue air quality to a much greater degree, the first step would be to hire an industrial hygienist. They would monitor the studio (est. cost for the test $100.00 to $180.00) to determine the level of particulate in the air. The information gathered from testing would then indicate the proper respirator type and filter.

Most pottery studios and commercial clay mixing operations will require an N95 respirator or an N100 respirator. The N95 and N100 are rated for protection against particles such as dry clay, dry glaze, and ceramic raw materials. There are other types of respirators, which filter out vapors. Both types are not interchangeable, and the potter must first determine which element in the studio has to be filtered. Listed are four respirators that will meet the NIOSH standards. These are just a few of the many available particle respirators that I field tested in my ceramics studio. They can also be purchased through your local ceramics supplier or any hardware store.

Willson Freedom 2000® Series respirator, Willson Valueair® Plus reusable respirator, 3M 8210 paper disposable respirator, 3M 8233 N100 paper disposable respirator.

All respirators are 42 CFR 84 approved by NIOSH.

Willson Freedom 2000 Series—"The No-Hassle Disposable Respirator"[2]

The distinctive feature of this lightweight respirator is the simple straightforward design and its lightweight feel on the face. It can be purchased in three face-piece sizes for an exact airtight fit on the face, which is a critical factor in any respirator design. The unit has an excellent P100 filter that is 99.97% effective in trapping particles down to .3 microns in size. This is the highest rating by NIOSH standards. The mask allows for eyewear and felt comfortable when I swept the studio or mixed dry glazes. However, the inability to replace the filter would be a major drawback if the potter were considering it for daily use in the studio. Replacing the entire mask and filter each time would be costly. To find your local distributor call Willson, (800) 345-4112. Retail price $18.55.

Willson Valuair Plus—"The Easy-Breathing, Economical Reusable Respirator"[3]

The P100 filter is 99.97% effective, which is the same as the Willson Freedom 2000 series mask. The ability to change the filter cartridges is a major benefit to this respirator. The obvious advantage being an easily replaceable filter that extends the service life of the unit. It also has a soft pliable face piece with adjustable straps to fit almost any face contour. From the first time I used it in my studio, it was very comfortable and there was low breathing resistance upon inhalation. Wearing eyeglasses will not prevent the mask from fitting your face. I would highly recommend the respirator for ceramics supply companies where extreme clay mixing operations take place every day. It can also function well in situations where there are heavy duty prolonged dry raw materials mixing in the studio. To find your local distributor call Willson, (800) 345-4112. Retail price $21.20.

3M 8210 and 3M 8110S N95 (smaller size)[4]

This respirator is commonly referred to as a paper dust mask (electrostatically charged micromedia fibers that allow airborne particles to be attracted and held in the filter) that is very lightweight and can be custom fit by a thin metal band on the upper part of the mask. Two elastic straps

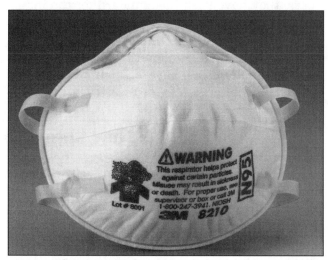

3M 8210

[2] Willson Division of WGM Safety Corporation, product information Form No. 9121C.
[3] Willson Division of WGM Safety Corporation, product information Form No. 9601.
[4] 3M Product information sheet #3044.

on each side of the mask hold it firmly against the face for an effective seal. I found the mask easy to use and lightweight on my face. The respirator was very comfortable when wearing glasses and, as an added benefit, had no parts to clean. It is priced low, which makes for reasonable replacement costs. Studies have proven this mask to be just as effective as rubber face piece respirators. I would buy a box of the respirators and replace them regularly (see next page, When to Change a Filter). It is rated at 95% filtration efficiency, which means the mask stopped 95% of the particles down to a .3-micron size. It can filter cobalt, copper, chrome, iron oxide, silica, and manganese. I would recommend the 3M 8210 and 3M 8110S N95 as low-cost effective respirators for dry materials encountered in the pottery studio. To find your local distributor call 3M, (800) 896-4223. Retail price $.78 cents, box of 20 $15.67.

3M 8233 N100[5]

This respirator is a paper dust mask (advanced electrostatically charged micromedia fibers) with a soft seal to conform to your face. It also has fully adjustable straps for a secure fit on the contours of the face. Also incorporated into the mask is a one-way "cool flow" valve, which makes breathing easier through the finer mesh filter. The respirator's efficiency is 99.97%, making it one of NIOSH's highest rated filters. OSHA recommends the respirator in situations where lead, cadmium, and arsenic are in the workplace. The respirator would function well when mixing dry glaze materials that contain cobalt, copper, chrome, iron oxide, silica, and manganese. The higher efficiency rating and high cost per mask is not required for protec-

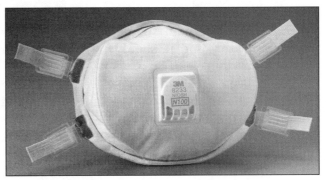

3M 8233 N100

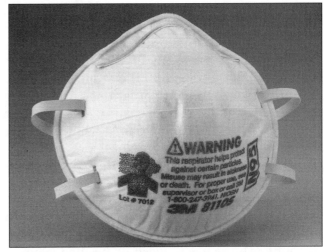

3M 8110S N95

tion against other ceramic raw materials. It could be used when sweeping up the pottery studio, or in ceramics supply companies' clay mixing operations, where exposure and concentration levels would presumably be higher than in an individual pottery studio. I would use this respirator only if lead, cadmium, or arsenic were present in the studio. To find your local distributor call 3M, (800) 896-4223. Retail price $6.03, box of 20 $120.69.

Respirator Fit

Fit is one of the most important considerations when choosing any respirator. Two factors are essential when placing a respirator on your face. A complete seal around the face is critical to keep secondary air from bypassing the filter. Simply make sure the mask conforms to your face so no outside air is drawn in when breathing. Men with beards must ensure that the mask forms an unbroken seal around their face; otherwise shaving the area is required. It

is especially important to obtain a secure fit with the paper dust masks, as they are held in place by thin rubber bands, which may not produce enough pressure against the face for a tight fit. The second factor is the comfort of the mask. If the particular mask is uncomfortable or heavy and it is not worn on the required occasions, it has offered no protection. If possible, potters should go to a ceramics supply store and try out several different styles of respirators to

---

[5.] 3M Product information sheet #3094.

ensure a comfortable useable fit. Every potter working in the studio should have his or her own respirator, and it should be stored in an easily accessible clean area.

The Willson Freedom 2000 series and Willson Valuair Plus respirators come with diagrams and instructions on how to wear the masks. Videos are also available to provide product information. The instructions on use and fit for the 3M 8210, 3M 8110S, and 3M 8233 N100 can be obtained from your local dealer or by calling the 3M technical service number, (800) 243-4630. Always read the instructions carefully on maintenance and the use of any respirator purchased, as there can be differences between each model and brand.

Respirators with higher efficiency (99.97% efficiency) filters can cause greater resistance when breathing, due to the use of finer filtering materials. High efficiency units have an exhalation valve in front to allow for easier breathing.

When to Change a Filter

The industry standard for changing filters occurs when any or all of the three Ds are encountered— Damage to the respirator, Dirty respirators, or Difficulty breathing through the respirator. While this measurement at first seems inexact, an explanation of what is taking place will explain the replacement strategy. During its use, as particles contact the respirator and penetrate below the outer surface of the filter, some filter holes are closed, causing a "caking" effect to occur. This causes the filter to become *more* effective in that an increased amount of holes are plugged up by the incoming particles. However, at some point, the heightened resistance needed to breathe causes unfiltered air to be drawn through the point of least resistance on the mask seal. Before this state is reached, the filter should be discarded. While this method might seem counterintuitive, meaning a dirty mask should be replaced immediately, the potter can apply whatever standard of replacement will serve his or her purpose. If the respirator or respirator filter is changed as soon as it appears dirty, or if the potter waits until there is too much resistance to breathe through it, it will not make a difference in the safety factor for capturing airborne particles. However, if the respirator becomes contaminated on the inside surface close to the face, it should be changed immediately.

Summary

All the respirators evaluated would exceed the respirator safety requirements of the studio potter. In addition, all of the units could be used in industrial applications where higher levels and longer exposure rates would be expected, as compared with an individual pottery studio or clay mixing operation. The higher efficiency units rated at 99.97% efficiency (Willson Freedom 2000, Willson Valuair Plus, and the 3M 8233 N100) would be very effective protection where lead or cadmium is present in the pottery studio. However, the 3M 8210 and 8110S N95 (smaller size) rated at 95% efficiency would also meet pottery studio requirements for safety.

Each respirator was comfortable and adaptable to fit my face, creating an effective seal. The 3M respirators, being only "paper like" fibers and elastic straps, were lighter in weight compared with the Willson respirators. Respirator cost is not a consideration when health and safety are involved, so deciding to purchase the lowest cost respirator was not a factor in the evaluation. For protection against airborne particles found in the pottery studio, the 3M 8210 and 3M 8110 S N95 respirators would be highly recommended. All the respirators tested would meet the requirements of potters, but the 3M respirators were lighter in weight, easily replaceable and comfortable. I do not think the 99.97% vs. 95% efficiency respirators would offer a much greater degree of protection for the materials found in pottery studios or commercial clay mixing operations. Keep in mind that there are other manufacturers of respirators that can fulfill the safety guidelines. It is the potter's responsibility to choose a respirator that will be safe, effective, and comfortable.

Willson Respirators
Dalloz Safety
2nd & Washington Streets
P.O. Box 622
Reading, PA 19603-0622
(610) 376-6161

3M Respirators
3M Occupational Health and
Environmental Safety Division
3M Center, Building 275-6W-01
P.O. Box 33275
St. Paul, MN 55133-3275
(800 896-4223

Chapter 8

Shielded Headgear, Eye & Face Protection

Several practices in the operation of a pottery studio require safety glasses or face shields. Both types of safety devices can prevent eye injury. The most potentially hazardous situations occur when scraping kiln wash or glaze drips off of kiln shelves. When using a chisel or any flat edge tool to remove kiln shelf debris, hard particles of glaze or kiln wash can cause cuts or other facial injures. Many potters use a high speed grinding wheel to remove glaze drips or rough surfaces from their pots. This becomes dangerous if hard projectiles are thrown off the spinning wheel, which can then hit soft body tissue. As an added safety measure, using some type of eye protection is advised for glaze mixing operations, since liquid glaze can spatter in all directions. Safety glasses offer eye protection but shielded headgear will give a greater degree of coverage for the entire face and neck. Either type of eye protection should be employed whenever there is a possible risk from liquid or solid flying objects. Most importantly, whether using safety glasses or shielded headgear, all safety equipment should be available in a central location within the studio. Even potters who strenuously believe in safe studios sometimes do not use safety equipment if it is not plainly in sight. The one time you do not use a safety device could be the accident waiting to happen.

The Wilson Headgear & Visor Set is only one of many eye and face protection systems offered by several companies that manufacture safety equipment for industry. Shielded headgear and safety glasses can also be purchased in hardware stores and ceramics supply companies throughout the United States and Canada. While safety glasses protect the eyes and are more comfortable than the shielded headgear, they do not offer adequate protection for the face and neck. I would recommend that, given a choice, potters purchase the full face and neck protection offered by the shielded headgear system.

Wilson Headgear & Visor Set

(Sheffield Pottery, Inc. Catalog # MR 25VNS Wilson Headgear & Visor Set)

Evaluation

At first, the Wilson Headgear & Visor felt a little top heavy, but after I adjusted the head strap it proved to be very comfortable. I have no doubt that any slight inconvenience of wearing the headgear and accompanying visor will be more than offset by the eye and face protection offered by this industrial quality safety equipment. The grading system for scratch resistance in visors includes poor, fair, good, and excellent ratings. The clear propionate visor has a rating of *good* for scratch resistance. The visor's resistance to scratch marks is an important value-added feature for a long service life. One potential defect of any visor or safety glasses is a lack of scratch resistance. The variety of substances within the pottery studio that can abrade or scratch *any* surface is considerable. Care must be taken to prevent any abrasive materials from contacting the safety glasses or face shields. Heavy scratches to the lenses make viewing more difficult, and the glasses are then less likely to be used in daily studio operations.

With the Wilson safety shield in place and wearing protective gloves, I used a high speed grinding wheel to smooth the bottom edges of fired pots. When I applied greater pressure against the grinding wheel, two 1/2" size chips flew off the pot. One landed about ten feet away and the other hit the bottom section of my face shield, bouncing off but causing no damage to the shield or my neck. After such "real life" testing, I would recommend the face and upper neck protection offered by the Wilson Headgear & Visor Set MR 25VNS. There are many situations within the ceramics studio that can cause flying debris—scraping fired glaze off a kiln shelf, scraping kiln wash off shelves, grinding glaze from the bottom of pots—all of which require that potters take precautions. Simply stated, if you work in the studio long enough, something will fly at high speed into your face, arms, legs, or body.

Wilson Headgear & Visor Set MR 25VNS Sheffield Pottery, Inc., U.S. Route 7, P.O. Box 399, Sheffield, MA 01257, (888) SPI-CLAY or (413) 229-7700. Catalog Item Code MR 25VNS price $24.99 + shipping.

All eye safety goggles and headgear shields should meet or exceed government OSHA/ANSI Z87.1 (Occupational Safety & Health Administration/American National Standards Institute) standards for eye protection. Look for the ANSI Z87.1-1989 label on the box, information/instruction page, or product. The label will ensure the safety device has been tested for impact and penetration resistance, corrosive factors, and optical clarity.

Eye protection from ceramic materials, whether in solid or liquid form, is easily assured by proper safety devices that have been tested and used by industry for years. This is one area where we as potters can benefit from big business' capital investment in safety. Government regulations have also prompted increased use of safety devices by industry, which potters can use when working with ceramic materials. Large industries have already done the research and implemented the eye safety tools such as infrared/ultraviolet protective glasses and face shields. As a whole, when working in any ceramics studio, there are some situations where eye protection is needed. Failing to use eye protection when required can place the potter in needless jeopardy. The percentage of potters who suffer eye damage, cuts, burns, or cataracts are extremely low, but if it happens to you, it's 100%.

Guidelines for Using Shielded Headgear and Safety Glasses

- Choose the whole face protection offered by a safety shield. It is better than the limited eye protection from safety glasses. The whole face protection devices will provide the additional coverage of the lower face and neck area.

- Keep eye safety shields or glasses in an easily accessible place. Common sense dictates that the easier it is to use a safety device the more use it will get in studio operations.

- Do not scratch the shield or safety glasses, as the best devices can easily be scratched by ceramic materials, tools, and mishandling.

- Always wear the eye or face shield when grinding or chipping fired glaze off of pots or kiln shelves. A respirator should also be used in any activity where dry particles are thrown into the air by the action of the grinding wheel. Grinding any fired surface by definition causes many small airborne particles, which can be thrown into the studio environment.

- Use safety glasses during the Raku firing process to prevent eye damage due to possible sparks or glaze shards coming off the pot.

- Use an eye shield in any activity where glaze liquids could splash into the face, as many glazes contain caustic ingredients, which can irritate unprotected eyes.

- Do not wear contact lenses in dry clay or dry glaze mixing operations. Clay or glaze particles can become trapped behind the contact lens, causing eye abrasions.

- To prevent brick chips or brick dust from entering the eyes, wear protective glasses when repairing or building kilns. During kiln building, small particles of soft or hard brick can become dislodged from the kiln. In any operation that creates brick dust from cutting bricks, a respirator should be used at all times.

Chapter 9

Eye Protection for the Studio Potter

Working with ceramic materials is not an inherently dangerous full time professional endeavor or part time amateur hobby. However, the pottery studio lends itself to a few potentially hazardous situations that can easily be avoided by using the proper safety equipment. A careful understanding of the principles involved in the multi-step process of making and firing pots will reveal several areas where eye protection is an essential part of ceramics. Fortunately, eye protection by special filter glasses or impact-resistant face shields has already been developed for use in several major manufacturing areas, such as foundries, steel mills, glass production, metal fabrication, and casting industries. In a practical way, potters can take advantage of an extensive range of safety products perfected for industry during the past twenty-five years. However, in actual practice, many safety devices, while available in the studio, are overlooked or used sporadically. There are many reasons for not using the proper eye protection glasses or, for that matter, any other devices that will protect the potter. In some instances, the equipment is not stored in a convenient location or the potter feels "just this once I don't need protection." One of the most often heard phrases after a studio accident is, "I didn't think it would happen to me." It is the potter's responsibility to incorporate all safety procedures and equipment whenever they are required by the task at hand. Just as it takes discipline to go into the studio and make pots, it takes discipline to apply the appropriate safety equipment.

Infrared/Ultraviolet Eye Protection

(IR and UV)

In the past, "glass blowers ailment" was a common eye problem among people who worked with hot glass. They were subjected to infrared and ultraviolet light when looking into high temperature molten glass tanks. After *years* of unprotected *high duration* exposure, the *cumulative* effect caused cataracts to develop in their eyes. Sometimes the exfoliation of the eye lens was a gradual process that went unrecognized until the damage was severe. Today, the causes of glass blowers' cataracts and the protective methods to prevent such eye damage have made this condition a historical curiosity.[1]

Both infrared and ultraviolet radiations are released during a kiln firing. Infrared radiation cannot be seen, as it is composed of wavelengths that are longer than visible light. Ultraviolet radiation is also invisible, consisting of shorter wavelengths than visible light. Both types of radiation are part of the electromagnetic spectrum, with visible light being just one segment of the entire range. The insidious characteristics of

---

[1] History of glass blowers' cataracts from an article by, B. Ralph Chou, "Optical Filters and Radiation Protection," published in *Eye Injury Prevention in Industry*, Second Edition, Edited by Edward McRace & Myrna Grimm, June 1994.

increasing cumulative damage and the invisibility of exposure were two factors that led the glass blowers into trouble over time. Learning from someone else's mistake is an inexpensive lesson as compared to having to endure an error personally. Simply stated, by using the proper kiln goggles or shaded glasses, potters can avoid potential long-term risk to their eyes. Many potters do not realize that they should be wearing the proper shade of eye protection, even at relatively low bisque firing temperatures (c/06—1830°F). As with the use of respirators for protection from airborne particles, eye protection should be used whenever looking into a firing kiln.

Listed are several safety devices that I have tested, along with my recommendations. When- ever choosing safety equipment, it is always best to try the equipment on before making a purchase. While a piece of safety equipment, such as glasses for protection against infrared/ultraviolet eye damage, will meet safety standards, it might not fit your face or feel comfortable in daily use. Always choose safety devices that can be used with comfort and reliability. There are many different manufacturers of protective eyewear and safety shield headgear available to potters throughout the United States and Canada. Manufacturers will offer various features with their products, however, the potter must make sure that all safety products adhere to or exceed government OSHA/ANSI Z87.1 standards.

Infrared/Ultraviolet Eye Protection Glasses

Cobalt Blue #5 Model MR 9140 glasses

Sheffield Pottery, Inc., U.S. Route 7, P.O. Box 399, Sheffield, MA 01257, (888) SPI-CLAY or (413) 229-7700. Catalog Item Code MR 9140. Price $43.99 + shipping.

The black frame Cobalt Blue #5 Model MR 9140 lenses filter out 70% of infrared light in the 780–2000 nanometer (unit of measurement, one billionth of a meter) ranges and 99.9% ultraviolet wavelength light. However, the polycarbonate lens has a darker tint than standard green shaded welding glasses. Green shaded welding glasses or goggles range from numbers 1.2 to 16, with the higher numbers offering greater degrees of protection against the infrared light spectrum.[2] At some point, a trade off has to be made, as higher shade numbers offer greater degrees of protection but viewing the pyrometric cones during the firing becomes more difficult due to increased light being blocked by the filter.

The cobalt blue #5 lens is rated on a different scale and does not correspond to the green shaded welding glasses #5. While this dual num- bering system might be confusing, overall the Cobalt Blue #5 Model MR 9140 glasses have an advantage over green shaded welding glasses #5, as they filter out a greater amount of the infrared light spectrum. As stated, higher filter levels result in higher degrees of eye protection. The important point being the Cobalt Blue #5 Model MR 9140 glasses offer eye protection up to 2700°F or approximately c/17, well above the temperatures reached by most potters. This model also meets or exceeds several industry standards for eye protection encountered in infrared and ultraviolet light conditions.[3]

I found the Cobalt Blue #5 Model MR 9140 glasses comfortable to wear with a flip up shade that reveals a set of clear lenses. This feature could be useful if the potter does not already wear glasses for vision correction. The glasses also have side shields that are an added eye protection safety feature. In actual practice, potters report problems when using dark colored glasses for infrared/ultraviolet eye protection. The lens is very dark and cuts out so much visible light to the eye that viewing the pyro-

---

[2] *Eye Injury Prevention in Industry*, Second Edition, Edited by Edward Mc Race & Myrna Grimm, June, 1994, Table 3, Transmission Specification for Filters, page 22.

[3] Cobalt Blue #5 Model MR 9140 glasses meet the standards for: ANSI Z87.1-1989 Standard ANSI, 11 West 42nd Street, New York, NY 10036, (212) 642-4980, www.ANSI.ORG.

Besides the ANSI requirements, another standard for infrared/ultraviolet eye protection is available from ASTM (American Society for Testing and Materials). For example, ASTM standards require: "Dark-shaded glasses from a safety supply house (shade number *1.7* to *3.0*) are recommended when looking into kiln peepholes . . ." From the 1999 Annual Book of ASTM Standards, Vol. 15.02, Designation: C 1023 Section X2.41, page 321. American Society for Testing and Materials, 100 Barr Harbor Dr., West Conshohocken, PA 19428-2959, (610) 832-9500, fax (610) 832-9555, www.astm.org.

CSA (Canadian Standards Association), 178 Rex Dale Boulevard, 80 B COKE, M9W1R3, Ontario, Canada, (416) 247-4000, (800) 463-6727, www.csa.ca/about_csa /index_loca.html.

metric cones clearly during the firing is difficult. When looking into the kiln with the Cobalt Blue #5 Model MR 9140 glasses, it was harder to see the pyrometric cones during the firing as compared with green shaded welders glasses.[4] There are however a few procedures to obtain better cone viewing while wearing the glasses.[5] While the Model MR 9140 glasses are more expensive than most other products of similar type, the extra protection was worth any price. Purchasing safety devices and implementing safety procedures are not areas to cut costs; specifically, potters should use eye protection at every appropriate opportunity.

When considering other infrared/ultraviolet eye protection glasses or goggles, make sure the product meets the ANSI standards. Always look for the ANSI Z87.1-1989 label on the glasses, instruction sheet, or box. However, note the ANSI set of standards for protective eyewear are extensive and some products with the ANSI Z87.1-1989 label might not be suitable for infrared/ultraviolet light protection. Therefore, look for a green shade designation of #5 or above.

The effects of infrared and ultraviolet light damage to the eyes are cumulative. Glass blowers were required to stare into a hot glass tank every day over a period of years. Eventually, because of prolonged unprotected exposure, they developed cataracts from the invisible radiation. The process of firing a pottery kiln contains the same elements of exposure to invisible radiation, but the duration of each exposure and cumulative rates of exposure are considerably less. Potters look into a firing kiln for seconds at a time. However, they should protect themselves from infrared and ultraviolet radiation despite short duration exposures, since the alternative of not using kiln glasses can result in potentially serious eye damage over a period of time. It's just not worth the risk, since wearing the proper eye protection can easily eliminate this hazard.

Guidelines for Using Infrared/ Ultraviolet Eye Protection Glasses

- Keep glasses clean and in a safe easily-accessible place.
- Do not scratch the lenses.
- *Always* wear glasses when looking into a firing kiln (bisque firing, Raku firing, or glaze firing).
- Keep a safe distance from the cone-viewing hole when using glasses. All types of firing kilns—electric, gas, wood, oil, Raku—create backpressure during firing. When viewing cones, the backpressure of flame and/or heat can extend a few inches or several feet from the open cone-viewing hole.

- Do not use regular sunglasses, as they will not offer safe levels of protection against infrared and ultraviolet light from the kiln. While sunglasses do shade sunlight, they are not designed to block the higher levels of infrared/ultraviolet light emitted from a kiln.

- Wear infrared/ultraviolet eye protection when doing any welding in the ceramics studio.

[4.] Cobalt Blue #5 glasses are rated at 0.2% VLT or visual light transmission, while green shaded #5 welders glasses are rated at 2% VLT. The lower VLT percentage, the less visible light that can be seen through the glasses. Cobalt Blue #5 Model #9140 glasses are a darker shade than most other kiln viewing glasses, causing the pyrometric cones to become less visible during the kiln firing. When loading the kiln, paint a kiln wash of flint and water onto a K-23 or G-23 soft brick and place the brick behind the pyrometric cones. The white background of the soft brick will offer a contrast to the cones during the firing.

[5.] Red iron oxide can be painted in vertical or horizontal stripes onto the soft brick, resulting in a contrasting background pattern for viewing the cones. Do not paint the cones with iron oxide or any contrasting coloring oxide, as it will interfere with the melting properties of the cone.

Horizontal or vertical 1/4" grooves can be cut into the soft brick, which will also offer a contrasting background pattern for viewing the cones.

Often shining a flashlight into the kiln will increase the visibility of the cones during the firing.

A different method of observing pyrometric cones during the firing is to carefully remove the cone-viewing plug and blow into the hole from a safe distance. Always wear protective heat resistant kiln gloves. Remember the backpressure gases and flame from the cone viewing port can easily cause burns to the face and eyes. If done correctly and safely, for a few seconds the cones will cool off leaving a dark outline of their shape, allowing for improved viewing.

I have included the following report by Edouard Bastarache M.D. (Occupational & Environmental Medicine) as an illustrative example of the in-depth information potters need in every area of health and safety. Please note the conclusion, as it offers specific information on the potential for eye injuries to potters due to radiation. I will not comment on the conclusion of the report but will let potters draw their own deductions from the analysis of the available medical information. The significant point being that many preconceived ideas on the possible dangers to potters must be thoroughly researched in order to concentrate our energies on the appropriate safety procedures for every aspect of working with ceramic materials in the pottery studio.

Eye Injuries Due to Radiation

1-Injuries Due to Ionizing Radiation:

X-rays, beta rays, and other radiation sources in adequate doses can cause ocular injury.

A. Lids:

The eyelid is particularly vulnerable to x-ray damage because of the thinness of its skin. Loss of lashes and scarring can lead to inversion or eversion (entropion or ectropion) of the lid margins and prevent adequate closure.

B. Conjunctiva:

Scarring of the conjunctiva can impair the production of mucus and the function of the lacrymal gland ducts, thereby causing dryness of the eyes.

C. Lens:

X-ray radiation in a dose of 500–800R directed toward the lens surface can cause cataracts, sometimes with a delay of several months to a year before the opacities appear.

2-Injuries Due to Ultraviolet Radiation:

A. Cornea:

Ultraviolet radiation of wavelengths shorter than 300nm (actinic rays) can damage the corneal epithelium. This is most commonly the result of exposure to the sun at high altitude and in areas where shorter wavelengths are readily reflected from bright surfaces such as snow, water, and sand. Exposure to radiation generated by a welding arc can cause welding flash burn, a form of keratitis.

B. Lens:

Wavelengths of 300–400nm are transmitted through the cornea, and 80% are absorbed by the lens, where they can cause cataractous changes. Epidemiological studies suggest that exposure to solar radiation in these wavelengths near the equator is correlated with a higher incidence of cataracts. They also indicate that workers exposed to bright sunlight in occupations such as farming, truck driving, and construction work appear to have a higher incidence of cataracts than those who work primarily indoors. Experimental studies have shown that these wavelengths cause changes in the lens protein, which leads to cataract formation in animals.

3-Injuries Due to Visible Radiation (Light):

Visible light has a spectrum of 400–750nm. If the wavelengths of this spectrum penetrate fully to the retina, they can cause thermal, mechanical, or photic injuries.

A. Thermal injuries:

They are produced by light intense enough to increase the temperature in the retina by 10–20°C. Lasers used in therapy can cause this type of injury. The retinal pigment absorbs the light epithelium, where its energy is converted to heat, and the heat causes photocoagulation of retinal tissue.

B. Mechanical injuries:

They can be produced by exposure to laser energy from a Q-switched or mode-locked laser, which produces sonic shock waves that disrupt retinal tissue.

C. Photic injuries:

They are caused by prolonged exposure to intense light, which produces varying degrees of cellular damage in the retinal macula, without a significant increase in the temperature of the tissue. Sun gazing is the most common cause of this type of injury, but prolonged unprotected exposure to a welding arc can also damage the retinal macula. There may be a permanent decrease in visual acuity. The intensity of light, length of exposure, and age are all important factors. The older ones are more sensitive, also those who have had cataract surgery because filtration of light by the lens is impaired.

4-Injuries Due to Infrared Radiation:

Potters may be exposed to this type of radiation.

Wavelengths greater than 750nm in the infrared spectrum can produce lens changes. La "cataracte des verriers" (glass blower's cataract) is an example of a heat injury that damages the anterior lens capsule among *unprotected artists*. Denser cataractous changes can occur in *unprotected* workers who observe glowing masses of glass or iron for *many hours a day*.

Another important factor is the *distance* between the worker and the source of radiation. In the case of arc welding, infrared radiation decreases rapidly as a function of distance, so that farther than 3 feet away from where welding takes place, it does not pose an ocular hazard anymore, but ultraviolet radiation still does. That is why welders wear tinted glasses and surrounding workers only have to wear clear ones.

Conclusion:

When we speak of *type of exposure,* potters look at their cone packs for very short periods of time in a repeated way, more often nearing the end of firing; and also according to the use of other methods for measuring temperature, like the concomitant use of a thermocouple and a reading device.

So, these *short-term* exposures, usually of a few seconds, are spaced by quite longer expo-sure-free periods, and the sum of the former does not correlate with the concept of *many hours a day*.

We have searched the literature pertaining to Occupational Health and Safety and have not found a single case of presumed *ceramicist's or potter's cataract*, even if the trade of potter is quite older than the one of glass blower.

Therefore, we do not think that any of the above types of radiation present a threat to potters.

It is a good thing, mainly at high temperature, to wear lightly tinted industrial grade safety glasses to better visualize cones (ocular ergonomics) and also to reassure those who are more worried.

These glasses also offer a better protection than typical sunglasses in case of projection of hot dust particles from a gas kiln when looking through the peephole in a soft brick door.

By the way, with aging, most, if not all of us, will suffer from cataracts of the *senile* type. The progress or change and the related reduction in vision are usually quite slow. Nuclear sclerosis—an increasing density in the central mass of protein—causes a myopic change that can be corrected by changing glasses for some years, in many instances, restoring vision to near normal.

Edouard Bastarache M.D.
(Occupational & Environmental Medicine)
Author of "Substitutions for Raw Ceramic Materials"
edouardb@sorel-tracy.qc.ca
http://www.sorel-tracy.qc.ca/~edouardb/

References:
Occupational & Environmental Medicine,
Joseph Ladoue & *al,* last edition.
Occupational Medicine, Zenz C., last edition.
Précis de Médecine du Travail, Desoille H., Scherrer J.,
Truhaut R., last edition. Oshline & Nioshtic
database.

Chapter 10

How to Read and Understand Material Safety Data Sheets

(MSDS Sheets)

In order to understand and eventually protect yourself, it is critical to know specifically about each raw material or product that enters the studio. A potter's education can come from many sources: books, product information sheets produced by mines, ceramics suppliers, equipment manufacturers, raw material processing plants, and experiential knowledge with a specific material or product. Without this knowledge, the potter and people who come in contact with the potter where he or she works, or the products the potter produces, are subject to potential health and safety problems. Ignorance of raw materials can be dangerous at most; at least it reveals a lack of honesty and integrity in pursuing one's craft.

One basic source of information is the MSDS, which contains several important characteristics of a raw material that the potter may come in contact with when working with clay or glazes. MSDS sheets contain a number of pieces of information regarding potentially hazardous materials used in the workplace. The information is divided into several sections (see example); information that cannot fit onto the sheet must be covered on a separate addendum section. Blank spaces on the sheet are not permitted. If any piece of information is not available from the manufacturer or mine, this must be

indicated by the word "unknown" or "unk." If the information does not apply to the material product under consideration, the letters "NA" (not applicable) should be inserted.

The MSDS sheets are prepared by the chemical manufacturers or mines that produce the materials. They must provide facts about the substances within a product along with how to handle the material safely; also listed will be first aid procedures and clean up measures to be taken if a spill or dispersion occurs. Distributors such as ceramics suppliers are required to issue a MSDS sheet with every material they sell to potters. Employers are also required to have MSDS sheets for the material they use in the production of their products, which must be available to their employees.

If chemical manufacturers become aware of a new hazard regarding the material, or ways to protect people that come in contact with the material, the MSDS sheet must be updated within three months. Potters can obtain MSDS sheets on the clays, feldspars, metallic coloring oxides, stains, and other ceramic raw materials they use in developing clay bodies and glazes. MSDS sheets are required to be on file for every raw material sold at ceramic supply stores. Potters should obtain an MSDS sheet for every raw material used in their studios. They can then use the guidelines listed to ensure a thorough knowledge of the material and the appropriate handling procedures for that material. Specifically, in the case of raw materials, knowledge is power. It gives potters a useful and needed tool to protect themselves and people who work in their studios. Always keep the MSDS information in a central easy-to-access location in the studio.

MSDS sheets must be in written in English and include the following information:

- The name of the chemical used on the container or bag label
- The specific chemical name and common names for the hazardous ingredients
- Physical and chemical characteristics of the material
- Physical hazards involved in handling the material
- Health hazards
- Primary route(s) of entry into the body
- OSHA, PEL, American Conference of Governmental Industrial Hygienists (ACGIH), Threshold Limit Value (TLV), and any other exposure limit
- Whether the chemical is listed as a confirmed or potential carcinogen by National Toxicology Program (NTP), International Agency for Research on Cancer (IARC), and/or OSHA
- Applicable precautions for safe handling and use
- Applicable control measures
- Emergency and first aid procedures
- Date of preparation or latest revision
- Name, address and telephone number of manufacturer, importer or other responsible party

---

PACER CORPORATION

MATERIAL SAFETY DATA SHEET

Date Issued: January 13, 1998

SECTION I: IDENTIFICATION OF PRODUCT AND PRODUCER

Producer: PACER CORPORATION P.O. Box 912, 35 S. 6th Street Custer, SD 57730	Telephone Numbers: 605-673-4419 7 am - 5 pm MST M-F FAX: 605-673-4459	Product Name: CUSTER FELDSPAR - 325 Mesh

Chemical Name: Feldspar CAS #68476-25-5

SECTION II: HAZARDOUS INGREDIENTS

Free Silica (Crystalline Quartz), Formula: SiO_2, Typically 3-10%, Respirable Silica 0.664%, CAS No. 14808-60-7
Feldspar is a naturally occurring inorganic, igneous rock. Formula: $K_2O \cdot Al_2O_3 \cdot 6SiO_2$

SECTION III: PHYSICAL DATA

APPEARANCE AND ODOR White and Odorless	SOLUBILITY IN WATER: Negligible	VAPOR PRESSURE N/A
BOILING POINT N/A	SPECIFIC GRAVITY 2.63	MELTING POINT 1450 C
PERCENT VOLATILE N/A		

SECTION IV: FIRE AND EXPLOSION HAZARD DATA

FLASH POINT Non Flammable Non Explosive	UNUSUAL FIRE & EXPLOSION HAZARDS N/A	FLAMMABLE (EXPLOSIVE) LIMITS (PERCENT BY VOLUME)
		Lower Limit: N/A Upper Limit: N/A
SPECIAL FIRE FIGHTING PROCEDURES None	FIRE EXTINGUISHING MEDIA N/A	

SECTION V: HEALTH HAZARD INFORMATION

HAZARD BY ROUTES OF EXPOSURE:

INHALATION: WARNING: Feldspar is not listed as a carcinogen by the International Agency for Research on Cancer (IARC), the National toxicology Program (NTP) or the Occupational Safety and Health Administration (OSHA). In October, 1996, an IARC working group re-assessing crystalline silica, a component of this product, designated crystalline silica as a Group 1 carcinogenic. The NTP indicates that crystalline silica is reasonably anticipated to be a Group 2 carcinogen. These classifications are based on sufficient evidence of carcinogenicity in certain experimental animals and on selected epidemiological studies of workers exposed to crystalline silica. These studies only rarely, however, include data on smoking, potential confounding exposures, and assurance of the comparability of referent population. Repeated prolonged inhalation of dust may cause delayed lung injury which may result in silicosis or pneumoconiosis.

INGESTION: Nausea may result from accidental ingestion.	EYE: Inflammation of eye tissue may occur from overexposure	SKIN CONTACT/ABSORPTION: Inflammation from contract with open cuts may occur.

SIGNS AND SYMPTOMS OF EXPOSURE:
Short term: Shortness of breath, coughing associated with inhalation of dust.
Long term: Steady and prolonged exposure to dust concentrations higher than TLV without approved respirator could cause silicosis, a chronic disease of the lungs marked by acute fibrosis, may cause cancer based on animal data.

EMERGENCY/FIRST AID PROCEDURES:
INHALATION/INGESTION: Consult physician and/or obtain competent medical assistance.
EYE CONTACT: Flush with water, consult physician and/or obtain competent medical assistance.
SKIN CONTACT: Wash thoroughly with water.

SECTION VI: REACTIVITY DATA

GENERAL REACTIVITY: N/A	INCOMPATIBILITY (Materials to Avoid) N/A
HAZARDOUS POLYMERIZATION: N/A	STABILITY: Feldspar is a stable material under ordinary conditions.

SECTION VII: PROCEDURES DISPOSAL REQUIREMENTS

STEPS TO BE TAKEN IN CASE MATERIAL IS RELEASED OR SPILLED:
Material is not dangerous if spilled. Wash away with water or vacuum with high efficiency (HEPPA) filter. If uncontaminated, recover and reuse. If contaminated, collect in suitable containers for disposal. Avoid creating dust. Avoid breathing dust. Wear a NIOSH/MSHA/OSHA approved respirator. Good housekeeping practices recommended.

WASTE AND CONTAINER DISPOSAL METHODS:
Disposal methods for non-hazardous materials should be complied with. May be buried in approved land disposal facility in accordance with Federal, State, and local regulations. Feldspar is not a hazardous waste under RCRA (40 CFR Part 261). Feldspar is not regulated by DOT.

SECTION VIII: SPECIAL PROTECTION INFORMATION

EYE PROTECTION: Safety glasses optional but recommended.	PROTECTIVE GLOVES: Optional, but recommended.

RESPIRATORY PROTECTION:
NIOSH/MSHA/OSHA approved respirator selection procedures. NIOSH approved dust mask.

VENTILATION:
Local exhaust required for dust removal. Refer to OSHA 1910.24, ASTM, and/or ANSI Standards. Do not exceed OSHA PEL or ACGIH TLV.

SECTION IX. SPECIAL REQUIREMENTS/PRECAUTIONS

STORAGE REQUIREMENTS:
Store in dry area. Do not breathe dust. Avoid creating dust in closed areas. Use adequate ventilation as recommended by NIOSH/MSHA/OSHA for crystalline silica.

The information contained herein is believed to be accurate, but Pacer Corporation makes no warranty with respect there to and disclaims responsibility for reliance thereon. This information applies only to the specific material described herein, and does not relate to use in connection with any other materials or in any process.

The Pacer Corporation makes no warranties, express or implied, concerning this product. No warranty of fitness for any particular purpose is made and we assume no responsibility whatever for any use of this product. This product should be used by properly trained personnel in compliance with applicable health and safety laws and regulations.

Reading and Understanding the Material Safety Data Sheet

The amount of information derived from each section of the MSDS sheet will in part depend on the specific raw material listed (i.e. Custer feldspar, iron oxide, cobalt oxide, dolomite, whiting, etc.) and the accuracy of information supplied by the manufacturer or mine. For example, the following MSDS sheet is for Custer feldspar, a potash feldspar widely used in clay bodies and glazes. *The explanation for each section appears in italics.*

Section I: Identification of Product and Producer

Chemical Identification

The initial section of the Material Safety Data Sheet lists the chemical manufacturer's name, address, emergency phone number, chemical name, chemical formula, and trade name.

When purchasing small amounts of a material (less than the original 50 lb. bag) from ceramics suppliers, the material is usually packaged in plastic or paper bags marked with the material name and safety information. The bags do not indicate any information on where the material originated. However, upon request the ceramics supplier has to supply the MSDS for each raw material that is repackaged and raw materials that are sold in their original package. The name and address of the original supplier will be listed on the MSDS. This is useful information and should be noted for future reference. When reordering the raw material, specify the material name and the original source supplier of the raw material; in this way, consistency of the material can be assured. In some situations, a ceramic supplier will change its source supplier of a raw material, which can lead to technical problems if the mesh size and chemical composition of the new material does not match the original material.

Producer

Pacer Corporation, P.O. Box 912, 35 S. 6th Street, Custer, SD 57730

Telephone Numbers

605-673-4419, 7 am—5 pm MST M-F, Fax 605-673-4459

The company phone numbers and fax numbers are also listed, as well as the days and times when an operator is available. If there is a question about the material, the potter can call or fax these numbers. Ask for a technical sales person to obtain any information you might need about the product. In some instances, the company will be able to send a free trial sample of their product for evaluation by the potter.

Product Name

Custer feldspar—325 mesh

The product name and its mesh size are useful information. In this case, 325 mesh Custer feldspar is the correct mesh size to use in glaze formulas. To ensure consistency, the same mesh size of Custer feldspar should be used for subsequent orders.

Chemical Name

Feldspar CAS #68476-25-5

The CAS number (Chemical Abstracts Service) Registry Number is a division of the American Chemical Society. It is a standard code that will identify a chemical substance. The number helps identify the vast number of chemical substances in use today. The society has compiled the largest database of chemical information. It has over 18 million document records from the chemical journal and patent literature. Occupational Safety and Health Administration does not require a CAS number on the MSDS sheets. However, suppliers of information to the MSDS sheets are allowed to add additional information such as CAS numbers.

Section II: Hazardous Ingredients

Free Silica (Crystalline Quartz), Formula: SiO_2, Typically 3–10%, Respirable Silica 0.664%, CAS No. 14808-60-7; Feldspar is a naturally occurring inorganic, igneous rock. Formula: K_2O Al_2O_3, 6 SiO_2

This section lists any dangerous characteristics or compounds of the chemical that can present a health or safety problem. Threshold Limit Values (TLV) and Permissible Exposure Limit (PEL) values can be listed in this section.

Taking Hints from Other Safe Studios

A well-organized and safe studio producing functional pottery or ceramic sculpture is an amalgamation of financial resources, physical space, studio location, and the potter's individual requirements. It is always a good idea, whether building your own or revising an existing studio, to incorporate the useful ideas of other potters' studios. Often the placement of equipment and supplies in other studios will offer ideas on how to accomplish an efficient placement within a new workspace. When possible, try to visit other studios and observe how the clay and glaze storage areas are positioned within the space. When surveying other studio situations, ask yourself these questions:

• Is the studio set up to reduce the amount of wasted movement when working with clay and glazes?
• Do the lighting fixtures add to a safe working environment?
• Are the appropriate safety devices in place and easily assessible?
• Is the kiln properly vented to eliminate fumes from the studio?
• Can the working spaces be easily cleaned after daily use?

It is essential to determine beforehand how the whole process of forming, glazing, and firing will function within a given space. Frequently the storage of tools and supplies is relegated to valuable floor space. Vertical storage space or wall space is often overlooked or underutilized. The common sense placement of equipment and supplies plays an important part in any studio set up.

Before building or revising a workspace, mentally figure out the flow of work through the studio. For example, if moist clay is purchased from a ceramic supplier, where is it delivered in the studio? Lifting 50 lb. boxes of moist clay many times from one location to another becomes physically and mentally tiring. It also increases fatigue and decreases the safety factor when working in the studio. Many potters have clay delivered near their wedging table, which should be placed close to the potter's wheel or handbuilding table. The sequence of moving clay from its bulk moist state to the fired pottery should be logically and carefully planned to reduce workload and stress. If properly planned, a safe studio does not have to be expensive to construct or maintain.

Potter's wheels should be located in a well-ventilated area. The height of the wheel head (see the aluminum head in the photo) should be at the same level as the seat of the chair. The level alignment will prevent back strain as upper body leverage and not total muscle power can be brought to bear on the moist clay during centering.

Sinks that are not adapted for the filtering of clay waste can use a bucket placed in the bottom of the sink to catch clay, glaze, and raw material debris before they enter the drain and sewage system. The heavier waste raw material sinks to the bottom of the bucket and can be cleaned out periodically.

Individual Studio

Connie Baugh, a professional potter has incorporated many health and safety features into her studio. Connie took the time before studio construction to carefully review and amend the floor plan of her workspaces. Each segment in the process of making and firing pottery has been planned with the goal of reducing unnecessary labor and fatigue.

The following are a series of photographs taken at Connie's studio, which will offer potters some ideas for the set up of their own work areas The Massachusetts College of Art has

An old barn converted into a pottery studio, the first floor contains the kiln room, wheel/handbuilding areas, raw material room, and storage shed. Each room can be cleaned separately for efficient use of the workspace. The second floor contains the pottery office and show room for finished ware.

Large sliding doors open, allowing maximum natural light into the main clay forming areas. The large sliding doors also allow for easy entry of equipment into the studio and the removal of finished pottery from the studio.

Storage shelves for green ware and the sink are positioned for natural and fluorescent lighting. A well-lit studio lessens the risk of slipping and falling, while also reducing eyestrain when working.

Wheel throwing areas are located near natural light, with tools placed within reach of the potter's wheel. Easy access to tools when working on the potter's wheel is an energy-saving measure.

A glaze storage area is used for stains with five-gallon glaze containers stockpiled under the worktable. Raw materials should be stored in sealed containers and properly labeled. Worktable surfaces should be non-absorbent and easily cleaned after dry and wet spills.

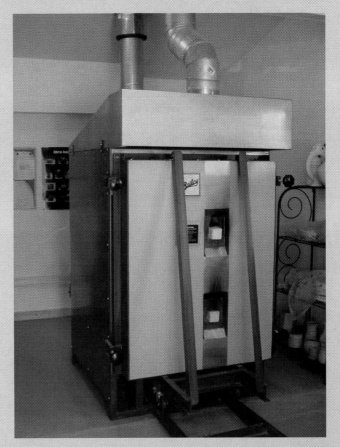

The propane-fueled gas kiln is placed in the rear of the pottery studio. Space around the kiln should be kept clear so the potter can inspect the kiln from all sides during the firing. All items must be removed from the floor around the kiln. It is common during a firing for a potter's attention to be directed only at the kiln, and an unsafe condition can exist if tools or supplies are left on the floor near the kiln.

A slab roller is conveniently located next to the wedging table, with moist clay stored under the table. Keeping the moist clay near the delivery door and under the wedging table prevents wasted motion when moving heavy clay around the studio. Potters should try to keep a logical and efficient progression of materials and supplies in the clay forming and firing process.

Glaze materials are neatly stacked near the glaze-mixing table. The table's stainless steel surface can be easily cleaned. It also serves a double function, as large quantities of raw materials are stored underneath for future use in glazes. Natural light enters the studio from two sources, which lessens eyestrain and helps visibility in clean-up operations.

The glaze mixing room has storage shelves for slip casting molds, with five-gallon wet glaze storage containers located under the worktable. Every space in the studio must be utilized, with tools and supplies placed in logical easy-to-find locations.

Five-gallon glaze storage containers on movable dollies help reduce heavy lifting, while enabling the glazes to be moved about the studio. The glaze container dolly should be constructed with heavy-duty wheels, and a sturdy base for the dolly. Lids on containers should fit tightly to prevent glaze spills. It is always easier to prevent spills than to waste time and energy cleaning up glaze room accidents.

Plaster mold storage shelves. Plaster slip casting molds can be heavy and should be stored in accessible locations to reduce the possibility of arm and back injury when moving molds around the studio.

A glaze spray booth is located near a portable ware cart. The air compressor, which powers the spray gun, is located under the spray booth. A small electric test kiln is located to the left of the spray booth. The ware can be spray glazed and placed on the ware cart and then loaded into the test kiln with a minimum of movement. The spray booth has a particle filter that captures excess atomized glaze. The spray booth fan also draws exhaust out of the studio.

The wheel throwing areas are located near a source of natural light. Artificial light is placed overhead to reduce shadows. Poor lighting conditions can eventually cause eyestrain. Tools are placed neatly and within reach to the left of the wheel. Plaster throwing bats are readily accessed behind the stool. The goal with tool placement is to have everything in reach when needed for the task.

Storage shelves are placed near the kiln. The storage of glazed and unglazed ware on the shelves will help in loading and unloading the kiln. Pottery is a labor-intensive activity and any reduction in the amount of steps needed to make pots or sculpture will pay off in extra time and energy saved for the potter. Many potential accident situations occur when the potter is tired and not paying attention to safety procedures.

Connie Baugh, professional potter, at work in the second floor office of the pottery studio.

College Ceramics Programs
Massachusetts College of Art

been a leading educational institution in the field of ceramics. It has developed an all-encompassing policy to ensure safe ceramics studios for faculty and students. While whole-room venting systems and multi-kiln exhaust venting systems might be cost prohibitive for the individual potter, there are many other safety devices that are low cost and easily maintained. Students and faculty at the college are thoroughly educated on studio and kiln firing safety practices, along with the regular academic art programs.

The following photos represent the placement of supplies and equipment in a school environment.

Massachusetts College of Art, Boston, Mass. Main entrance to the school.

Pottery wheels are lined up near a source of natural light with properly spaced overhead fluorescent lighting. Good lighting reduces shadows over wheel-thrown forms and lessons eye strain. A well-lit studio also helps prevent potters from tripping or falling over unseen objects and equipment. Adjacent worktables are kept clean and free of clay scraps and powder, which can be released into the studio atmosphere.

Each graduate student has a workspace that is well lit and kept clean. Shelving adjacent to the workspace is used to store supplies.

The students clean the pottery studio in the undergraduate area after every class. Worktables in the rear of the room have venting systems to actively pull any clay dust from the table area.

The glaze mixing room is well organized, with dry raw materials neatly stored on shelves. Glaze buckets are centrally located for easy access. The tables are placed near the glaze buckets, which prevents glaze spills and allows for an efficient glazing operation. The studio is well lit with overhead florescent lights.

Dry raw materials are stored under the glaze mixing tables for easy access when weighing out glaze formulas. Each raw material bin is clearly and accurately labeled. It is important to keep the distance between the raw material storage areas and weighing out scales as short as possible to prevent spillage. Each workstation is individually vented to remove any airborne raw material as it is weighed out for the glaze batch.

The glaze room sink is located close to the glaze-mixing table. Individual venting stations draw airborne raw materials out of the room. A sign listing health and safety practices informs all students on the correct way to handle raw materials.

Glaze buckets, tools, sieves, and other glaze mixing equipment are cleaned in the sink. Note the vertical pipe (lower left area of sink), which is attached to the sink drain. Standing water in the sink allows for all solid material to fall to the bottom of the sink where it is periodically cleaned out and removed. This low cost system of drainage can be incorporated into most studio sinks.

Clay and glaze materials are carefully stored on shelving. It is essential to stock raw materials in a clean well-organized area. A sink is available for any clean up operation. The floor should be kept clean at all times so raw materials do not become airborne.

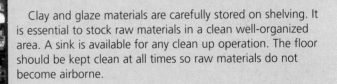

The glazing room has clean tables and is well lit with portable shelving to ensure an efficient safe workspace.

Close up view of the gas kiln venting system in the kiln room. Pots are neatly stacked and are waiting to be fired in the kiln. A well-organized kiln room is a major safety factor in any ceramics studio.

The ware racks are loaded with pots to be fired in the kilns. The kiln room floor is clean, and kiln shelves are neatly stacked near the kilns.

The kiln room has gas and electric kilns with each one vented to remove any kiln exhaust from the building. Kiln posts and shelves are carefully stored in shelving to reduce the possibility of accidental falls and mishaps.

Electric kiln venting

A system of booths has been constructed that captures and removes electric kiln exhaust fumes. During bisque firing, organic materials are released from the clay. In the glaze firing, organic gums and binders are volatized and removed by the venting system. Both types of firing require adequate kiln venting to remove any fumes and vapors from the studio area.

Electric kiln venting

A central exhaust hood vents three small electric test kilns. When the kilns are firing, the exhaust venting system is turned on, removing volatized particles from the studio atmosphere. The venting system actively draws vapors out of the kiln room.

Additional Safety Tips

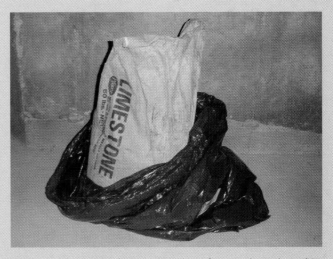

Large quantities of raw material should be stored in a low moisture space, easily accessible to the glaze mixing area. Any raw material spills should be wet mopped up completely when they occur. Plastic bags should have a clear label identifying the raw material. While raw materials will remain useable indefinitely, soluble materials such as Gerstley borate, Colemanite, Borax, Potassium carbonate (Pear Ash), and soda ash should be kept in very low moisture areas and sealed tightly, as they can take on moisture in storage and present future glaze problems.

Larger quantities of raw material are frequently packaged in 50 lb. bags from the mine or processing plant. The bags are paper and they can tear and leak raw material. Some bags have a series of perforations to allow excess air to escape during the filling process at the mine. It is not uncommon for a completely sealed bag to puff out airborne raw material when moved about the studio. The raw material bags should be kept in double heavyweight plastic bags to prevent accumulation of excessive moisture and prevent material leakage.

Smaller stocks of raw materials that cannot be stored in large bins, can be kept in plastic containers with lids. All containers should be carefully labeled with the material name. If possible, materials used for glaze mixing should be kept close to scales, screens, water, and glaze mixing equipment.

Glass storage jars are not recommended in the ceramics studio, due to the ease with which they can slip out of the potter's hands and break on the studio floor. Plastic non-breakable jars with secure lids will hold raw materials securely.

Soot or carbon can be deposited on the outside surfaces of hydrocarbon fueled (natural gas, propane gas, wood, coal, oil) kilns. When the amount of gas exceeds the amount of air at the burners, a reduction (carbon monoxide) kiln atmosphere is created within the kiln. Carbon is a byproduct of incomplete combustion. While some carbon is normal during a kiln firing, excessive carbon can be deposited on floors, walls, storage racks, and other kiln room surfaces. Carbon can cause air quality problems, due to the small lightweight particle size of the material that can be blown around the kiln room.

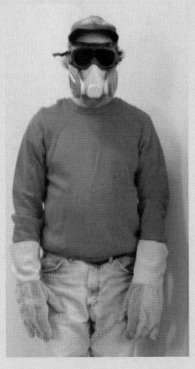

Raku safety clothing

The high temperature insulated leather lined gloves stop burns from hot kilns and pots. The kiln goggles prevent eye damage when looking into kilns. A "paper type" respirator is used when mixing dry glazes. A cartridge type approved respirator is designed for use when taking pots out of the reduction medium, which can cause heavy black smoke.

Raku clothing

The correct clothing is essential for a safe Raku firing. Always wear long-sleeved shirts, head protection, long Raku gloves, a respirator, and kiln goggles. When looking into a firing kiln, use the approved shaded goggles to protect your eyes from infrared and ultraviolet light. When unloading the kiln, always wear impact-resistant goggles or shielded head gear to protect the eyes and neck from a potential pot exploding.

A small test electric kiln with refractory ceramic fiber placed in spaces between lid and main body of the kiln. Refractory ceramic fiber in the bulk form is often used to seal leaks and open spaces in pottery kilns. It has superior insulation qualities and is very flexible, which makes it an ideal refractory material to fit into small open spaces between kiln bricks.

Fiber Blanket

Refractory ceramic fiber is formed into blankets, boards, loose bulk fiber, and other shapes, which can be used for many different areas where high temperature insulation is required. Isofrax ™ refractory ceramic fiber is produced by Unifrax Corporation. The fiber has outstanding insulating properties with extremely low lung biopersistence. The ceramic fiber consists mainly of magnesia and silica.

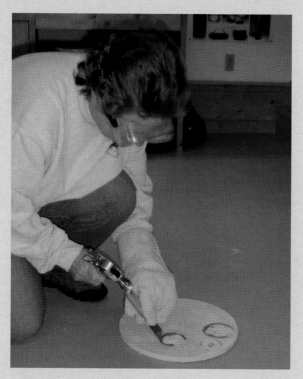

Cuts

Fired glazes can have very sharp edges, either due to the irregular surface qualities of the clay underneath or from cracked ware. The safe way to unload a glaze kiln is with a pair of gloves. Not only do they protect the hands from any residual heat in the kiln but the gloves prevent glaze cuts on the hands. Hand injuries from cuts and burns are a major cause of ceramics studio accidents.

Cuts

Wear protective eye goggles and gloves when chipping fired glaze drips from the kiln shelf. Glaze debris on the kiln shelf can become razor sharp and fly about the room when hit with a chisel. Always clean up the entire area after chipping glaze off kiln shelves.

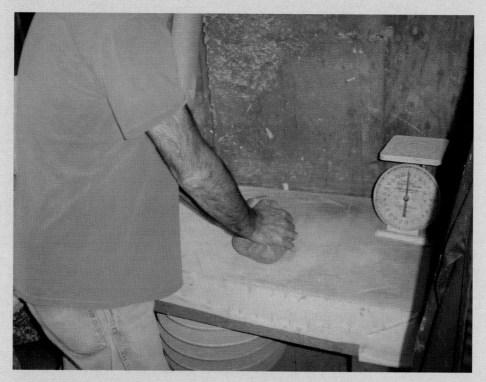

Back and Hand Protection

The height of the wedging table is critical in eliminating back stress. The ideal height of the table should be based on the dimensions of the potter using the table. When the potter is standing up next to the table, his or her hands should comfortably rest on the tabletop. In this way, upper body leverage over the moist clay can do most of the wedging, which will rely less on muscle power to move the clay. Excessive bending over or reaching up to wedge the clay can cause muscle problems in the back and upper arms. Back pain is one of the leading causes of health problems for the studio potter.

Back Protection

To reduce back strains, adjust the height of the wheel seat so it is level with the height of the wheel head. It will be easier to center the moist clay, as the potter can use upper body leverage when leaning over the moist clay. Avoid prolonged repetitive throwing, as it can potentially cause back, hand, and wrist injuries.

Eye Injury and Burns

Hot exhaust flames and vapors can be ejected from the kiln (back pressure) whenever the cone viewing bricks are removed during the firing. Do not stand close to the kiln when removing cone-viewing bricks. Always wear protective goggles to prevent potential eye injuries due to infrared and ultraviolet light emitted from gas or electric kilns.

Wheel Clutter

One possible source of studio accidents, or more frequently confusion and irritation, is a cluttered studio space. While some potters enjoy having many items in their working area, such as tools, brushes, buckets, bricks, glaze containers, etc. it can make for a disorganized environment. Time spent looking for a misplaced tool can disrupt a steady work schedule, resulting in frustration and delay. Occasionally, a bucket tips over or a potter's knife is left in a position that can lead to a cut hand. Good studio organization depends on all tools and equipment being in the right place for easy access when they are needed.

Hard bricks (lower brick) are frequently used in the studio and can be found in the construction of many types of gas kilns. Each hard brick weighs over 5 lbs. and if dropped on an unprotected foot or finger, it will cause disabilities. Always wear heavy-duty protective shoes and handle the hard bricks with care.

Soft bricks (top brick) are used in the construction of gas and electric kilns. A fine particle dust coats the surface of the soft brick. Always wear a respirator when handling or cutting soft brick.

Kiln Clutter

Firing kilns can give off radiant heat. The kiln should be placed away from any combustible materials. All items should be removed from the area around the kiln area to prevent a fire hazard and the more frequent hazard of tripping over things left around the kiln. The potter should be able to walk around the kiln unimpeded to inspect the entire kiln during the firing process.

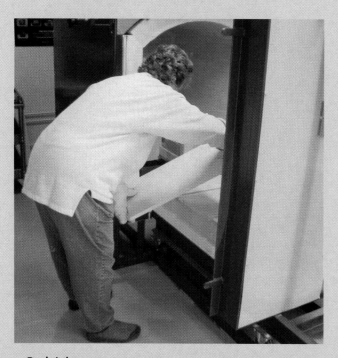

Back Injury

Never bend over when lifting heavy kiln shelves. Do not lean over or twist the body.

Always lift heavy kiln shelves with a straight back. To increase stability, place feet together near the kiln shelf.

Both terms express the airborne concentration levels of a chemical a worker can be exposed to during an eight-hour workday. The C.A.S. numbers (Chemical Abstract Service) can also be listed in this section. The C.A.S. number identification system can identify individual chemicals, according to information published by the American Chemical Society.

The chemical and common names of all ingredients, which have been determined to be reportable health hazards, are listed in this section. The common names listed should be those ordinarily in use for that product such as feldspar. If the chemical is a mixture, which has not been tested as a whole, the chemical and common names are listed for all ingredients that are:

- *Hazards to health comprising 1% or more of the mixture*
- *Identified as carcinogens and present at 0.1% or greater*
- *Determined to be a physical hazard when present in a mixture*

Respirable silica is determined to be a health hazard in Custer feldspar.

Section III: Physical Data

This section tells what the material or mixture is and how it reacts. This information can help in deciding on a ventilation system when using the material. It can also be used to formulate adequate fire and spill containment procedures. The section lists physical properties such as the chemical's boiling point, vapor density, percent volatility, appearance, and odor as well as other chemical characteristics. The information will help in judging the potential hazards with the chemical in various work environments. For example, vapor density is the weight of a vapor relative to an equal volume of air (air=1). Chemicals with vapor densities greater than 1 are heavier than air and will fall to the ground.

Appearance and Odor
White and Odorless

Custer feldspar is white in its raw color and is odorless. The appearance and odor of a substance may help you identify the substance you are working with. However, keep in mind many ceramic materials are either white or off white in raw or unfired color. Do not rely on odor to indicate whether there is a hazardous concentration of the substance in the air. Some substances can reach hazardous levels and not have a noticeable odor.

Solubility in Water
Negligible

Solubility in water is the percentage by weight of the substance, which can be dissolved in water. Solubility may be given in weight percent, or the following terms may be used in MSDS.

Negligible .... less than 0.1 percent solubility
Slight .... 0.1 to 1 percent solubility
Moderate .... 1 to 10 percent solubility
Appreciable .... more than 10 percent solubility
Complete .... soluble in all proportions.

The solubility of any material is an important factor in its removal when it is bound up with water. An appreciably soluble or completely soluble raw material used in a glaze formula, aside from causing potential technical problems in the glaze, can also cause disposal problems if the glaze is poured down a sink. The solid part of the waste glaze can block a private septic field and the soluble component of the glaze can affect local ground water and vegetation.

Vapor Pressure
N/A (not applicable)

Vapor pressure tells how much vapor the material may give off. It refers to the pressure of saturated vapor above the liquid and is usually measured at 20^0 C (68^0 F) and given in millimeters of mercury (mm Hg). The vapor pressure and the temperature where measured are listed. A high vapor pressure indicates that a liquid will evaporate easily.

Boiling Point
N/A (not applicable)

The temperature at which a liquid boils, in degrees F or C, under ordinary atmospheric pressure (1 atmosphere = 760 mm Hg). If the material is a mixture, a boiling range may be given.

Specific Gravity
2.63

The specific gravity indicates the ratio of the weight of a volume or liquid to the weight of an equal volume of water at a specified temperature.

1.0......the material is the same weight as water
Above 1.0..... the material is heavier than water
Below 1.0.......the material is lighter than water

Custer feldspar has a specific gravity of 2.63 which means it is heavier than water and will sink when placed in water.

Melting Point

1450 C

Melting point indicated the temperature at which Custer feldspar melts. Custer feldspar when heated will go into a glass at 1450 C.

Percent Volatile

N/A (not applicable)

Percent volatility is the rate at which the material evaporates. If a material has an evaporation rate of greater than one, it evaporates more easily than the chemical it is compared to; if the rate is less than one, it evaporates more slowly than the chemical it is compared to.

Section IV: Fire and Explosion Hazard Data

Flash Point

Non Flammable, Non Explosive

Custer feldspar cannot be ignited or explode.

Flash point is the lowest temperature at which a liquid gives off enough vapor to make an ignitable mixture of vapor in air in a test container. Flash point and auto ignition should be listed in degrees Fahrenheit or Centigrade, or both. Chemicals that catch fire at or above 100^0F are classified as combustible; those that catch fire below 100^0F are classified as flammable. This section lists the chemical's upper and lower flammability limits and the correct type of fire extinguishing media.

Unusual Fire and Explosion Hazards

N/A (not applicable)

This section lists any properties of the material that will create any fire or explosion hazard when handling or storing the material.

Flammable (Explosive) Limits

(Percent by volume)

The range of gas or vapor concentrations (percent by volume of air) that will burn or explode if an ignition source is present. Lower and upper limits are noted. Knowledge of the lower limit will aid in determining the volume of ventilation needed for an enclosed space to prevent fires and explosions.

The units used in measuring concentration and the temperature at which the test was conducted are given. If the material tested was in the form of a dust in air, this fact is also noted. This information will aid in the safe handling of hazardous or unstable substances. Instability or incompatibility with common substances such as water, direct sun, and metals used in piping or containers, acid, alkalis, etc. should be listed.

Lower Limit N/A

(not applicable—see above statement)

Upper Limit N/A

(not applicable—see above statement)

Special Fire Fighting Procedures

None

Special fire fighting procedures and unusual fire and explosion hazards would need to be described for any combustible material. Some concentrated corrosives, calcium carbide, or reactive metals must not have water applied in case of fire. Always check to see if the material is a catalyst, and check for reactivity with water and polymerization in water or air.

Fire Extinguishing Media

N/A (not applicable)

Extinguishing media identifies what kind of fire extinguisher to use. If the substance is not flammable and/or is completely inert, the MSDS should say so. Otherwise this line must always be filled out on the MSDS sheet.

Section V: Health Hazard Information

Hazard by routes of exposure:

Inhalation: Warning: Feldspar is not listed as a carcinogen by the International Agency for Research on Cancer (IARC), the National Toxicology Program (NTP) or the Occupational Safety and Health Administration (OSHA). In October, 1996, an IARC working group reassessing crystalline silica, a component of this product, designated crystalline silica as a Group 1 carcinogenic. The NTP indicates that crystalline silica is reasonably anticipated to be a Group 2 carcinogen. These classifications are based on sufficient evidence of carcinogenicity in certain experimental animals and on selected epidemiological studies of workers exposed to crystalline silica. These studies only rarely, however, include data on smoking, potential confounding exposures, and assurance of the comparability of referent population. Repeated prolonged inhalation of dust may cause delayed lung injury, which may result in silicosis or pneumoconiosis.

While this statement at first appears contradictory, claiming Custer feldspar is not listed as a carcinogen, it does however go on to state that the crystalline silica, which is a part of the feldspar can possibly cause cancer. Crystalline silica has shown to be a cancer-causing factor in workers and experimental animals. The studies for the most part do <u>not</u> include data on workers who smoke or who are exposed to other materials in the workplace. However, repeated long-term exposure to crystalline silica can cause lung injury (silicosis or pneumoconiosis) over a period of time. It is strongly recommended to use a respirator whenever Custer feldspar is in the dry state.

The section on health hazards tells of the effects associated with overexposure to chemicals through inhalation, ingestion, skin and eye contact. The information may include: acute (immediate) and chronic (long-term) effects of overexposure to the chemical. It can also list if the chemical is a cancer-producing agent. Listed will be emergency and first aid procedures to follow in case of overexposure. If workers are in an area where overexposure to a harmful material is possible, safety equipment may be required in the workplace.

Ingestion:
Nausea may result from accidental ingestion.

Self-explanatory. Custer feldspar should not be ingested.

Eye:
Inflammation of eye tissue may occur from overexposure.

Self-explanatory. Eye irritation can occur if Custer feldspar particles come in contact with the eyes. Safety glasses are required when mixing any dry material.

Skin Contact/Absorption:
Inflammation from contact with open cuts may occur.

Self-explanatory. Use gloves and/or wash hands after using Custer feldspar.

Signs and Symptoms of Exposure:
Short term: Shortness of breath, coughing associated with inhalation of dust.
Long term: Steady and prolonged exposure to dust concentrations higher than TLV (Threshold Limit Value—The airborne concentration of the substance which represents conditions under which it is believed that nearly all workers may be repeatedly exposed day and day without adverse effects.) without approved respirator could cause silicosis, a chronic disease of the lungs marked by acute fibrosis, may cause cancer based on animal data.

This section lists common effects by route of exposure or entry, usually inhalation or absorption by skin contact. It includes chronic and acute effects, as well as information on carcinogencity, teratogenicity, or mutagenicity.

The combined estimate of the hazard of the total product. This might be stated as a time weighted average concentration, PEL or TLV. Includes chemicals that are carcinogens, toxic or highly toxic agents, reproductive toxins, irritants, corrosives, sensitizes, hepatotoxins, nephrotoxins, neurotoxins, agents which act on the hematopoietic system, and agents which damage the lungs, skin, eyes or mucous membranes.

Signs and symptoms of exposure indicate relevant signs, symptoms, and disease that could result from acute and chronic exposure to the hazardous substance.

Emergency/First Aid Procedures:
Inhalation/Ingestion: Consult physician and/or obtain competent medical assistance.
Eye Contact: Flush with water, consult physician and/or obtain competent medical assistance.
Skin Contact: Wash thoroughly with water.

Emergency first aid procedures offers treatment information that could be used by paramedics and individuals trained in first aid.

Section VI: Reactivity Data

General Reactivity: N/A (not applicable)
Incompatibility: N/A (not applicable)
Hazardous Polymerization: N/A (not applicable)
Stability: Feldspar is a stable material under ordinary conditions.

This section will aid in the safe handling of hazardous or unstable substances. Instability or incompatibility with common substances such as water, direct sun, and metals used in piping or containers, acid, alkalis, etc. should be listed. Chemicals that are unstable or reactive may burn, explode, or release toxic substances under certain conditions. The stability or instability of a material is also listed.

Stability
Unstable (reactive) means a chemical that in the pure state or as produced or transported will vigorously polymerize, decompose, condense, or become self-reactive under conditions of shock, pressure, or temperature. Custer feldspar, when used as a glaze or clay body material, is stable.

Incompatibility
Common materials or contaminants that the specific material could be expected to come in contact with and which could produce a reaction should be listed in this section. Conditions to avoid should also be listed.

Hazardous Decomposition or Byproducts
Products released if the substance is exposed to aging, heating, burning, oxidation, or allowed to react. The product's shelf life should also be listed in this section when applicable. Although some materials are innocuous in their original form, when they are exposed to conditions such as aging, burning, etc., they may form hazardous products.

Hazardous Polymerization
A reaction with extremely high or uncontrolled release of energy. If this section is checked, the condition under which it could occur should be explained.

Section VII: Procedures Disposal Requirements

Steps to be taken in case material is released or spilled: Material is not dangerous if spilled. Wash away with water or vacuum with high efficiency (HEPA) filter. If uncontaminated, recover and reuse.

If contaminated, collect in suitable containers for disposal. Avoid creating dust. Avoid breathing dust. Wear a NIOSH/OSHA approved respirator. Good housekeeping practices recommended.

Waste and disposal methods: Disposal methods for non-hazardous materials should be complied with. May be buried in approved land disposal facility in accordance with Federal, State, and local regulations. Feldspar is not a hazardous waste under RCRA (40 CFR Part 261). Feldspar is not regulated by DOT.

Waste disposal methods are listed if labeling and special handling of cleanup residue is necessary; that should be stated along with the appropriate method of disposal—for instance, sanitary landfill, incineration, etc.

In the handling and storage section, any special precautions to be taken in storage and handling are listed, such as avoiding reaction hazards with oxidizing agents, acids, etc. Conditions for storage such as temperature, ventilation, and no smoking or other sources of ignition are also given. When applicable, the safe storage life is indicated. Additional precautions are listed. Custer feldspar can be disposed of in landfill sites. It is always recommended to show the MSDS sheet to the local landfill operator before attempting to use the landfill.

Section VIII: Special Protection Information

Eye Protection:
Safety glasses optional but recommended.

Safety glasses can keep unwanted Custer feldspar from entering the eyes when using it in the dry form.

Protective Gloves:

Optional, but recommended.

Latex or rubber gloves can be worn when using Custer Feldspar.

Respiratory Protection:

NIOSH/MSHA/OSHA approved respirator selection procedures. NIOSH approved dust mask.

In glaze mixing or clay body mixing operations, Custer feldspar particles can be released into the studio environment. An approved respirator must be used when Custer feldspar is in the dry form.

Ventilation:

Local exhaust required for dust removal. Refer to OSHA 1910.24, ASTM, and/or ANSI Standards. Do not exceed OSHA PEL or ACGIH TLV.

This section must give information on protection against any or all of these kinds of exposures.

Eye protection covers first aid procedures, such as flooding with water. If splashes may occur, eye protection and eyewash facilities should be recommended. Included in this part are other health or safety concerns that have not already been mentioned in other sections of the MSDS.

Protective gloves must be worn if the skin is a primary route of exposure. If gloves are recommended, the type should be specified. A check of the chemical family of the material will tell if the proper gloves are recommended.

Check the respiratory protection section to see if inhalation is a probable means of overexposure. Check to see how volatile the material is to determine the potential degree of hazard.

- *If respirators are required or recommended, the type and class should be stated, such as "supplied air" or "organic vapor cartridges," or "suitable for dust no more toxic than lead," etc.*

- *If protective clothing is required, the type and material of that clothing should be indicated.*

Ventilation should not exceed OSHA, PEL, or ACGIH standards.

Other protective clothing, equipment, special suits, clothing of special material and/or construction, and any other special handling that may be required for personal protection should be indicated in this section of the MSDS.

Example of raw material label—Custer Feldspar Ceramic Supplier, Ceramic Supply of NY/NJ

The information listed on the label states the ceramics supplier's name, material name, weight, and safe handling procedures. The CAS number for each component of Custer feldspar is listed along with a recommendation to use an approved respirator. There is also a limited liability statement, which indicates the ceramic supplier will only replace the material if defective. The label also states the material is limited for use in the ceramic industry and arts.

Example of raw material label—Custer feldspar Ceramic Supplier, Sheffield Pottery, Inc., Mass.

The safety information might be slightly different on each ceramics suppliers label, but the basic product and safety recommendations should be clearly visible. Note the statement on the bottom of the label, "ALWAYS READ CURRENT MATERIAL SAFETY DATA SHEET (MSDS)." This sheet is available with every raw material sold by the ceramics supplier. When in doubt about how to handle a material, call or write your ceramics supplier for the MSDS sheet. Sheffield's label lists the company name, address, and phone number.

Example of raw material labels—
Custer feldspar
Great Lakes Clay & Supply Company, Ill.
Lists the safety precautions for using a raw material and the appropriate safety equipment. The label also lists the clean up procedures when using a raw material. Many ceramic supply companies state on raw material labels they are not responsible for mishandling or misuse of the material by the user of the raw material. Potters therefore should assume full responsibility for handling and testing any raw material.

NOTICE ON CLAY SAFETY

All clays and glaze materials contain silica and many of these materials are toxic in other ways. Continued breathing of silica could lead to silicosis and a respirator should be worn when handling dry clays. Please refer to our glossary of materials on pages 40-42 for the toxicity of certain materials.

Great Lakes Clay can assume NO responsibility for the handling or mishandling of any dry clays and glaze materials.

Material Safety Data Sheets are available on ALL raw materials upon request.
ALL RAW MATERIALS CONTAIN SILICA, WHICH CAN BE HARMFUL IF BREATHED IN CONTINUOUSLY
WEAR AN OSHA/NIOSH APPROVED RESPIRATOR

"Contains: Respirable quartz when in dry form. Damp mop after use." Please wear proper clothing and use an OSHA or NIOSH approved respirator when working with <u>any</u> dry clay.

Section IX: Special Requirements/Precautions

Example of raw material label—
Custer feldspar
Ceramic Supplier, Laguna Clay Company, Calif.
The warning and safety information supplied on the label applies to anyone using Custer feldspar in the United States. California has one of the most stringent safety labeling regulations, and Laguna Clay Company is located in this state. The label lists the Ceramic Supply Company name, address, and phone number, name of the material, net weight, a cancer warning, recommendations for using an approved NIOSH respirator, protective clothing, proper ventilation, and a phone number for further information on Custer feldspar along with a warning not to use Custer feldspar with food or beverage.

Storage Requirements:

Store in dry area. Do not breathe dust. Avoid creating dust in a closed area. Use adequate ventilation as recommended by NIOSH/ MSHA/OSHA for crystalline silica (*refer to Section II*).

Custer feldspar should be stored in a dry area. Since the feldspar is not reactive with water, this recommendation is more suited to water being absorbed into a paper storage bag and weakening the container. As with other dry raw materials in the pottery studio, it is not recommended to breathe the dust. Wearing the appropriate respirator will protect against the warning concerning the crystalline silica component of Custer feldspar

The information contained herein is believed to be accurate, but Pacer Corporation makes no warranty with respect thereto and disclaims responsibility for reliance thereon. This information applies only to the specific material described herein, and does not relate to use in connection with any other materials or in any process.

The Pacer Corporation makes no warranties, express or implied, concerning this product. No warranty of fitness for any particular purpose is made and we assume no responsibility whatever for any use of this product. This product should be used by properly trained personnel in compliance with applicable health and safety laws and regulations.

Pacer Corporation has supplied the available information they have on hand to the best of their knowledge. The information is limited only to Custer feldspar listed on the MSDS sheet and not to any other material or process in using that material.

Pacer Corporation does not guarantee, assure, or promise Custer feldspar for any purpose. Pacer does not take responsibility for the use of Custer feldspar, and only properly trained persons operating under the appropriate health and safety regulations should use it.

MSDS information supplied by Contact Lab Safety Supply, P.O. Box 1368, Janesville, WI 53547-1368, (800) 356-0783.

Raw Material Labeling Information:

Most raw materials used in ceramics, such as feldspars, flint, dolomite, whiting, talc, and various dry clays, are shipped to the ceramics supplier in 50 lb. bags or larger dry bulk containers. Whenever possible, the potter should purchase the entire 50 lb. bag of raw material as the price per/lb. will decrease as compared with ordering lesser amounts of the material. It also increases the accuracy of re-ordering the raw material as the original source manufacturer or mine will have their company name on the bag. However, some raw materials cannot realistically be ordered in their original large-weight shipping containers, as with cobalt oxide or tin oxide, which are prohibitively expensive. The potter is then left with the option of ordering a raw material in less than full bag quantities, which the ceramics supplier will re-bag for sale to potters.

However, there is always the chance of mislabeling the re-bagged material. Keep in mind a great many ceramic raw materials are white to off-white in color. In situations where the potter is handling a raw material that is not in its original container, look for the ceramics supplier's own label on the bag. It will offer valuable information on the safety procedures, which can be used when working with the material.

The bag label can list several specific pieces of information:

- The ceramics supplier's name and address
- The raw material name and mesh size where applicable
- The bag weight of the raw material
- Warning information and a listing of safety information

- CAS (Chemical Abstracts Service) number identifying material (can also be listed on the MSDS sheet)
- Listing of the most predominant substance in the raw material by percent
- Statement suggesting testing the material before using
- Statement of limited liability—ceramics suppliers are liable for only replacing the defective or substandard material
- Statement that the material only be used in ceramic industry and arts
- Do not use around food or drink
- Provide adequate ventilation

Listed are several examples of different ceramic supply companies' labels used on their bags of raw material. There is no standard label format that applies on a national level. However, several states do have specific regulations on raw material packaging and labeling. Always make sure the labels are firmly attached to the raw material bag. Sometimes when bags are stored for long periods of time in differing moisture conditions, a label can come off the bag. At that point the potter is left guessing which white powder is in the unmarked bag. It is often more efficient at that point not to test the raw material but to simply dispose of the material and the bag. When in doubt as to a raw material label or how to handle the material in a safe manner, first call the ceramic supplier where the material was purchased. If further information is needed, call the phone number on the MSDS sheet for that raw material.

Chapter 11

Ceramic Raw Materials

Airborne, Dermal Absorption, Ingestion

There are potentially over 90 clays and more than 120 commercially available raw materials that a potter can conceivably come in contact with when working in ceramics. This vast number does not include local clays and raw materials that potters choose to mine themselves. Various raw materials and clays can be found in prepared clay body and glaze formulas or can be encountered in their individual forms, which potters use in their studios. For example, a potter might use a clay body formula containing several individual clays, feldspar, flint, and a grog component, all of which are contained in a moist pliable mixture of clay. Glaze formulas can include clay, feldspar, flint, talc, and metallic coloring oxides such as chrome oxide or cobalt oxide, which contribute color to the fired glaze. Potters have the option of choosing an individual material or any combination of clay and glaze formulas.

Individual clays, feldspars, flint, talc, or other raw materials can also be used during any number of ceramics studio projects. Whether clays and raw material are used in combination or individually, the potter's primary responsibility is to know how to safely handle each raw material used in the studio.

The major but not only source of danger to one's health is inhaling raw materials during everyday ceramic activities. To a lesser degree, several raw materials can cause skin irritation in their dry or wet form when they come in contact with exposed skin. Potters' skin sensitivity is variable depending on the sensitivity of the individual. The permeability of some raw materials through the skin resulting in toxicity in the body is not fully researched as it pertains to potters. Ingestion of raw materials is the third method of entry into the body.

Listed are the most commonly available commercial Clays, Flints, Feldspars, and Raw Materials, which are distributed by many ceramics supply companies in the United States and Canada. Keep in mind most commercial clay body formulas are composed of two to six raw materials. In over 80% of glazes, the same ten to twelve raw materials are used in differing ratios depending on the firing temperature, color, texture, and kiln atmosphere in which the glaze functions. While the raw material choices and combinations are almost infinite in variety, the actual number of raw materials used in clay and glaze formulas is fairly small. With this reality in mind, it is important to know how to handle safely only a relatively small number of raw materials.

Potters should educate themselves on raw materials, clays, feldspars, flints, metallic coloring oxides, and stains. When receiving any raw material into the studio always refer to the MSDS. The Material Safety Data Sheet for each raw material purchased can be obtained from the ceramics supplier who sells the material. Do not stop with this piece of useful information. If in doubt on how to protect yourself, call the ceramic supplier and locate the original manufacturer of the material. Suppliers of raw materials will have a product stewardship information hotline or customer service line dedicated to helping their customers use the material safely. There is often additional information on a raw material from a manufacturer's Web page.

Clays

Clays are found in many clay body formulas and glaze formulas.

Individual Clays:

#1 Glaze Clay
#6 Tile Clay
A.P.G. Missouri fireclay 28M
Ajax P
Albany Substitute
Alberta Slip
Alberta Slip
Alberta Slip Clay
Apache Fire Clay
Bandy Black Ball Clay
Barnet Clay
Bentonema
Bentonite B
Bentonite, Western 200M
Bentonite, Western 325M
Black Charm Ball Clay
Blackbird (Barnard)
C- Red
C-1 Clay
Calcined Glomax LL
Cedar Heights Bonding
Cedar Heights Goldart
Champion Ball Clay
Cherokee Fireclay
Christy Mineral Fireclay
CP #7 Ball Clay
D'Arvor Kaolin
DB Float Kaolin
Delta
Dresden Ball Clay
English Grolleg
EPK Kaolin (Florida)
F-2 Clay
Foundry Hill Creame
Georgia Diamond Kaolin
Georgia Kaolin
Gold Label
H.C. Spinks C&C
Hawthorn Bond 20M, 35M, 50M
HC-5 Ball Clay
HCVC Ball Clay
Helmar Kaolin
HPM-20 Bentonite
HTP Ball Clay
Huntington Clay
Ibex-200 Bentonite
Jackson Ball Clay
Kaiser

Kaolex D-6
Kaolex D-6
Kaopaque 10 kaolin
Kaopaque 20
Kentucky OM #4
Kentucky Special
Kentucky Stone
Kingsley
KT-1-4 Ball
Laguna #1
Laterite
Lincoln Fireclay 60
Lincoln Greenstripe
Lizella
McNamee
MH 77 Ball Clay
Mississippi M& D
Newman #7
Newman Red
North American Fireclay
Old Hickory #5 Ball Clay
Old Hickory M-23
P.V. Clay
Peerless Kaolin
Pioneer Kaolin
Ranger Red
Ranger Red Shale

Redart
Roseville Stoneware
Salt Lick
Sapphire
Sheffield Slip Clay
Snocal 707
SPG #1 Ball Clay
Starcast Ball Clay
Sterling Lump
Sutter 200
T-7 Kaolin
Tennessee #1, #5, #9, #10
Thomas Ball
Treviscoe Kaolin
Velvacast
XX Sagger
Yellow Banks #401
Yellow Banks #401
Zamek Ball Clay

The inventory of clays listed and clays that are not listed should be subject to the following safety procedures.

Potters should use a respirator anytime there is the potential for dry raw materials to be deposited into the studio atmosphere. Safety standards require potters to wear a respirator any time the studio is cleaned, when raw material bags are opened, and during clay or glaze mixing operations.

Protection Procedures

Airborne:

Dry clays can contain varying amounts of free silica. The danger with silica in any form is its ability to become inhaled into deep recesses of the lungs. Breathing silica over a long period of time can cause silicosis, a disease of the lungs that can lead to shortness of breath and susceptibility to other respiratory ailments. China clays or kaolins can cause kaolinosis, when sub micron size particles become imbedded in lung tissue, causing disruption of normal lung function. The symptoms are similar to silicosis but also lead to emphysema. The inhalation aspects of clays can be brought under control by concentrating on keeping a clean studio and using a respirator with the material. Always wear a NIOSH approved respirator when mixing dry clays. Wet mop the studio and wipe down work surfaces with a wet sponge to remove dry clay. Wear clothes that will not attract or hold clay particles, and wash the clothes frequently after working in the studio. Do not eat, drink, or smoke in the studio.

Dermal Absorption:

Clay entry through the skin barrier has not proven to be a health risk. Under some circumstances, clay contact with the skin can cause a rash in certain individuals. Keep in mind that clay is used as a base in many cosmetics and skin medicines. Clay is often applied as a poultice to draw out excess moisture from the skin. If the skin is sensitive to dry or moist clay, a good quality hand lotion should be applied before and after using clay, or use rubber gloves to protect the hands. Always wash and dry hands thoroughly after working in the studio. Any cuts or abrasions on the skin should be protected with rubber gloves before using clay in any form.

Ingestion:

Under normal studio operations, potters would not be susceptible to eating clay. However, always closely monitor any children working in the pottery studio. Small children should be under direct adult supervision at all times. While clay should never be eaten, a commonly available medicine for stomach ailments is Kaopectate, which contains 95% kaolin.

Flint

Flint or silica is found in many clay body and glaze formulas, it is also associated with clays and other raw materials as free silica.

Individual Flints:

Flint 200x mesh, 270x mesh, 325x mesh, and 400x mesh
INSIL A-25 Silica
Amorphous Silica

Protection procedures

Airborne:

As the silica component (free silica) in clays can cause silicosis after prolonged and high concentration exposure, silica or flint has a higher concentration of silica, which can also cause potential health problems. As stated, many clays, feldspars, and other ceramic materials contain silica as part of the material; therefore, always wear a NIOSH approved respirator whenever opening bags of silica or other raw materials.

Dermal Absorption:

Silica or flint has shown no proven hazard when in contact with the skin. Whenever there is a cut on the hand, wear rubber gloves. If the hands develop a rash or irritation, use skin

The studio floor should be wet mopped daily to prevent clay particles from being stirred into the air. The wet mop captures raw material particles and transfers them to a water bucket.

lotion, hand cream, or rubber gloves before using flint in the dry form. After using flint, wash the hands thoroughly with soap and water and apply hand cream.

Ingestion:

Silica or flint has shown no proven health hazard but should not be ingested. It is inconceivable that a rational person would eat silica or flint. However, small amounts can be accidentally ingested if food or drink is allowed in the pottery studio. Under these circumstances, someone placing food on a table that has flint on it could ingest the material by accident. To prevent this type of health concern, do not eat or drink in the studio.

Feldspars

Feldspars are found in clay body and glaze formulas; they can also contain free silica.

Indvidual Feldspars:

Custer feldspar
Minspar 4
G-200 feldspar
Nepheline syenite 270x, 400x
Cornwall Stone
Kona F-4
Primas P
Primas S
Spodumene
NC-4 Feldspar

Protection Procedures:

Airborne:

Feldspars contain varying amounts of free silica (crystalline quartz); some individual feldspars typically contain 6% to 10%. Respirators should always be used in the presence of free silica and/or any dry raw materials to prevent micron size particles from entering the lungs. As with silica/flint, and clays, always wet mop the studio and maintain good housekeeping procedures when using feldspars.

Dermal Absorption:

Feldspars have not proven to be a health hazard when in direct contact with the skin. If a skin rash or irritation develops, protect the hands by using hand lotion or rubber gloves when handling the dry material. Wash hands thoroughly after coming in contact with feldspar.

Ingestion:

Feldspar has shown no proven health hazard but should not be ingested. It is inconceivable that a rational person would eat feldspar.

Rubber or latex gloves can be worn when mixing wet glaze ingredients. Gloves should always be used when the potter has cuts or abrasions on his or her hands.

However, small amounts can be ingested if food or drink is allowed in the pottery studio. Under these circumstances, someone placing food on a table that has feldspar on it could ingest the material by accident. To prevent this type of health concern, do not eat or drink in the studio.

Individual Raw Materials

Additive A—increases clay body plasticity

Inhalation: always use a respirator when handling material in the dry form

Dermal Absorption: wash hands thoroughly after using

Ingestion: do not ingest

Alkatrol (pyrax substitute)—used in clay bodies

Inhalation: always use a respirator when handling material in the dry form

Dermal Absorption: wash hands thoroughly after using

Ingestion: do not ingest

Alumina, Calcined 325M—used in glazes/kiln shelf wash

Inhalation: always use a respirator when handling material in dry form

Dermal Absorption: wash hands thoroughly after using

Ingestion: do not ingest

Alumina Hydrate—used in glazes/kiln shelf wash

Inhalation: always use a respirator when handling material in dry form

Dermal Absorption: wash hands thoroughly after using

Ingestion: do not ingest

Alumina Oxide (Calcined)—used in glazes/ kiln shelf wash

Inhalation: always use a respirator when handling material in dry form

Dermal Absorption: wash hands thoroughly after using

Ingestion: do not ingest

Antimony Oxide—used in glazes

Inhalation: always use a respirator when handling material in dry form, can turn into vapor during firing

Dermal Absorption: contact can cause an abnormal change in the skin or lesions, irritation to eyes and skin

Ingestion: do not ingest; can cause vomiting, pulmonary congestion, and liver/kidney damage by hemorrhage; carcinogenic

Ashes (any wood ash)—used in glazes

Inhalation: always use a respirator when handling material in dry form

Dermal Absorption: caustic to the skin; wear protective gloves when using in a glaze

Ingestion: do not ingest; caustic when combined with water

Barium Carbonate (German, Chinese)— used in clay bodies and glazes

Inhalation: always use a respirator when handling material in dry form; can cause eye and nose irritation; can cause Baritosis and lung damage

Dermal Absorption: partially soluble; may cause skin irritation on people with sensitive skin, but has no proven toxicity when in contact with the skin

Ingestion: do not ingest; can cause convulsions and cardiac or respiratory failure; affects nervous and circulatory system

Barium Sulfate—used in clay bodies and glazes

Inhalation: always use a respirator when handling material in dry form

Dermal Absorption: can cause skin irritation; wash hands after using

Ingestion: do not ingest

Bismuth Sub nitrate—used in glazes as a luster

Inhalation: always use an approved respirator for vapors

Dermal Absorption: can cause skin irritation; wash hands after use

Ingestion: do not ingest

Bone Ash, Natural—used in glazes and some clay bodies

Inhalation: always use a respirator when handling material in dry form; can cause slight irritation

Dermal Absorption: slight irritation

Ingestion: do not ingest

Bone Ash, Synthetic—used in glazes and some clay bodies

Inhalation: always use a respirator when handling material in dry form; can cause slight irritation

Dermal Absorption: slight irritation

Ingestion: do not ingest; can cause slight gastric upset

Boraq—glaze material

Inhalation: always use a respirator when handling material in dry form

Dermal Absorption: repeated contact can cause skin irritation

Ingestion: do not ingest

Borax, Powdered—used in glazes

Inhalation: always use a respirator when handling material in dry form; inhalation can cause vomiting, stomach pain, nausea

Dermal Absorption: can cause skin irritation or burns

Ingestion: do not ingest; can cause gastric illness, kidney damage, nausea

Borax, Granular—used in glazes

Inhalation: always use a respirator when handling material in dry form; inhalation can cause vomiting, stomach pain, nausea

Dermal Absorption: can cause skin irritation or burns

Ingestion: do not ingest; can cause gastric illness, kidney damage, nausea

Boric Acid, Granular—used in glazes

Inhalation: always use a respirator when handling material in dry form; inhalation can cause vomiting, stomach pain, nausea

Dermal Absorption: can cause skin irritation or burns

Ingestion: do not ingest; can cause gastric illness, kidney damage, nausea

Cadmium—glaze material

Inhalation: always use a respirator when handling material in dry form

Dermal Absorption: can cause skin irritation

Ingestion: do not ingest; can cause kidney disorders, bronchitis, anemia

Cadycal 100 Borate—glaze material

Inhalation: always use a respirator when handling material in dry form

Dermal Absorption: repeated contact can cause skin irritation

Ingestion: do not ingest

CMC—glaze additive

Inhalation: always use a respirator when handling material in dry form

Dermal Absorption: can cause skin irritation; use protective gloves when handling material in the dry form

Ingestion: do not ingest; however, certain types of CMC are found in fast food milk shakes

Calcium Chloride—not commonly used in glazes

Inhalation: always use a respirator when handling material in dry form

Dermal Absorption: can cause skin ulcers; wear rubber gloves when handling

Ingestion: do not ingest; can cause gastric upset

Chrome Oxide—glaze material

Inhalation: always use a respirator when handling material in dry form, can cause respiratory irritation

Dermal Absorption: contact can cause skin allergies

Ingestion: do not ingest; poisonous; destructive to cells in the human body; causes cancer in animals; can cause liver and kidney disorders; affects digestive system

Cobalt Carbonate—glaze material

Inhalation: always use a respirator when handling material in dry form; can cause asthma and lung irritation

Dermal Absorption: can cause skin allergies; wear protective gloves

Ingestion: do not ingest; can cause vomiting and stomach upset

Cobalt Oxide—glaze material

Inhalation: always use a respirator when handling material in dry form; can cause asthma and lung irritation

Dermal Absorption: can cause skin allergies; wear protective gloves

Ingestion: do not ingest; can cause vomiting and stomach upset

Cobalt Sulfate—glaze material

Inhalation: always use a respirator when handling material in any form

Dermal Absorption: can cause skin allergies; wear protective gloves

Ingestion: do not ingest

Copper Carbonate—glaze material

Inhalation: always use a respirator when handling dry material

Dermal Absorption: can cause skin irritations and skin allergies

Ingestion: do not ingest; can cause stomach irritation and vomiting; can cause Wilson's disease

Copper Oxide Black—glaze material

Inhalation: always use a respirator when handling dry material

Dermal Absorption: can cause skin irritations and skin allergies

Ingestion: do not ingest; can cause stomach irritation and vomiting; can cause Wilson's disease

Copper Oxide Red—glaze material

Inhalation: always use a respirator when handling dry material

Dermal Absorption: can cause skin irritations and skin allergies

Ingestion: do not ingest; can cause stomach irritation and vomiting; can cause Wilson's disease

Cordierite—clay body material

Inhalation: always use a respirator when handling dry material

Dermal Absorption: can cause skin irritation in large particle sizes

Ingestion: do not ingest

Cryolite—glaze material

Inhalation: always use a respirator when handling dry material; inhalation can cause lung irritation; can give off fluorine gas during firing; always vent kilns

Dermal Absorption: can cause skin irritation and skin allergies

Ingestion: do not ingest; can cause anemia, silicosis, bone defects

Darvan #7—slip casting clay body additive

Inhalation: avoid atomized spray of liquid

Dermal Absorption: can cause skin irritation; wash hands after using

Ingestion: do not ingest

Darvan #811—slip casting clay body additive

Inhalation: avoid atomized spray of liquid

Dermal Absorption: can cause skin irritation; wash hands after using

Ingestion: do not ingest

Dolomite—clay body material

Inhalation: always use a respirator when handling dry material

Dermal Absorption: wash hands after using material

Ingestion: do not ingest

Epsom Salts (Magnesium Sulfate)—glaze additive

Inhalation: always use a respirator when handling dry material

Dermal Absorption: can cause skin irritation; wash hands after using

Ingestion: do not ingest

Excelopax—glaze material

Inhalation: always use a respirator when handling dry material; prolonged exposure can cause silicosis

Dermal Absorption: can cause skin irritation and allergic reactions; wash hands after using material

Ingestion: do not ingest

Flourspar—glaze material

Inhalation: always use a respirator when handling material in dry form; can cause lung irritation, anemia, bone defects; gives off fluorine gas during firing; always vent kilns

Dermal Absorption: skin irritant or allergic reactions with prolonged use; always wash hands after using

Ingestion: do not ingest; may cause stomach problems, intestinal disorders, and nervous system problems

Frits (all brands of non-lead frit)—glaze material

Inhalation: always use a respirator when handling material in dry form

Dermal Absorption: wash hands after using material

Ingestion: do not ingest; depending on the frit and its solubility, it can cause intestinal disorders

Frits (all brands of lead frit)—glaze material.

Some frits can still leach lead into the atmosphere, or release lead from the fired glaze. Due to special precautions and the toxic effects of lead, it is not recommended for use in the pottery studio.

Inhalation: always use a respirator when handling material in dry form, inhalation can deposit lead in the lungs

Dermal Absorption: toxic lead can leach from the glaze; always wash hands after using any lead frit

Ingestion: do not ingest; stomach acids can break down ingested frit causing lead poisoning, which can result in chronic indigestion, anemia, headaches, malaise, pain in joints, kidney damage, and possibly birth defects

Gerstley Borate—glaze material

Inhalation: always use a respirator when handling material in dry form

Dermal Absorption: repeated contact can cause skin irritation

Ingestion: do not ingest

Gillespie Borate—glaze material

Inhalation: always use a respirator when handling material in dry form

Dermal Absorption: repeated contact can cause skin irritation

Ingestion: do not ingest

Grogs (all mesh sizes)—clay body additive

Inhalation: always use a respirator when handling material in dry form

Dermal Absorption: repeated contact can cause skin irritation

Ingestion: do not ingest

Gum Arabic—glaze additive

Inhalation: always use a respirator when handling material in dry form; can cause respiration allergies in atomized form

Dermal Absorption: can cause skin irritation

Ingestion: do not ingest

Ilmenite, Granular—clay body additive

Inhalation: always use a respirator when handling material in dry form

Dermal Absorption: repeated contact can cause skin irritation

Ingestion: do not ingest

Ilmenite, Powder—glaze material

Inhalation: always use a respirator when handling material in dry form

Dermal Absorption: repeated contact can cause skin irritation

Ingestion: do not ingest

Iron Chromate—glaze material

Inhalation: always use a respirator when handling material in dry form; inhalation can cause respiratory allergies and lung cancer

Dermal Absorption: can cause allergies, ulcers, and skin irritation

Ingestion: do not ingest; can cause poisoning, muscle cramps, and kidney damage

Iron Oxide, Black—glaze material

Inhalation: always use a respirator when handling material in dry form

Dermal Absorption: if rash develops; wear protective gloves

Ingestion: do not ingest

Iron Oxide, Black 5999—glaze material

Inhalation: always use a respirator when handling material in dry form

Dermal Absorption: if rash develops; wear protective gloves

Ingestion: do not ingest

Iron Oxide, Brown 521- glaze material

Inhalation: always use a respirator when handling material in dry form

Dermal Absorption: if rash develops; wear protective gloves

Ingestion: do not ingest

Iron Oxide, Red NR4284 Red—glaze material

Inhalation: always use a respirator when handling material in dry form

Dermal Absorption: if rash develops; wear protective gloves

Ingestion: do not ingest

Iron Oxide, Spanish Red—glaze material

Inhalation: always use a respirator when handling material in dry form

Dermal Absorption: if rash develops wear protective gloves

Ingestion: do not ingest

Iron Oxide, Yellow #5060 Red—glaze material

Inhalation: always use a respirator when handling material in dry form

Dermal Absorption: if rash develops; wear protective gloves

Ingestion: do not ingest

Iron Sulfate (Copperas)—glaze material

Inhalation: always use a respirator with the appropriate filter when handling this soluble material

Dermal Absorption: can cause irritation to the skin, eyes, nose, and throat

Ingestion: do not ingest; can be poisonous if ingested

Kryolite—clay body additive

Inhalation: always use a respirator when handling material in dry form

Dermal Absorption: repeated contact can cause skin irritation

Ingestion: do not ingest

Kyanite (all mesh sizes)—clay body additive

Inhalation: always use a respirator when handling material in dry form

Dermal Absorption: repeated contact can cause skin irritation

Ingestion: do not ingest

Laguna Borate—glaze material

Inhalation: always use a respirator when handling material in dry form

Dermal Absorption: repeated contact can cause skin irritation

Ingestion: do not ingest

Lead Bi-Silicate—glaze material
(not recommended for use in pottery)

Inhalation: lead inhalation can poison the gastrointestinal tract, causing anemia, neuromuscular damage in the fingers, ankles, and other organs; proven to cause birth defects; may vaporize during firing

Dermal Absorption: wash hands after using material

Ingestion: do not ingest; can cause loss of red blood cells, irritability, malaise, kidney damage, and liver damage

Lead Carbonate—glaze material
(not recommended for use in pottery)

Inhalation: lead inhalation can poison the gastrointestinal tract, causing anemia, neuromuscular damage in the fingers, ankles, and other organs; proven to cause birth defects; may vaporize during firing

Dermal Absorption: wash hands after using material

Ingestion: do not ingest; can cause loss of red blood cells, irritability, malaise, kidney damage, and liver damage

Lead Monosilicate—glaze material (not recommended for use in pottery)

Inhalation: lead inhalation can poison the gastrointestinal tract, causing anemia, neuromuscular damage in the fingers, ankles, and other organs; proven to cause birth defects; may vaporize during firing

Dermal Absorption: wash hands after using material

Ingestion: do not ingest; can cause loss of red blood cells, irritability, malaise, kidney damage, and liver damage

Lead Oxide Red—glaze material (not recommended for use in pottery)

Inhalation: lead inhalation can poison the gastrointestinal tract, causing anemia, neuromuscular damage in the fingers, ankles, and other organs; proven to cause birth defects; may vaporize during firing

Dermal Absorption: wash hands after using material

Ingestion: do not ingest; can cause loss of red blood cells, irritability, malaise, kidney damage, and liver damage

Lead Oxide Yellow (Litharge)—glaze material (not recommended for use in pottery)

Inhalation: lead inhalation can poison the gastrointestinal tract, causing anemia, neuromuscular damage in the fingers, ankles, and other organs; proven to cause birth defects; may vaporize during firing

Dermal Absorption: wash hands after using material

Ingestion: do not ingest; can cause loss of red blood cells, irritability, malaise, kidney damage, and liver damage

Litharge 100Y—glaze material (not recommended for use in pottery)

Inhalation: lead inhalation can poison the gastrointestinal tract, causing anemia, neuromuscular damage in the fingers, ankles, and other organs; proven to cause birth defects; may vaporize during firing

Dermal Absorption: wash hands after using material

Ingestion: do not ingest; can cause loss of red blood cells, irritability, malaise, kidney damage, and liver damage

Lithium Carbonate—Granular—glaze material

Inhalation: always use a respirator when handling material in dry form; can irritate the throat, eyes, and nose

Dermal Absorption: always wash hands after using the material; can be corrosive in water

Ingestion: do not ingest; partially soluble; can cause vertigo and gastric upset; corrosive to internal organs

Lithium Carbonate—Powdered—glaze material

Inhalation: always use a respirator when handling material in dry form; can irritate the throat, eyes, and nose

Dermal Absorption: always wash hands after using the material; can be corrosive in water

Ingestion: do not ingest; partially soluble; can cause vertigo and gastric upset; corrosive to internal organs

Macaloid (Vee Gum T)—glaze additive

Inhalation: always use a respirator when handling material in dry form; can irritate the throat, eyes, and nose

Dermal Absorption: can cause skin irritation; use rubber gloves when handling dry material

Ingestion: do not ingest; can cause gastrointestinal disorders

Magnesium Carbonate—glaze additive

Inhalation: due to its low density, always use a respirator when handling material in dry form; can irritate the throat, eyes, and nose

Dermal Absorption: can cause skin irritation; use rubber gloves when handling dry material

Ingestion: do not ingest; can cause gastrointestinal disorders

Manganese Carbonate—glaze material

Inhalation: always use a respirator when handling material in dry form

Dermal Absorption: can cause skin irritation; use rubber gloves when handling dry material

Ingestion: do not ingest; can cause manganese poisoning by inhalation or ingestion, symptoms include spasms, headaches; can affect motor function; can cause brain impairment

Manganese Dioxide—Granular Powdered—glaze material

Inhalation: always use a respirator when handling material in dry form

Dermal Absorption: can cause skin irritation; use rubber gloves when handling dry material

Ingestion: do not ingest; can cause manganese poisoning by inhalation or ingestion, symptoms include spasms, headaches; can affect motor function; can cause brain impairment

Manganese Dioxide—Powdered—glaze material

Inhalation: always use a respirator when handling material in dry form

Dermal Absorption: can cause skin irritation; use rubber gloves when handling dry material

Ingestion: do not ingest; can cause manganese poisoning by inhalation or ingestion, symptoms include spasms, headaches; can affect motor function; can cause brain impairment

Molochite porcelain grog (all mesh sizes)— clay body additive

Inhalation: always use a respirator when handling material in dry form

Dermal Absorption: repeated contact can cause skin irritation

Ingestion: do not ingest

Mullite (all mesh sizes)—clay body additive

Inhalation: always use a respirator when handling material in dry form

Dermal Absorption: repeated contact can cause skin irritation

Ingestion: do not ingest

Murray's Borate—glaze material

Inhalation: always use a respirator when handling material in dry form

Dermal Absorption: repeated contact can cause skin irritation

Ingestion: do not ingest

Nickel Carbonate—glaze material

Inhalation: always use a respirator when handling material in dry form; can cause irritation of the respiratory system and lung cancer

Dermal Absorption: use protective rubber gloves when handling the material in dry form; can cause skin allergies and eye irritation

Ingestion: do not ingest; can cause stomach irritation and injury; carcinogen; affects central nervous system

Nickel Oxide Black—glaze material

Inhalation: always use a respirator when handling material in dry form; can cause irritation of the respiratory system and lung cancer

Dermal Absorption: use protective rubber gloves when handling the material in dry form; can cause skin allergies and eye irritation

Ingestion: do not ingest; can cause stomach irritation and injury; carcinogen; affects central nervous system

Nickel Oxide Green—glaze material

Inhalation: always use a respirator when handling material in dry form; can cause irritation of the respiratory system and lung cancer

Dermal Absorption: use protective rubber gloves when handling the material in dry form; can cause skin allergies and eye irritation

Ingestion: do not ingest; can cause stomach irritation and injury; carcinogen; affects central nervous system

Nylon Fiber—clay body additive

Inhalation: always use a respirator when handling the material

Dermal Absorption: can cause skin irritation; use rubber gloves when handling the material

Ingestion: do not ingest; can cause stomach irritation

Ochre Yellow—glaze material

Inhalation: always use a respirator when handling the material

Dermal Absorption: can cause skin irritation; use rubber gloves when handling the material

Ingestion: do not ingest; can cause stomach irritation

Pearl Ash (Potassium carbonate)—glaze material

Inhalation: always use a respirator when handling the material; can cause lung disease

Dermal Absorption: corrosive when in contact with skin, nose, or eyes; always use rubber gloves when handling the material in the wet or dry form; can form caustic solutions

Ingestion: do not ingest; can cause injury to the mouth; can be fatal

Petalite—glaze material

Inhalation: always use a respirator when handling the material; can contain free silica, which can cause silicosis with prolonged exposure

Dermal Absorption: use rubber gloves when handling the material; non-toxic to skin contact

Ingestion: do not ingest; no specific toxicity

Plaster (all types)—used in wedging tables and pottery bats, molds

Inhalation: always use a respirator when handling the material

Dermal Absorption: prolonged use can dry out hands

Ingestion: do not ingest

Potassium Bi-Chromate—glaze material

Inhalation: always use a respirator when handling the material; can cause respiratory allergies

Dermal Absorption: can cause allergies and skin ulcers; use rubber gloves when handling the material

Ingestion: do not ingest; can cause poisoning, kidney damage, stomach cramps

Pyrophyllite (Pyrax HS, Pyrotrol)—clay body additive

Inhalation: always use a respirator when handling

the material; can contain free silica, which can cause silicosis with prolonged exposure
Dermal Absorption: non-toxic to skin contact
Ingestion: do not ingest; no specific toxicity

Raw Sienna, Yellow Ochre—glaze material
Inhalation: always use a respirator when handling the material
Dermal Absorption: use rubber gloves when handling the material; non-toxic to skin contact
Ingestion: do not ingest

Red Crocus Martis Ochre—glaze material
Inhalation: always use a respirator when handling the material
Dermal Absorption: use rubber gloves when handling the material; non-toxic to skin contact
Ingestion: do not ingest

Rutile, Dark Milled—glaze material
Inhalation: always use a respirator when handling the material
Dermal Absorption: use rubber gloves when handling the material; non-toxic to skin contact
Ingestion: do not ingest

Rutile, Granular Ceramic—clay body additive
Inhalation: always use a respirator when handling the material
Dermal Absorption: use rubber gloves when handling the material; non-toxic to skin contact
Ingestion: do not ingest

Rutile, Light Ceramic—glaze material
Inhalation: always use a respirator when handling the material
Dermal Absorption: use rubber gloves when handling the material; non-toxic to skin contact
Ingestion: do not ingest

Selenium—glaze material
Inhalation: always use a respirator when handling the material
Dermal Absorption: use rubber gloves when handling the material in dry form; can cause irritation to the mucous membranes and dermatitis
Ingestion: do not ingest; affects nervous system

Silica Sand (all mesh sizes) Kryolite—clay body additive
Inhalation: always use a respirator when handling material in dry form; fine particles can cause silicosis with repeated exposure
Dermal Absorption: repeated contact can cause skin irritation
Ingestion: do not ingest

Silicon Carbide (all mesh sizes)—glaze additive
Inhalation: always use a respirator when handling the material

Dermal Absorption: use rubber gloves when handling the material; non-toxic to skin contact
Ingestion: do not ingest

Silver Nitrate—glaze additive
Inhalation: always use a respirator with an approved filter for this type of vapor
Dermal Absorption: can stain the skin; caustic; can burn the unprotected skin
Ingestion: do not ingest; soluble

Soda Ash—glaze additive
Inhalation: always use a respirator when handling material in dry form
Dermal Absorption: Alkali is corrosive; can cause skin, eye, and mouth irritation
Ingestion: do not ingest; soluble; can be fatal in high dosages

Sodium Bicarbonate—glaze additive
Inhalation: always use a respirator when handling material in dry form
Dermal Absorption: can cause skin irritation; wear protective gloves when handling dry or wet material
Ingestion: do not ingest; soluble

Sodium Nitrate—glaze additive
Inhalation: always use a respirator with an approved filter for this type of vapor
Dermal Absorption: can cause skin irritation; wear protective gloves when handling material
Ingestion: do not ingest; poisonous

Sodium Silicate (water glass)—casting slip additive
Inhalation: no respirator needed
Dermal Absorption: can cause skin irritation; wear protective gloves when handling material
Ingestion: do not ingest

Sodium Silicate Dry—casting slip additive
Inhalation: always use a respirator when handling material in dry form
Dermal Absorption: can cause skin irritation; wear protective gloves when handling material
Ingestion: do not ingest

Sodium Sulfate Nitrate—glaze additive
Inhalation: always use a respirator with an approved filter for this type of vapor
Dermal Absorption: can cause skin irritation; wear protective gloves when handling material
Ingestion: do not ingest; poisonous

Stannous Chloride—glaze additive
Inhalation: always use a respirator with an approved filter for this type of vapor

Dermal Absorption: skin, eye, lung irritant; use protective gloves
Ingestion: do not ingest

Strontium Carbonate—glaze material
Inhalation: always use a respirator when handling material in dry form
Dermal Absorption: not toxic to the skin
Ingestion: do not ingest

Talc (all talcs)—clay body and glaze material
Inhalation: always use a respirator when handling material in dry form; some talcs can contain free silica, which can cause silicosis; some talcs can contain asbestos, which can cause lung cancer
Dermal Absorption: use protective gloves when handling the material in dry form
Ingestion: do not ingest; ingestion can cause intestinal cancer if asbestos is present in talc

Tin Oxide—glaze material
Inhalation: always use a respirator when handling material in dry form; can irritate nose
Dermal Absorption: not toxic to the skin but can irritate eyes
Ingestion: do not ingest

Titanium Dioxide—glaze material
Inhalation: always use a respirator when handling material in dry form
Dermal Absorption: not toxic to the skin
Ingestion: do not ingest

Tri-Calcium Phosphate (Bone ash)—glaze material
Inhalation: always use a respirator when handling material in dry form
Dermal Absorption: not toxic to the skin
Ingestion: do not ingest

Ultrox—glaze material
Inhalation: always use a respirator when handling material in dry form
Dermal Absorption: not toxic to the skin
Ingestion: do not ingest

Umber, Burnt—glaze material
Inhalation: always use a respirator when handling material in dry form
Dermal Absorption: not toxic to the skin
Ingestion: do not ingest

Uranium Oxide—glaze material (not recommended for use in the ceramics studio)
Inhalation: always use a respirator when handling material in dry form; exposure can cause emphysema, lung cancer, kidney damage, and nerve damage
Dermal Absorption: toxic; do not touch
Ingestion: do not ingest; poison

Vanadium Pentoxide—glaze material
Inhalation: always use a respirator when handling material in dry form; exposure can cause pulmonary edema, asthma, kidney damage, nerve damage, intestinal and heart damage
Dermal Absorption: use protective gloves when handling the material in dry or wet form; can cause skin allergies, eye and skin irritation
Ingestion: do not ingest, can cause intestinal and heart problems

Vee Gum CER—glaze additive
Inhalation: always use a respirator when handling material in dry form
Dermal Absorption: use protective gloves when handling the material in dry form
Ingestion: do not ingest

Volcanic Ash—Pumice—glaze material
Inhalation: always use a respirator when handling material in dry form; can contain free silica
Dermal Absorption: use protective gloves; can cause skin rash and irritation
Ingestion: do not ingest

Whiting—glaze material
Inhalation: always use a respirator when handling material in dry form
Dermal Absorption: non-toxic
Ingestion: do not ingest

Wollastonite—glaze material
Inhalation: always use a respirator when handling material in dry form
Dermal Absorption: non-toxic
Ingestion: do not ingest

Zircon, G Milled—glaze material
Inhalation: always use a respirator when handling material in dry form
Dermal Absorption: use protective gloves; can cause skin irritation
Ingestion: do not ingest

Zinc Oxide—glaze material
Inhalation: always use a respirator when handling material in dry form
Dermal Absorption: non-toxic
Ingestion: do not ingest

Zirconium Silicate—glaze material
Inhalation: always use a respirator when handling material in dry form; can cause silicosis with prolonged exposure
Dermal Absorption: use protective gloves; can cause skin irritation
Ingestion: do not ingest

Zircopax Plus—glaze material

Inhalation: always use a respirator when handling material in dry form; can cause silicosis with prolonged exposure

Dermal Absorption: use protective gloves; can cause skin irritation

Ingestion: do not ingest

Summary of Ceramic Raw Material Hazards

Ceramic materials primarily enter the body in three ways—inhalation, dermal absorption, and ingestion. A common sense approach to good housekeeping procedures within the studio will also ensure a lower risk of health problems whenever working with ceramic related equipment or materials. While this fact is deceptively simple to comprehend, it is sometimes hard to practice on a daily basis. It is only human nature to take short cuts whenever rushed in the work cycle or when physically or mentally tired. Statistically, such situations produce the most accidents in any human activity whether driving a car too fast or opening bags of dry clay without the use of a respirator.

For most ceramic raw materials that are inhaled, the negative health effects can take years to present themselves. Because of the delayed reaction time, a potter can be under the false assumption that each unprotected exposure is harmless. It is only after repeated exposures over years that the damage to the respiratory system can happen. Obviously, if a potter opened a bag of flint without a respirator and suddenly died, a cause and effect situation would warn others immediately. Potters should always think of a delayed inhalation reaction to raw materials, which the consistent use of a respirator will prevent. It is also within our power to educate ourselves on other ceramic hazards we encounter in our daily activities and enact protective measures to deal with the potential hazards. Protection in the ceramics studio starts with understanding how raw material can enter the human body.

The human body is marvelously constructed to filter foreign material and to neutralize it if it gets into the system. However, preventive measures are always to be enacted. The most prevalent, and potentially the most harmful, point of entry into the body is inhalation of raw materials or kiln exhaust. Every potter has seen the fine particles of clay move in the air when they have opened a bag of dry clay or smelled the acrid fumes that fill the studio when firing a bisque kiln. These are the obvious signs of studio environment compromise. The unseen micron size particles of clay, raw materials, and kiln exhaust vapors are also to be considered. It is for these reasons that the proper planning and implementation of air filtering measures will be critically important for the potter to master.

Breathing draws oxygen into our systems, and since it is impractical to hold one's breath when working with clay, glazes, and firing kilns, several protective measures should be considered to keep inhalation of ceramic materials to a minimum. Whole room venting systems, if correctly designed and fitted to the workspace, should be considered in educational institutions or craft centers. The optimum place for such units is where numerous students with varying degrees of safety conscious abilities are enrolled. It is assumed that not every student will thoroughly clean the room or, specifically, their individual work area. Often the reasons for such lax behavior are not intentional but merely caused by a lack of knowledge on how to protect themselves and others from possible contamination by raw materials. However, room venting systems, while effective, can be expensive purchases for the average individual potter, which makes other less expensive preventive measures all the more important.

As the Ceramic Raw Material Hazard list indicates, when handling any dry raw material or clay, a properly approved respirator is required. Avoid prolonged exposure to dry materials when not wearing a respirator. While this advice is seemingly a simple safety directive, it is important to use a respirator on every occasion where a small particle size material might be released into the studio environment. The use of venting and the appropriate respirator is absolutely required when using lusters, which are metallic alloys suspended in oil-based solvents. They are most frequently applied to already glazed surfaces and then refired, causing the oil-based solvent to be driven off as a vapor, leaving the metallic color to bond to the underlying glazed surface. During the first part of the luster firing, vapors leave the kiln, which have caused health problems for potters. This fact was determined by "The Potter's Health & Safety Questionnaire" (page 141).

Another common directive is the use of rubber or latex protective gloves when handling dry materials or the materials in the wet form, such as found in glazes. The use of gloves is recommended for people with sensitive skin, cuts on the hand, skin rashes, or any skin sensitivity. Keep in mind potters have not reported or have not experienced major health or skin diseases when they have not worn gloves in glaze mixing or glaze application procedures. The overall recommendation is to wash the hands thoroughly after any glazing operation and before leaving the studio at the end of a work session. As an added safety measure, it is always a good practice to have a separate set of studio clothes, which can be cleaned on a regular basis. In this way, any ceramic raw material will not travel out of the studio and into other locations.

While the statement, "Do not eat ceramic materials," might seem obvious, in some instances a straightforward directive applies to a critical safety issue. It is hard to conceive of a situation where an adult would consciously go into a pottery studio and ingest any of the raw materials contained in storage jars. However, by not eating, drinking, or smoking in the studio, the potter reduces the risk of even a minor accidental ingestion of a raw material. The Ceramic Raw Material Hazards recommendations can be summarized by a few basic concepts, namely a clean studio goes a long way to protect a potter's health and safety. A good respirator used whenever dry materials are encountered reduces the risk of potential health problems. Obtaining and using an appropriate kiln venting system will also protect the air quality within the studio.

Children and infants are highly susceptible to any contaminant in whatever the form, and they will require additional safety measures, or they should be removed from the ceramics studio work area. Children who are old enough to work with clay and glazes should be monitored by an adult on a *continuous* basis while in the studio. Many times children will ingest materials that an adult with a higher reasoning power and experience will automatically not place anywhere near their mouth. A consistent application of the safety procedures on a daily basis and knowledge of ceramic materials will ensure a low-risk studio environment.

Chapter 12

Is Barium Carbonate Safe?

The investigation of barium carbonate was originally printed as a chapter in my book, *What Every Potter Should Know* (Krause Publications, 1999). In the past few years, there have been increased discussions in the ceramics community concerning the use of barium carbonate in the studio.

Barium carbonate is a common glaze material and is often used in low fire red clay bodies to neutralize soluble salt scumming in the fired ware. The toxicity of barium carbonate is not in question. However, at present there is no statistical medical and occupational data to indicate barium poisoning in the population of potters. Furthermore, there is no evidence of barium release from fired glazes that have caused health problems in the general public. The raw material, barium carbonate, is characteristic of a number of ceramic materials that are potentially hazardous to potters. There is also the potential for some high barium glazes to leach after firing. However, we do not know if these adverse health effects are actually taking place. Potters in many studio situations have used similar potentially hazardous materials for years on a daily basis with no difficulty. During this time, they have employed stringent to non-existent degrees of safety precautions when handling and firing raw materials.

Barium carbonate requires an in depth comprehensive study to determine its actual toxic effects on potters. The results of which will indicate if a wider range of handling procedures should be considered when using it in clay and glazes. Unfortunately, there is little or no current information on ceramic toxicity as it relates to the small pottery population. The economic reality does not support health research, as there are not enough potters or people who buy "handmade" pottery to fund such a toxicity study. Conversely, the commercial dinnerware industry, employing thousands of people who manufacture pottery in larger volumes than the small "garage" potters, has carefully documented conditions in the workplace along with stricter requirements for the release of toxic materials from their pottery products.

The central question asked by potters has been, "Is barium carbonate safe?" Yes, provided you don't go into your studio and eat barium carbonate, or directly inhale this white powder. While this statement cannot be definitively proven at this point, it is important to remember that the history of barium carbonate when used by potters does not indicate a problem material. However, a complete knowledge of barium carbonate, especially in its raw form, is vital to a potter's health and safety. That is the short answer to a controversial issue raised by many in the field of ceramics.

Barium carbonate has a long history of use in clay bodies, glazes, and casting slips. It serves several functions when used in clay bodies or glaze formulas. Regardless of its history, today many potters are removing barium from their studios, fearing the toxic potential of this material. As the general population has become more aware of health and safety issues, every material is being examined for its potentially harmful effects in our lives. Understandably, potters do not want to jeopardize themselves when handling ceramic raw materials. They also do not want to place their customers at risk when using fired clay and glaze products. With such legitimate health and safety concerns why use barium carbonate?

Barium Carbonate in Clay Bodies

We have all noticed surface deposits of white powder developing on exposed parts of common red building brick. The soluble salts in the clay migrate to the brick surface, crystallizing and causing white scumming. When barium carbonate is added to the clay body (1/4% to 2% based on the dry weight of the clay body), it reacts with calcium and/or magnesium salts found in clays. It changes them into calcium carbonate and barium sulfate, which do not produce soluble salt scumming. By eliminating soluble salts in the clay body, subsequent firing discoloration is reduced. Some red earthenware clays are more susceptible to soluble salt problems, but even so called "clean" clays can occasionally have high levels of troublesome salts. Consequently barium carbonate is found in many different types of clay body formulas.

Barium Carbonate in Casting Slips

Ball clays used in casting slip formulas sometimes contain soluble salts. If the ball clay was left untreated, it would require excessively high amounts of deflocculant to transform it into a casting slip. Barium carbonate reacts with soluble salts found in clays, changing them into insoluble barium sulfates, which in turn reduces the deflocculant requirement for the slip. In low fire white clay bodies where the amount of ball clay can be as much as half the clay body formula, the level of barium carbonate required can be .03% to .05% based on the dry weight of the clay body formula. The actual amount used will depend on the soluble salt levels found in the clay. In stoneware and high iron content casting slips, barium carbonate is needed to facilitate good casting properties in the slip and can be as high as 2% based on the dry weight of the clay body formula.

Barium Carbonate in Glazes

Barium carbonate can be classified as an alkaline earth that is very refractory. Small percentages in low temperature glazes will result in dry matt-fired surfaces. At higher temperatures, barium carbonate is mostly known for producing soft, buttery, glaze textures. It can also yield intense blue colors when combined with copper in reduction glazes. Barium causes unique glaze colors and surface qualities that are very difficult to obtain when using alternative glaze materials.

Barium Carbonate Alternatives

Sometimes if less than 6% barium carbonate is used in high temperature (above c/6 or 2232^0F) glaze formulas, and it is not needed to promote color or glaze texture, it can be removed without changing the fired nature of the glaze. In such situations, barium is acting as a marginal flux. Its absence from the formula will not appreciably affect the fired glaze result. In glazes containing barium carbonate in amounts greater than 6%, barium is probably contributing to unique qualities of opacity and glaze color, and removing it would substantially change the glaze.

Strontium carbonate goes into a melt more actively than barium carbonate. It has been used in place of barium (strontium carbonate 3/4 parts to barium carbonate 1 part) but it does not yield an adequate match in glaze color, opacity, and texture. Another ineffective barium carbonate substitute, barium sulfate (insoluble and non toxic), which is the form of barium used for medical procedures, has not been an adequate alternative in glazes or clay bodies. Sulfate fumes are released as it reacts with the increasing kiln temperature, causing blisters or pinholes in glazes and bloating in clay bodies.

Facts about Barium Carbonate

The actual material that potters use in clay and glazes, barium carbonate, is never found in nature in its elemental form but is mined from barite ore that contains barium sulfate. Barite is a naturally occurring mineral used in the oil- and gas-drilling industries. About 5% of barite is processed into barium carbonate, barium chloride, and barium hydroxide. Barium carbonate is used in the manufacture of glass for television and computer screens, due to it capacity to absorb X-rays generated when the image is produced. Barium carbonate is also blended with iron oxide to form ceramic magnets used in many products. Various industries in the United States use approximately 50,000 tons of barium carbonate every year. [1]

---

[1] Toxicology and Carcinogenesis Studies of Barium Chloride Dihydrate (Drinking Water Studies), U.S. Department of Health and Human Services (CAS NO. 10326-27-9), pages 13–16.

Toxic Effects of Barium Carbonate

A search of the relevant medical literature and journals reveals two kinds of problems associated with toxic reactions to raw barium carbonate. Barium carbonate can be accidentally ingested/inhaled, or it can be intentionally ingested to commit suicide.

Ingestion

The effects of ingestion take place when barium carbonate changes in the presence of stomach acid (hydrochloric acid found in the stomach), yielding soluble barium chloride. The first symptoms can be vomiting, skeletal and muscle twitching, or muscle paralysis. Small amounts of ingested barium carbonate (13 grams) can be lethal.

One woman attempted suicide by eating 40 grams of barium carbonate. The patient required mechanical ventilation after her respiratory muscles were paralyzed. She recovered fully within one week. [2] Another example of ingestion occurred when seven people in one family accidentally consumed rodenticide (barium carbonate) and required treatment at their local hospital. [3]

An intentional ingestion of barium happened when a person went on a "spree drinking" episode of binging on ethanol for one week then ingested about 13 grams of barium chloride, with intent to commit suicide. He developed paralysis involving the extremities, his respiration became paralyzed, and he was placed on mechanical ventilation. Magnesium sulfate was administered. The patient made a rapid recovery after an 11-day hospital stay. [4] Such cases are significant in that barium ingestion was by intent and not an accident

Most barium that enters the body is eliminated within one to two weeks. [5] Barium is not a cumulative substance in the body where at some point a toxic level could be reached. Past information about barium causing cumulative central nervous system damage is not supported by the Environmental Protection Agencies toxicological evaluation of soluble barium. [6] However, just on a common sense level, it would still not be a good idea to rush into your studio and eat barium carbonate. Yet, accidents do happen in every area of life. What could prevent an accidental dose of barium carbonate from being swallowed? Use a dust mask when mixing barium in glazes. Not eating or smoking in your studio would cut the risk of ingesting *any* foreign substance including barium. Also, placing barium carbonate in a covered jar would be a prudent step in handling this material.

Inhalation

Breathing particles of *any* substance found in the pottery studio should be prevented. Whenever clay and glaze materials are handled in the dry state, small particles can become airborne. Wearing a dust mask in situations where bags of dry material are opened or mixed is a safeguard against inhalation of the particles.

In the medical literature, one case demonstrates what types of problem potters are *not* having with barium carbonate. A 22-year-old man, who was new on the job, caused barium carbonate to blow back into his face by dumping barium into another material and causing an explosion. He inhaled a considerable amount of powder but did not swallow much. The industrial worker was not wearing a dust mask. He experienced cramps and nausea, and his feet and hands felt heavy and weak. At the hospital he was treated with potassium intravenously and had a complete remission in the next five days. [7] Potters are not likely to encounter a case where barium carbonate is involved in an explosive reaction, but it does illustrate the need for a dust mask.

While such cases are sensational and thought provoking they do not reflect potters' experience with barium carbonate. For more than forty years, potters in the United States have been using bar-

[2] Phelan, D.M.; Hagley, S.R.; Huerin, M.D. "Is Hypokalemia the Cause of Paralysis in Barium Poisoning?" *British Medical Journal*, Volume 289: page 882, 1984.

[3] Johnson-CH; Van Tassell-VJ; Ann-Emerg-Med 1991, Oct.; 20 (10): 1138-42.

[4] Wetherill, S.F.; Guarino, M.J.; Cox, R.W.; "Acute Renal Failure Associated with Barium Chloride Poisoning?" *Annals of Internal Medicine;* Volume 95; No. 2; pages 187-188; 1981.

[5] "Toxicological Profile for Barium"; U. S. Department of Health and Human Services; Public Health Service; Agency for Toxic Substances and Disease Registry; PB 93-110658.

[6] Environmental Protection Agencies report, Federal Register, Vol. 62 No. 2 Friday, January 3, 1997, pages 368-370.

[7] Shankle, R.; Keane, J.R.; "Acute Paralysis from Inhaled Barium Carbonate"; *Archives of Neurology,* Volume 45; pages 579-580; May 1988.

ium carbonate in their studios and have sold functional pottery containing barium in their glazes. The medical records do not show any reports of toxic reactions to barium carbonate used in pottery studios or toxic levels of barium released from glazes.[8] This lack of information can indicate a few possibilities. Potters are receiving toxic doses of barium carbonate in their studios, and their symptoms (vomiting, paralysis, etc.) are not recognized or reported. Another possibility is that potential toxic reactions concerning barium carbonate are not happening. The absence of evidence concerning potters' misapplication of the material is one factor in considering the continued use of barium carbonate.

An occupational exposure study reports no adverse health effects related to workers exposed to high levels of barium carbonate dust for periods of 7 to 27 years.[9] Clearly such diverse information about barium carbonate is confusing to anyone contemplating using the material in his or her studio. However, protection from inhalation by wearing a dust mask is a precautionary step that would remove the potter from any short- or long-term hazard due to inhalation and ingestion. Thoroughly cleaning the pottery studio on a regular basis would be a further safety measure in the use of any ceramics related material.

Handling Barium Carbonate in the Studio

Essentially, the same safety precautions should be in effect when handling any raw material. Whenever possible, purchase clean unopened bags of raw material and store them in a place where they cannot be broken. As a safety and studio hygiene measure, place raw material bags in covered jars or large heavyweight plastic garbage bags with twist top closures. During glaze mixing or clay mixing operations, any unused raw material is returned to the covered jar or storage bag. In this way, bags will not accidentally be broken open causing small particles of raw material to be spread throughout the studio. When opening a raw material bag or mixing dry materials, always wear a cartridge respirator or a paper dust mask. Paper masks should be discarded after use, and extra masks should be kept in a sealed container. Cartridge masks should have their filters changed regularly.

Mixing Barium Carbonate in Glazes

Barium carbonate has a limited solubility in pure water. Any solubility of barium carbonate in glaze water is marginal. Solubility varies with glaze water pH levels. If the glaze water is acidic (low pH levels), some barium carbonate changes to barium chloride with levels in the water of 15.3 to 45 p.p.m. (as a comparison 1 p.p.m. would be equivalent to 1 minute in a 2 year period). Such amounts are well below any toxic concern for penetrating the skin even with an open wound on the hand. While mixing a wet or dry glaze with your hands is not recommended, barium carbonate in the glaze *will not* cause a health risk, providing you do not drink large quantities of the glaze. The medical literature does not contain any reports of barium carbonate migrating through wounds in the skin, as might occur in a glaze mixing operation. By way of comparing the relative risks in glazing operations, mixing highly alkaline and soluble wood ash glazes with bare hands is more harmful as this *will* cause a health risk through skin irritation and/or burns. Regardless, washing your hands after any glazing operation is always best.

Barium Release Levels in the Environment

In the past, long-term exposure to low levels of barium was thought to cause health problems, but the data does not support this belief. The National Toxicology Program Study by the U.S. Department of Health and Human Services conducted tests where they fed animals water containing up to 700 p.p.m. levels of barium. At this level of constant daily consumption, the water was considered safe to drink and did not produce harmful effects. The medical assumption in this method of testing is that animals respond similarly to humans. The purpose of this study was to predict the possible long-term effects of daily ingestion of barium in humans.

Barium in its different forms is commonly found in food, water, soil, and even the air we breathe. It is one of the most abundant materials found in the earth. We are in a barium-laden environment. The Toxicology and Carcinogenesis Studies Report issued by the U.S. Department of Health and Human Services states that the drinking water in some United States cities

---

8. Databases searched, BIOSIS (toxicological aspects of environmental health), TOXLIT (toxicology literature), RTECS (Registry of Toxic Effects of Chemical Substances), and MEDLINE.
9. Essing, H.G.; et al.; "Exclusion of Disturbances to Health from Long Years of Exposure to Barium Carbonate in the Production of Steatite Ceramics" (translated from German); *Arbeitsmedizin Sozialmedizin Praventimedizin*; Volume 11; No. 12 pages 299-302; 1976.

can exceed 20 p.p.m. of barium. This amount of barium reflects what people are consuming daily without ill effects; it does not tell us what amount greater than 20 p.p.m. people *could* consume with no ill effects!

Humans ingest barium on a regular daily basis. It is found in many foods, including tea, coffee, and fruits. Dietary consumption of barium from foods is from 300 to 1,770 mg/day. Barium is also found in bran flakes (3.9 p.p.m. barium release), eggs (7.6 p.p.m. barium release), sea water (5.2 p.p.m. to 25.2 p.p.m. barium release), beets (2.6 p.p.m. barium release), and Brazil nuts (1000 p.p.m. barium release). However, the chances of eating enough Brazil nuts to achieve a toxic level of barium are remote, as the stomach and digestive system could not hold that volume of nuts.

Barium Release Levels in Glazes

Barium carbonate decomposes when heated and changes to barium silicate or barium salts in the fired glaze, after which the glazed surface can be soluble when it contacts weak acids contained in foods. Release levels of pottery glazes containing barium can range from 0 p.p.m. to more than 1250 p.p.m. However, many glazes tested are within the 20 p.p.m. barium release ranges.

It is always prudent and useful to test for barium-release levels on functional pottery glazes that come into direct contact with food or drink. Choose a laboratory that is familiar with the testing procedure. If the test is done correctly, the accuracy rate is 99%.[10]

Commonly, high barium release levels in glazes can be substantially decreased by firing the glaze one or two cones higher in temperature or adjusting the glaze formula. If you are unsure of how to adjust the glaze, seek guidance. Experimenting on your own without a basic understanding of glaze materials can be fun but it can also be time consuming.

As potters, we should educate ourselves about the safe use of any raw material in our studio. We should then use this knowledge to protect ourselves and our customers from the potentially harmful effects of the ceramic process. However, we are often asked to make decisions about ceramic materials based on incomplete facts. In the past, unchallenged claims, unfounded dire projections, and generalizations about raw materials hazards brought more drama to the issues than useable facts. In some circumstances, the information published is not relevant to how we as potters use the material. An ongoing effort to increase our knowledge of questionable materials will yield a realistic evaluation of their hazards. Often a valid disagreement exists on which materials are truly dangerous. Such differing opinions are needed, as they contribute to discussions, testing, and greater research in ceramic raw material toxicology as it directly relates to potters.

The ongoing health and safety issues concerning potters' use of barium carbonate fall into two primary areas of concern: The accidental or intentional ingestion/inhalation of the material in the studio, and its potential release in fired glazes. To prevent accidental inhalation/ingestion, wear a dusk mask when mixing or handling barium carbonate. Sometimes a simple recommendation is not considered valuable or effective because it is too easy to believe. As for the intentional ingestion of barium carbonate, that is beyond the scope of this article.

The second area of health worry relates to the potential release of barium used in clay bodies, casting slips, and fired functional pottery glazed surfaces. The low percentages of barium carbonate used in clay bodies and casting slip formulas and its potential release is considerably below any level of concern regarding health and safety. In glazes, the ideal situation would be an inert, stable, non-leaching fired surface. In the real world, this situation is not necessary for barium as it should be for lead and other heavy metals, which are highly toxic and can accumulate in the body.

With the level of barium release in some communities' drinking water approaching 20 p.p.m. with no ill effects in the population, a 20 p.p.m. or lower release of barium for functional pottery glazes should be a conservative goal. This amount takes into consideration various factors, which can cause variable barium release levels in glazes, such as glaze thickness, kiln-firing atmosphere, end point firing temperature, time to temperature, re-firing glazes, and marginal glaze testing inaccuracies. The

---

[10.] For testing of barium release or other elements in glazes (i.e., antimony, manganese, vanadium, lead, etc.), send a fired sample of the glaze on a cup or bowl to: Office of Sponsored Programs, New York State College of Ceramics, Alfred University, Alfred, NY, 14803, (607) 871-2486, fax (607) 871-3469, or, The Alfred Analytical Laboratory, 4964 Kenyon Road, Alfred Station, NY 14803, (607) 498-8074, fax (607) 478-5324, ats@infoblvd.net. There is a $30.00 charge per element tested.

drinking water study (Toxicology and Carcinogenesis Studies of Barium Chloride Dihydrate) is significant because it relates to a barium consumption level in water (20 parts per million) that humans drink every day over a prolonged time. This is the closest approximation to people drinking or eating from barium-release glazed surfaces for an extended time. It also assumes the worst case situation where a glaze releasing barium will continue to release the same amount of barium every time it contacts food or drink

Barium carbonate is not an easy material to classify concerning safety issues. It requires respect and effort to understand how to use it safely. Potters can always take the recommendations of "experts," but the real information comes from building up a base of knowledge from many sources. Disregarding raw material warnings is irrational just as believing in the "poison of the month" theory is excessive. Both extremes are inaccurate and offer ignorance instead of insight. Potters must do some hard work and look into the literature and toxicity statistics on this common glaze material. On some level, we calculate the relative risk factor in all daily events. How dangerous is flying? Not as dangerous as driving to the airport. How dangerous is barium carbonate as used by potters? Not as dangerous as driving to your studio, or as high a risk as back pain from lifting kiln shelves, or carpal tunnel syndrome (repetitive motion injury from throwing, wedging, lifting), or retina damage from looking into a firing kiln without eye protection. Proper protection and knowledge will prevent accidents in these known potential areas of risk. The same principle should be applied to barium carbonate.

What to Do

Wear a dust mask when mixing barium carbonate. Keep barium carbonate in a covered storage container. Test *only* barium glazes that come into *direct* contact with food. If the barium release level is higher than 20 p.p.m., adjust the glaze or test an alternative barium glaze. Often the most efficient method is to obtain several barium glaze formulas that have already been tested.

Health and Safety Recommendations for Handling Raw Materials

- Obtain a MSDS from your ceramics supplier for each raw material used in the studio. It will list the control measures for safely handling the material.
- Never eat, drink, or smoke in the pottery studio.
- Always wet mop the studio floors every day or every other day to remove raw material dust. Use a dust mask during this operation.
- Always wear a dust mask when mixing dry glaze or clay body materials.

- Always put all dry glaze and clay materials in double plastic bags or sealed containers.
- Clean up any raw materials spills on the floor or tables when they occur.
- Place a doormat outside the pottery studio to catch dry materials.
- Wear a separate set of clothes in the studio, and clean your studio clothes frequently.
- Clean eyeglasses after leaving the studio.
- Label all raw materials in the studio.
- Wipe down worktables with a wet sponge before leaving the studio.
- The use of a small particle air filtration unit in the studio will improve air quality.
- Supervise children at all times in the studio.
- Do not ingest or inhale any raw materials.
- Wash hands before leaving the studio.
- Do not store food in the studio.
- All dry and wet materials should be stored in containers with lids or in closed plastic bags.

Chapter 13

Talc and Asbestos

The historical association between talc and asbestos is an extremely unfortunate one. Precipitated in large measure by the use of overly broad asbestos definitions and nonspecific analytical techniques, the idea that asbestos is commonly and intimately associated with talc is simply not correct.[1]

In the early 1970s, news articles appeared claiming that trace amounts of asbestos had been found in some "off-the-shelf" baby talcum powders. The accuracy of those reports was later disputed as asbestos analytical techniques improved and rigorous quality control practices were instituted throughout the talc industry as an extra margin of caution. However, the geologic conditions under which talc and asbestos form are dissimilar—they are not commonly found together.

Perhaps the biggest contribution to this faulty asbestos in talc perception involved technical and regulatory confusion over one specific unique industrial grade talc mined exclusively by R.T. Vanderbilt Company in upstate New York. Before describing the basis of that interesting controversy, it is important to note that talc represents a major ceramic raw material in clay bodies and glazes. In low fire clay bodies c/06 to c/04 (1830^0F to 1940^0F), it can make up 50% of the clay body formula. In fact many low fire moist white clays used in schools are composed of 50% talc and 50% ball clay. Talc helps the glaze to ensure a more compatible fit on the fired clay body. It reduces or eliminates crazing (a fine network of lines in the glaze where the glaze contracts more than the clay body during the cooling cycle of the kiln) in low fire glazes. In glazes talc contributes much needed silica and magnesia to the formula, with high percentages of talc producing a matt opaque glaze surface. Potters have used talc as a primary ingredient in clay body and glaze formulas for over fifty years, and talc has had a longer and greater function in the sanitary and commercial dinnerware industry.

As noted, for decades there has been a controversy surrounding talc and its possible asbestos content. Asbestos has been linked to pulmonary cancer among certain types of industrial workers. It is an accepted medical fact that excessive exposure to asbestos can cause harm to humans. The actual term asbestos denotes a commercial name applied to a group of fibrous silicate minerals that can be separated into long thin fibers and woven into a cloth. In fact, asbestos fibers were commonly woven into cloth, which was used in heat-protective clothing and gloves. Asbestos fibers were also incorporated into floor tile and pipe insulation found in the basements of many old houses. Most people think of asbestos as a single entity. However, asbestos can be found in any one of six minerals: chrysotile/white asbestos, crocidolite/blue asbestos, amosite/brown asbestos, anthophyllite, actinolite, and tremolite. Each of the minerals listed comes in asbestiform and non-asbestiform varieties. The confusion and misunderstanding that improperly linked asbestos to Vanderbilt talc was due in large measure to the fact that several minerals have the same name but all are not asbestos.

In 1972, OSHA set its first asbestos standard in which it listed serpentine chrystile, crocidolite, amosite, anthophyllite, actinolite, and tremolite under the generic term "asbestos."

---

[1]."Talc: Occurrence, Characterization, and Consumer Applications" by Zazenski, R. et al; *Regulatory Toxicology and Pharmacology* 21, 218-229 (1995).

Tremolite is the mineral that makes up 50% of R.T. Vanderbilt talc. However, the tremolite in R.T. Vanderbilt talc is non-asbestiform. In this configuration, no scientific study or medical evidence has associated non-asbestiform tremolite with asbestos. There is an essential difference between the fibers of an asbestiform mineral as compared to the non-fibrous non-asbestiform mineral. The dissimilarity between the asbestiform tremolite and non-asbestiform tremolite lies in their physical structure. The asbestiform tremolite forms in a single line, resembling long thread-like filaments. It does not fragment or break but does bend and arch. The non-asbestiform tremolite grows in many directions in random prismatic patterns much like random crystal growth. When pressure is applied, it breaks, fragmenting into prismatic subdivisions.

The start of the difficulty with Vanderbilt talc was not with tremolite but with OSHA setting a standard that consolidated tremolite into one group without understanding the mineralogy. In effect, the regulatory agency seemed to understand what asbestos was but did not understand what it wasn't. Many people are still under the misunderstanding that all tremolite is asbestiform and therefore dangerous. The National Bureau of Standards, the Bureau of Mines, and the U.S. Geological Survey have questioned this lack of specificity concerning tremolite by OSHA. In 1992, OSHA formally corrected their original definition of asbestos. It would not treat non-asbestiform tremolite as asbestos. OSHA could find no evidence that would support their original classification of tremolite.

More to the point, the animal and human medical studies do not reveal any relationship between R.T. Vanderbilt talc and cancer. One epidemiological study in particular illustrates this point. In this study, Vanderbilt talc workers were compared with talc workers in Vermont. The study compared both mining populations with similar exposure years and similar overall dust exposure levels. The comparison showed that the overall lung cancer mortality is no different in both groups. Vanderbilt talc miners and millers are among the most studied in the world, and they are subject to a very active medical surveillance program at the talc plant.

The medical data does not indicate that workers exposed to the talc are at risk for developing asbestos-related cancer or asbestos-related general pulmonary disease.[2]

It is also interesting to place this information in perspective as it pertains to potters. Workers at Vanderbilt daily come in contact with talc throughout the mining and milling operation. The material is taken from an open pit mine, loaded on trucks, and taken to the milling operation where it is ground down into a powder. Talc is moved around the plant through discharge shoots, conveyor belts and pulleys, all of which are maintained periodically by mechanics and technical staff, who come in contact with the talc daily. The final processing involves the powder dropping into 50 lb. paper bags. At every step, workers are exposed to varying levels of airborne particles, with the bag packers receiving the highest percentages of particles per/cu. ft of air. Packers sit in front of a machine that loads approximately four bags per minute, five days a week. It is reasonable to assume Vanderbilt talc workers receive many times more exposure than a potter opening a bag of talc in his or her studio. If there is no asbestos risk demonstrated among those workers (also supported by animal studies involving this talc), it's hard to imagine how such a risk might then exist for pottery workers using this talc.

Throughout the United States, there are many different deposits of talc, some of which have not been the focus of the asbestos controversy. Each talc deposit has individual characteristics in terms of particle size, particle shape, trace materials, and fired color. It is always the best course of action to test a new talc when making a talc substitution in a clay body or glaze formula.

Some potters will feel more comfortable with the option of using a pre-mixed moist clay body formula that does not contain any talc. Recently ceramic supply companies have formulated low fire, no talc, moist clay bodies. Several ceramics suppliers now selling moist low fire white clays are: Laguna Clay Company, 1400 Lomitas Ave., City of Industry, Calif. 91746-0305, (800) 452-4862; Tucker's Pottery Supplies, Inc., 15 West Pearce St., No. 7, Richmond Hill, ON Canada L4B 1H6, (800) 304-6185; Standard Ceramics, P.O. Box 4435, Pittsburgh, Pa. 15205, (412) 276-6333.

2."Asbestos, Health Risk and Tremolitic Talc: The Never Ending Saga" by Kelse, J.W. (R.T. Vanderbilt Company, Inc.) Paper presented at The Environmental Information Association Conference, New Mexico, March 27, 2001—Session 15.

Chapter 14

Toxicity Issues of Refractory Ceramic Fiber

Refractory ceramic fiber is a product of the space age. It offers a low density, high insulation value material capable of maintaining its physical dimensions at high temperature. The fiber is made by heating alumina and silica to a molten state after which it is fiberized and fast cooled. The chemically inert fiber can be rolled into a variety of sized blankets, papers (high temperature gasket materials), ropes, boards, and is also manufactured in bulk form, which looks very much like white cotton. The material can withstand temperatures up to 2300⁰F. The blanket and bulk form of the fiber is frequently used to close up cracks in refractory brick kilns. For the past several years, fiber pottery kilns have been constructed using the blanket or block form of the heat resistant lightweight material, which has resulted in lower fuel costs per kiln firing. Potters have been using refractory ceramic fiber for over thirty years from several different manufacturers, Fiberfrax ™ and Kaowool ™ being two trade names of refractory ceramic fiber product.

In recent years, the use of refractory ceramic fibers has come under review by industrial hygienists as to their potential human toxicity. Much work has been done to examine the potential toxicity of refractory ceramic fiber in animal studies. Tests have shown that animals exposed to respirable fiber, over the life of the animal, can develop disease. Recently the use of refractory ceramic fibers has come under review by industrial hygienists as to their potential toxicity in humans. Epidemiological studies and medical evaluations are being conducted by the University of Cincinnati, which monitor the primary manufacturing sector of industry workers producing the fiber. To date, their findings indicate no adverse health effects to humans from occupational exposure to refractory ceramic fibers. Under such conditions, the exposure concentrations and the duration of exposure in industry workers would be many times higher than encountered by individual potters.

A new generation of high temperature fibers has been developed by Unifrax Corporation, 2351 Whirlpool Street, Niagara Falls, NY, 14305-2413, (716) 278-3800, www.unifrax.com, Unifrax Information Hotline (800) 322-2293. The company has created a new magnesium silicate fiber, Isofrax™, which is a soluble alternative to refractory ceramic fibers. The product has extremely low lung biopersistence and low durability, which means if inhaled it is rapidly dissolved and removed from the lungs. Conversely, a high durability level in a material means it stays in the body longer, which increases the risk of future health problems. The relative solubility of the fiber is measured by a continuous flow-leaching test, which simulates a lung fluid environment. Fibers are exposed to a constant flow of fluid for a specific period of time. After exposure, the fluid is analyzed to determine the amount of dissolved material. Dissolution rate is expressed as the mass of all dissolved components per surface area of the sample per hour. The fiber has passed the short-term inhalation biopersistence test as defined in EU Directive 97/69/EC protocol ECB/TM26 Rev 7 and as a result is not classified as a potential carcinogen. Isofrax consists primarily of magnesia and silica spun into a high temperature fiber, which can be formed

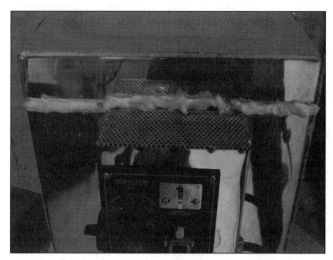

A small test electric kiln with refractory ceramic fiber placed in spaces between the lid and main body of the kiln. Refractory ceramic fiber in the bulk form is often used to seal leaks and open spaces in pottery kilns. It has superior insulation qualities and is very flexible, which makes it an ideal refractory material to fit into small open spaces between kiln bricks.

into various dimensions of boards, blanket, papers, and bulk fiber. One of the properties of the fiber is its ability to maintain its physical dimensions at temperatures up to 2300^0F.

Potters can utilize this product much as they have used other refractory ceramic fiber products. As with any form of loose fiber or breathable dust, a respirator should be worn when handling the material.

Rates of Exposure

Potters do not have enough information about the materials they work with on a daily basis. The lack of information as it pertains to potters has contributed to confusion and misunderstandings on a whole range of raw materials used in ceramics. There is a strong need for an organization to monitor potentially hazardous materials in pottery studios. The tests would determine the degree rate of exposure to various raw materials that potters encounter when working with clay, glazes, and kilns. The rate of exposure to any raw material in the workplace can be monitored. In fact it is examined in a range of industries across the industrialized world. What is measured among other factors is the rate of exposure per material over a workday. The study is further broken down by how much exposure a specific worker encounters in his or her individual job.

While the majority of potters do not have the financial ability to monitor any raw material in their workplace to determine what concentrations they are exposed to, theoretically they can use the information gathered on specific raw materials that have been monitored in similar industries. For example, in the ceramics industry approximately 80% of the measurements taken on industrial exposure to ceramic refractory material fall below .5 f/cc (fiber per cubic centimeter of air). This number is significant in that 300 f/cc has been shown to cause cancer in animal studies. However, it is highly unlikely on a practical level for a potter to come in contact with 300 f/cc of fiber in the daily use of the material.[1]

Many items we come in contact with on a daily basis, such as gasoline and artificial sweeteners like saccharin, can cause cancer or toxicity in unrealistically high concentrations over long durations of exposure. The issue of perspective comes into focus when looking at the substances we come in contact with in our daily life, namely that many are found to cause toxicity at high levels. However, at the levels we use them and the duration of their use, we accept small risks. As with other aspects of our daily life, the risk and benefits have to be judged and the primary tool for this task is an informed consumer.

Fiber Blanket Description
Refractory ceramic fiber is formed into blankets, boards, loose bulk fiber, and other shapes, which can be used for many different areas where high temperature insulation is required. Isofrax ™ refractory ceramic fiber is produced by Unifrax Corporation. The fiber has outstanding insulating properties with extremely low lung biopersistence. The ceramic fiber consists mainly of magnesia and silica.

[1.]"New Magnesium Silicate Fiber Isofrax™ is a soluble alternative to refractory ceramic fiber (RCF)," information obtained from a paper by Dean E. Venturin, Director, Health, Safety and Environment, Unifrax Corporation.

Chapter 15

Common Ceramics Studio Hazards

The four most frequent health concerns expressed by potters working in the ceramics studio are back pain, carpal tunnel syndrome, cuts, and burns. Back pain develops from incorrectly lifting heavy items, such as moist clay, kiln shelves, raw materials, and assorted pottery equipment. Potters are constantly lifting heavy boxes of finished pots or large sculpture pieces. Another common ailment affecting potters is carpal tunnel syndrome or repetitive motion syndrome. Any activity repeated constantly over a period of time can cause nerve damage in the hands and wrist. Cuts and burns are frequent mishaps in the pottery shop. Potters often reach into a hot kiln and either burn their hands on the pots or the still-hot kiln shelves. Pottery can be fairly warm to the touch, but the kiln shelves, having more thermal mass, remain hotter longer, resulting in many burns. Potters can also get severe cuts from fired glazed surfaces.

To prevent cuts, potters should not reach into a kiln unless they are wearing protective gloves. Always have emergency phone numbers for fire and health services available by the studio phone. An adequate first aid kit should be placed in a central location and be readily available to treat minor cuts and burns. Fire extinguishers should be placed throughout the studio in visible locations. The fire extinguisher in the kiln room should be placed in an easily accessible location in relation to the kiln.

To prevent carpal tunnel syndrome, reduce the amount of repetitive activities done at one time.

For example, instead of wedging 50 balls of clay at one time, break up this activity into several segments while doing other studio tasks.

One of the most common forms of injury in the pottery studio is caused by incorrectly lifting kiln shelves or other heavy objects such as boxes of bricks or finished ware. Before lifting any heavy object, follow the simple suggestions for lifting and, if possible, have another person help. Working with clay does involve a lot of lifting. Moist clay is shipped in 50 lb. boxes, which should be stored near the clay forming areas. Kiln shelves have to be lifted in and out of the kiln. Pots have to be unloaded and packed or stored. All of these activities involve lifting heavy objects repeatedly. It is a good idea to sit down in the studio and mentally figure out the flow of materials during a normal production cycle. Some planning at this stage will save energy when actually doing the work later.

A major concern of all potters is the fundamental question of studio safety. No one knowingly wants to work in a potentially dangerous environment or expose others to uncertain materials. Ceramic materials, the forming process, and the subsequent glazing and firing processes are not in themselves inherently dangerous, but knowledge of the materials and care in their use are essential factors in a safe workplace. In any pottery-making situation, there are procedures that once known will produce a clean safe ceramics studio. The best tool for a safe studio is a basic knowledge of the materials and how to use them sensibly.

Kiln Room

Safety Tips

Most kiln room accidents are caused by burns from unloading hot kilns, cuts from fired glazes on the kiln shelf, or back injury caused by incorrectly lifting kiln shelves. Always lift heavy objects with a straight back and do not lean over to place shelves in the kiln. Place your feet near the object being picked up and lift while bending the knees. Try not to twist your body when lifting and have a clear path to where the object can be set down carefully. Taking a few extra minutes to get help will save many weeks of pain from a back injury. Some kiln room accidents happen when potters trip over bricks, posts, and other supplies left on the kiln room floor. All items, especially around the kiln, should be removed or placed on shelves. The floor around the kiln should provide easy access to all sides of the kiln.

- Read carefully all the manufacturer's instructions on the burner system of your kiln. When using electric kilns, read the instruction booklet completely before firing the kiln.

- Have a qualified electrician or the local gas company inspect the kiln before it is operational.

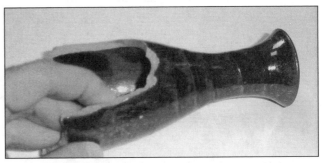

Fired glazes can have very sharp edges, either due to the irregular surface qualities of the clay underneath or from cracked ware. The safe way to unload a glaze kiln is with a pair of gloves. Not only do they protect the hands from any residual heat in the kiln but the gloves prevent glaze cuts on the hands. Hand injuries from cuts and burns are a major cause of ceramics studio accidents.

- Read the start-up procedures for the kiln burners.

- Store bricks, posts, and kiln room equipment in their proper areas.

- Keep the kiln room floor clean.

- Wear a respirator and eye protection when scraping kiln shelves.

- Do not unload a hot kiln. Always wear protective gloves when unloading the kiln.

- During a firing, the kiln cone viewing holes often emit flames and hot gasses; wear protective goggles and gloves when looking through the cone viewing holes during a firing.

- Do not bend over when lifting kiln shelves; use proper lifting techniques.

- Do not wear easily combustible clothing when firing the kiln (synthetic clothing can ignite when exposed to direct flame); wear cotton clothing.

- Do not eat, drink, or smoke in the kiln room.

- Wet mop any dry material spills immediately after they occur.

- Wear the proper shade goggles or eyeglasses when looking into any kiln during the firing. Sunglasses will not stop exposure from infrared or ultraviolet light damage to the eyes. It is essential to wear shaded goggles even at relatively low bisque firing temperatures. After the firing, do not unload the kiln until the pots are cool to the touch. Many potters receive burns from hot pots, kiln shelves, and kiln posts in their rush to see the fired results.

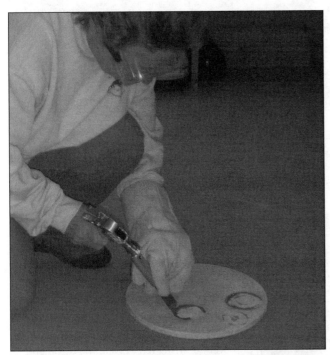

Wear protective eye goggles and gloves when chipping fired glaze drips from the kiln shelf. Glaze debris on the kiln shelf can become razor sharp and fly about the room when hit with a chisel. Always clean up the entire area after chipping glaze off kiln shelves.

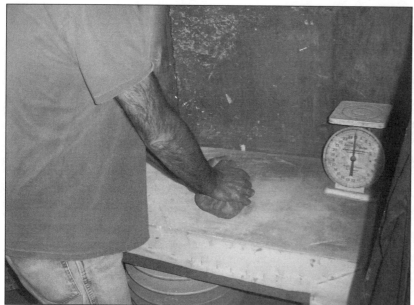

The height of the wedging table is critical in eliminating back stress. The ideal height of the table should be based on the dimensions of the potter using the table. When the potter is standing up next to the table, his or her hands should comfortably rest on the tabletop. In this way, upper body leverage over the moist clay can do most of the wedging, which will rely less on muscle power to move the clay. Excessive bending over or reaching up to wedge the clay can cause muscle problems in the back and upper arms. Back pain is one of the leading causes of health problems for the studio potter.

To reduce back strains, adjust the height of the wheel seat so it is level with the height of the wheel head. It will be easier to center the moist clay, as the potter can use upper body leverage when leaning over the moist clay. Avoid prolonged repetitive throwing, as it can potentially cause back, hand, and wrist injuries.

Hot exhaust flames and vapors can be ejected from the kiln (back pressure) whenever the cone viewing bricks are removed during the firing. Do not stand close to the kiln when removing cone-viewing bricks. Always wear protective goggles to prevent potential eye injuries due to infrared and ultraviolet light emitted from gas or electric kilns. Kiln gloves should also be worn to prevent burns when viewing the pyrometric cones within a firing kiln.

Inefficient work table and organization of tools

One possible source of studio accidents, or more frequently confusion and irritation, is a cluttered studio space. While some potters enjoy having many items in their working area, such as tools, brushes, buckets, bricks, glaze containers, etc., it can make for a disorganized environment. Time spent looking for a misplaced tool can disrupt a steady work schedule, resulting in frustration and delay. Occasionally, a bucket tips over or a potter's knife is left in a position that can lead to a cut hand. Good studio organization depends on all tools and equipment being in the right place for easy access when they are needed.

Incorrect kiln area

Firing kilns can give off radiant heat. The kiln should be placed away from any combustible materials. All items should be removed from the area around the kiln area to prevent a fire hazard and the more frequent hazard of tripping over things left around the kiln. The potter should be able to walk around the kiln unimpeded to inspect the entire kiln during the firing process. When the kiln is firing, the potter's full attention should be on the kiln and not stepping over objects in the kiln firing area.

Always lift heavy kiln shelves with a straight back. To increase stability, place feet together near the kiln shelf.

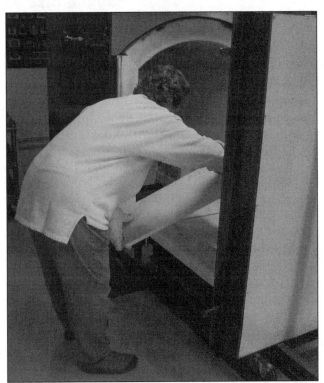

Never bend over when lifting heavy kiln shelves. Do not lean over or twist the body.

Hard bricks (lower brick) are frequently used in the studio and can be found in the construction of many types of gas kilns. Each hard brick weighs over 5 lbs. and if dropped on an unprotected foot or finger, it will cause disabilities. Always wear heavy-duty protective shoes and handle the hard bricks with care.

Soft bricks (top brick) are used in the construction of gas and electric kilns. A fine particle dust coats the surface of the soft brick. Always wear a respirator when handling or cutting soft brick.

When constructing a kiln fired by a hydrocarbon fuel (natural gas, propane, wood, sawdust, coal, oil), the kiln stack is the device that exhausts the hot gases from the firing chamber of the kiln. A common mistake made by beginning kiln builders is to physically attach the kiln stack to a combustible roof member. When the kiln stack heats during the firing, it can ignite any combustible material that is in contact with the stack. In this photo, the wooden roof-supporting beam is a safe distance away from the hot kiln exhaust stack.

Combustible materials are kept away from direct contact with the kiln stack, allowing for secondary cooling air to carry away the products of combustion that can leak through spacing in the kiln stack bricks.

Glaze Mixing Room

Safety tips

It is always easier and safer to mix glaze materials in the wet stage. Most glazes should be placed through an 80x sieve three times before the final application to the pot. This procedure serves to mix the glaze without creating dust. Label each glaze container carefully, as the fired color cannot be discerned in the liquid state. It is a good idea to keep an accurate representation of the fired glaze by attaching a fired glaze sample to the corresponding glaze bucket.

- Carefully read all safety information on commercial glaze containers.
- Turn on the venting system in the glaze mixing room or area.
- Wear an approved respirator before opening or mixing raw materials.
- Wet mop and clean up immediately any raw material spill.
- Replace any unused materials and seal the containers after using.
- Wear rubber or latex gloves if there are any cuts or open wounds on the hand.
- Do not eat, drink, or smoke in the glaze mixing room.
- Do not ingest or inhale raw materials.
- Wipe down worktables with a wet sponge before leaving the glaze mixing room.
- Wash hands before leaving the glaze mixing room.
- Clean eyeglasses after leaving the glaze mixing room.
- The processing and washing of highly alkaline wood ash (used as a glaze raw material), along with soda ash, pearl ash and potassium dichromate, can cause skin irritation to unprotected hands. Wear rubber or latex gloves when mixing any caustic material.

Glazing Application Room

Safety tips

Some potters have an allergic reaction to moist clay or liquid glazes when they contact their skin. Small bumps or irritations on the hands and forearms are noted after working with these materials. Apply hand lotion to the arms before working with moist clay or glazes. The lotion will often eliminate a sensitive skin reaction. At times under the right conditions, mold can occur on moist clays (which can increase the clay's plasticity). Mold can also grow in stored wet glaze containers. A few drops of household bleach per gallon of glaze will eliminate mold growth.

- Carefully read all safety notices posted on spray booths, respirators, and glaze application equipment.
- Use the correct respirator when mixing dry glaze materials.
- Do not inhale or ingest raw materials.
- Wipe down glaze mixing tables with a wet sponge before leaving the glazing room.
- Clean eyeglasses before leaving the room.
- Do not eat, drink, or smoke in the room.
- Do not use glass containers in the glazing room, as they can easily break into sharp pieces.
- Clean up any glaze spills when they occur.
- Wash hands before leaving the room.

Raw Material Storage Areas

Safety tips

The most often asked question about studio safety is, "what amount of clay dust in the air will cause a harmful effect on the human body?" The practical answer is to keep all work areas free from any airborne materials. It's not the clay floating around the studio that is potentially harmful. The nose and lungs filter most of these large particles. It's the micron size invisible particles that can get past our natural filtering mechanisms and can cause lung and respiratory irritation and possible permanent damage. The best policy is to keep all levels of airborne material as low as possible. Following proper cleaning procedures in the ceramics work area and the use of common sense in handling dry materials will be very effective strategies in maintaining a safe environment.

- Read carefully all safety notices posted on raw material storage containers and bags.
- Wear an approved respirator when opening raw material bags.
- Clean up any raw material spills on the floor or tables when they occur.
- Do not ingest or inhale raw materials.
- Do not eat, drink, or smoke in any raw material storage areas.
- Close raw material containers when finished with the material.
- Wash hands before leaving raw material storage areas.

Pottery Studios

Safety tips

Potters can damage nerves in their hands from the repetitive motion of wedging clay or throwing pots. The best way to prevent this type of injury is to break up the work activities associated with making pots into small segments, minimize repetition, reduce speed, and rest your hands in all shop activities. Do not wedge a hundred pounds of clay at once or sit at the potter's wheel making pots for hours on end. As a further example, throwing twelve pots on the wheel should not be followed by making another twelve but by trimming pots that are leather hard or loading the bisque kiln for the next firing cycle. Working with ceramic materials involves a series of separate tasks to complete fired ceramic objects. Shifting from one task to another in the construction process avoids prolonged repetitive motion situations.

- Carefully read all safety notices attached to pottery wheels, slab rollers, extruders, or any studio equipment.

- Do not store food, eat, drink, or smoke in the pottery studio.
- Wipe down tables with a wet sponge when a raw material spill occurs.
- Wear a separate set of clothes in the studio, and clean your studio clothes frequently.
- Wear clothes that can be easily cleaned and do not have pockets which can trap particles.
- Immediately clean up any raw materials that drop to the floor.
- Clean eyeglasses before leaving the studios.
- Wash hands before leaving the studios.

Another leading cause of studio injury is carpal tunnel syndrome (CTS), which develops when too much pressure is exerted on the nerve that runs through the carpal bone in the wrist. When the nerve is compressed against the bone, the hand and fingers can be affected. Symptoms of vise-like pressure and tingling can frequently progress to permanent nerve damage. Any type of repetitive hand motion can cause CTS. Factory workers on the production line, typists, dentists, roofers, auto body shop repairers, or any person involved in any repetitive hand motion over a prolonged time can experience CTS. Carpal tunnel syndrome can be successfully treated if diagnosed early. To prevent injury, take breaks from the repetitive work every half hour, stretch your hands, and alternate tasks in the workplace.

Chapter 16

Glaze Testing Services

At some point, anyone who has made functional pottery or has used handmade pottery might have wondered, "Is this glaze non-toxic" or "Will the glaze leach poisons into my food or drink when in use?" We have all heard news reports of tourists buying pottery in a foreign country, and then taking it home and getting sick from drinking out of a juice cup.

While a fired glaze does often look hard and durable to the eye and to the touch, it can be "soft." The term refers to glazes that can be easily scratched, and/or are capable of releasing part of their oxide content into food or drink. A soft leachable glaze will exhibit several characteristics that are most evident when an acid based food or drink is placed on the glazed surface. Often within an hour, a stain or discoloration is noticed where the food or drink comes into direct contact with the glaze. Wine, tomato sauce, grapes, orange juice, or any food with an acid base can facilitate the leaching out of metallic coloring oxides from a glaze, much like bleach can leach out the color on clothing.

A soft glaze can also come under chemical attack showing discoloration or pale areas after being placed in a dishwasher. Dishwasher cleaning agents have a higher degree of caustic content than regular soaps, which can accelerate the attack on exposed glaze surfaces. In some instances, the glaze can slowly fade after years of daily use and washing by hand. While discoloration of the glaze surface is an indication of a soft or leachable glaze, some glazes that have high percentages of heavy metal or metallic oxide release do not show any visible signs of this condition. Both visible and invisible leaching glazes need to be tested to ensure the glaze is safe for functional pottery.

The first step in having a glaze tested for any metal release is to locate a testing service that has a good reputation and a high accuracy rate for this particular kind of testing. There are many testing laboratories; however, some are not familiar with the specific test or do not perform the test enough to ensure the degree of accuracy needed. The test itself involves carrying out a few procedures but as with any testing service it pays to find a certified laboratory that performs the test on a regular basis. The Alfred Analytical Laboratory, 4964 Kenyon Road, Alfred Station, NY 14803, (607) 478-8074, fax (607) 478-5324, email ats@infoblvd.net, has been testing glazes for potters and is a nationally certified laboratory.

In order to achieve an accurate test result, the potter should glaze all the surfaces of a small cup that will come in contact with food or drink. It is important to fire the glaze under the same glaze application, clay body, and kiln-firing conditions as will be carried out in future production glazes (see "Variability of Test Results" later in this chapter). The pot with the glaze to be tested should be carefully packed for the US mail, UPS, or FEDEX delivery. If the samples are to be returned, add the same amount that it costs to ship the pot to Alfred Station, NY. Each piece tested will be given a computer identification number, which is marked on the bottom of the pot.

Summary of the Testing Method

Glazes are composed of oxides, such as silica, alumina, calcium, boron, magnesium, zinc, and various others found in their raw form (such as silica found in flint), or they can be combined with other oxides in nature (as is found in wollastonite, a common glaze material that combines silica and calcium). Metallic coloring oxides and their carbonate forms give glazes color and in some instances texture. Some commonly used oxides are cobalt oxide, chrome oxide, iron oxide, manganese dioxide, copper oxide along with other metallic coloring oxides that are combined in nature as are found in iron chromate (iron and chrome), and rutile (iron and titanium). Metallic oxides or their carbonate forms can contain varying amounts of trace oxides along with their primary oxide. For example, one brand of copper oxide (not all copper oxides are the same in analysis) can contain trace amounts of zinc, silica, lead, and nickel. Whatever the metallic oxide combination within the glaze, it is important to note the specific oxide level if it is being leached out of the fired glaze. The goal should be to reduce the oxide release to safe levels or eliminate the release completely.

For example, one glaze can contain both cobalt oxide and chrome oxide and can leach both oxides above the Maximum Contamination Level (MCL). To find out if leaching is taking place, metals are extracted from the glaze by leaching with a 4% acetic acid for 24 hours at 20 to 24^0C and are measured by an atomic absorption spectrophotometer. Each sample is tested by a modified standard method of ASTM C738 (American Society for Testing and Materials), which is used to generate a leachate. The vessel is first cleaned with a detergent wash and then rinsed with tap water, followed by a distilled water rinse. The dried sample is then filled to within 6 to 7 millimeters from the top with a 4% acetic acid solution. The volume is recorded and the pot is covered with an opaque glass plate so that the extraction is carried out without the presence of light. The glass also prevents the evaporation of the leaching acid within the pot. Contact between the cover and the leaching solution has to be avoided to ensure accuracy of the test results. The pot and leachate are left for 24 hours at room temperature: 20 to 24^0C. The acetic acid mimics acidic foods that interact readily with glazed surfaces on functional pottery.

The sample is then preserved with nitric acid to a pH of less than 2.0. Instrumental methods of analysis involve the use of an Atomic Absorption Spectrophotometer, which measures metals in a solution by their different wavelengths of visible and ultraviolet light. The greater absorption of light that occurs, the higher the concentration of metals. The results were once recorded in p.p.m. but have been changed to mg/L, (milligrams per liter), although it means basically the same thing. When measuring blood chemistry, a more exact standard requires the use of only mg/L, but p.p.m. is a workable standard for metal release in glazes.

Glazes contain many metals, which are used as fluxes (to cause the glaze to melt at an appropriate temperature) or to produce colors. Heavy metals have the capability of producing beautiful colors in glazes, but they can be toxic. Glaze testing can be accomplished on glazes containing cadmium, chromium, lead, copper, cobalt, nickel, manganese, barium, zinc, boron, and iron. The metals that require testing are the ones used in the largest amounts and the ones that are considered most toxic. In some instances, it is possible for the potter to determine which metals need to be tested for just by looking at the color of the glaze, manufacturer's literature, MSDS, or reference books. For example, a bright blue glaze color is most likely caused by cobalt oxide or cobalt carbonate in the glaze. If the potter is formulating his or her own glazes, the metallic coloring oxide will be apparent in the list of raw materials used in the glaze.

The U.S Food and Drug Administration regulates the amount of lead and cadmium that may leach from glazes. However, all the other toxic metals may leach into food or drink. While the Food and Drug Administration has stated its concern about these other metals, they have not yet set standards for them. Until there are standards for them, the Alfred Analytical Laboratory will use the Maximum Contamination Levels or Suggested Maximum Contamination Levels for drinking water set by the Environmental Protection Agency (EPA).

The following tables give the maximum allowable level of contamination or the Maximum Contamination Level (MCL). When the law is not specific, the Suggested Maximum Contamination Level (SMCL) is used. The MCL is set at a level at which no known or anticipated adverse health effects occur. SMCL are not health related and are not enforceable. The SMCL are set at a level that will not adversely affect the public welfare.

Testing Glazed Ceramic Surfaces

Scope: This test covers the precise determination of chemical substances extracted from glazed ceramic surfaces. The resulting leachate is tested using primarily an Atomic Absorption Spectrophotometer. The leaching method used is under the jurisdiction of ASTM Committee C-21 with a fixed designation C738, which is the standard test method recommended for Lead and Cadmium extracted from glazed ceramic surfaces.

Below are listed the leachate tests, followed by the MCL in mg/L.

Antimony	0.005	Arsenic	0.05
Barium	2.0	Beryllium	0.004
Cadmium	0.005	Chromium	0.1
Copper	1.3	Lead	0.015
Mercury	0.002	Nickel	0.1
Sodium	20	Selenium	0.05
Thallium	0.002		

Secondary test with Suggested Maximum Contamination Levels (SMCL)

Aluminum	0.2	Iron	0.3
Silver	0.1	Zinc	5.0

Maximum Contamination Standards

The Maximum Contamination Standards are based on the EPA standards for drinking water in the United States. Whether this is the appropriate standard for evaluating the level of toxic metal release in a glaze is a question that is open to controversy and debate. The central issue is one of equivalency, or to state the concern another way, "Do people drink water at the same rate as a heavy metal will be released from a glaze?" If the exposure rates are different, the current standards will have to be amended and based on more accurate data reflecting the subject being tested. Unfortunately, at this time there is no definitive database to draw maximum contamination standards from that relates to heavy metal release from glazes.

While it is a desired goal to set maximum contamination standards for heavy metal

release in glazes, it is more important to use the correct standard. A false standard set too high or too low serves no useful purpose and can give a false sense of security. While some people state there can be no such thing as a maximum contamination standard set too high, why should pottery glazes not be subject to the same risk assessment protocols as other aspects of public safety? The current philosophy behind adhering to the Maximum Contamination Standard for heavy metal release in glazes is that it makes sense for glazes not to contaminate our food and drink at levels in excess of those that are allowed in drinking water.

Variability of Test Results

While it would seem that testing a glaze for any possibility of leaching would offer the definitive solution to the goal of producing a safe glaze, the test results can be elusive and open to interpretation. The reasons for the lack of a clear-cut heavy metal release on any given glaze are not in the testing procedure, provided you have chosen a reputable testing laboratory. They revolve around several other factors, some of which the potter cannot control (accurate Maximum Contamination Standards—previous paragraph) and some of which the potter can control if they are aware of kiln firing and glaze application techniques.

Consistency is the most important factor in obtaining the best test results for a glaze. A true representative sample of the glaze is important. The glaze should be fired on the same clay body and in the same size kiln as the potter intends to use throughout the production run of the glaze. Needless to say, once a favorable test result is achieved the glaze formula and all operations related to applying and firing the glaze should remain unchanged. Listed are some possible variables that can alter a glaze test result.

End point temperature—is the absolute temperature reached in a kiln firing. The higher the end point temperature the more the glaze melts. A mature glaze has the greatest chance of tying up the heavy metal content held within the glaze.

Time to temperature—is the amount of time it takes to reach the end point temperature in a kiln firing. Firing at too fast a rate can cause a glaze to be immature with the possibility of leaching heavy metals. An immature glaze can also be "soft" and easily abraded or scratched by knives when in daily use.

Underfiring—is when a glaze does not reach its end point temperature or reaches its end point temperature with too fast a heat increase. An immature glaze can leach heavy metals due to its silica content not fully binding with the heavy metal content of the glaze.

Overfiring—occurs when a glaze is fired past its end point temperature. At that point, it can cause the glaze surface to become unstable, releasing its heavy metal content.

Kiln venting (electric)—Heavy metals can vaporize as the glaze reaches maturity. If the kiln is not actively vented by air being drawn into the kiln, the glaze vapor can be deposited on the fired glaze surface, causing a high metal release level when the glaze is tested.

Gas kiln—Firing a gas kiln can present a diverse combination of atmospheres taking place within the kiln in a single firing or over a number of individual firings, all of which can affect the heavy metal release in a glaze.

Glaze thickness—Thicker glaze applications can increase the amount of heavy metal release from any unstable glaze.

Kiln stacking—In electric kilns, pots stacked close together can prevent or limit the circulation of kiln atmosphere, allowing heavy metal vapor to remain on the pots during the glaze firing.

Overlapping glaze—When two or more different glazes overlap, their total heavy metal release can increase. Do not assume because each individual glaze has been tested successfully that an overlapping combination will be safe. All overlapping glaze combinations should be tested.

Size of kiln—A glaze firing in a small test kiln might produce a different heavy metal test result than the same glaze fired in a larger kiln. The lower thermal mass of small kilns can speed up the heating and cooling cycle on a glaze with a greater potential for heavy metal release due to an immature glaze.

Heating and cooling cycle—Changing the rate at which a glaze kiln heats and cools can adversely affect heavy metal test results. Fast kiln firings can cause immature glaze results with the potential of decreasing the ability of the glaze to contain any heavy metal in a stable glaze matrix.

Re-firing glaze—Re-firing a glaze can increase its heavy metal release due to the re-fired glaze's increased porosity and surface area.

Particle size of raw materials—Using a larger particle size raw material in a glaze formula can change the heavy metal release of a glaze due to an incomplete glaze melt. For example, using flint 200x mesh in place of flint 400x mesh decreases the surface area of the silica, which can prevent a more complete melting action in the glaze.

Second test can increase glaze oxide release—In a situation where a glaze has to be re-tested for heavy metal release, the release rate can be higher due to the testing acid increasing the fired glaze's porosity.

Underglaze colors—Metallic coloring oxides, metallic coloring carbonates, or stains applied to a bisque pot with a covering glaze can occasionally release heavy metals in the fired glaze.

Overglaze colors—Metallic coloring oxides, metallic coloring carbonates, or stains used over an existing glaze can sometimes release heavy metals in the fired glaze.

Lusters/decals—can contain high levels of potentially toxic heavy metals. Since they "ride" or are fired on top of an existing glaze, they can remain unstable in terms of their release of heavy metals.

Fuming—is a process where metallic salts—stannous chloride, bismuth sub nitrate, silver nitrate, cobalt sulphate, copper sulphate, iron sulphate—are introduced into a kiln at a low temperature where they volatize, producing iridescent luster colors on fired glazed surfaces. The iridescent surface fuming can release high levels of heavy metal on the glaze surface.

With any glaze, there are many potential factors that can invalidate a test result. However, the potter should try to eliminate the factors under their control, such as kiln size, kiln atmosphere, kiln firing cycle, ware stacked in the glaze kiln, consistency of glaze raw materials, glaze application, and clay body. Once the potter is aware of factors that can influence a test result, he or she can begin to work towards producing a consistent glaze sample for the greatest possibility of an accurate test.

Many potters will use a liner glaze on the inside of pots or eating surfaces that has no possibility of leaching heavy metals, or they will use a liner glaze that has been tested successfully. It is safest to use an *underglaze* wash or coloring oxide or stain on a bisque pot and then use a safe liner glaze over the wash. While any combination of *underglaze/overglaze* can release unsafe levels of heavy metals, this combination offers the lowest risk as compared to applying an *overglaze* wash of coloring oxide or stain to a glaze surface. The *overglaze* wash area can release heavy metals from the glaze. The best policy is "when in doubt, test the glaze."

To date, glaze testing still offers the most effective safety measure for determining the heavy metal release of any glaze. Aside from the fact of glaze testing being a good advertising point, in many instances potters who sell to retail stores will need to have proof that their glazes are non-toxic.

Potters Formulating Their Own Glazes

When potters formulate their own glazes from raw materials, a greater flexibility is possible in adjusting the glaze in terms of surface texture, light transmission, glaze viscosity, temperature range, application method, and glaze color. In such instances, if the potter is producing functional ware, it is the potter's responsibility to assure the public that the glaze is safe and non-toxic. Another important factor in knowing the actual glaze formula is the ability to adjust or change the formula entirely depending on the glaze test results. If a known glaze formula containing nickel is tested and exceeds the MCL, the potter always has the option of making adjustments to the glaze, which will produce a lower safer level of release, or they can change the formula so it does not release any nickel.

Many potters work from a single base glaze (base glazes do not contain metallic coloring oxides, metallic coloring carbonates, or stains) and add different amounts of coloring oxide or stain. While this system of glaze formulation can generate several good glazes, each variation should be tested for heavy metal release, as the percentage and type of coloring oxide, carbonate, or stain, can influence the release rate of a base glaze. Knowledge and experience in developing glaze formulas always yields a greater

Test pot
An example of a small teacup with the glaze to be tested on an eating or drinking surface.

range of ways to overcome potential toxicity issues when evaluating glaze test results.

Commercial Glazes

All commercial glazes labeled Non-Toxic must conform to the ASTM D-4236 standard. The American Society for Testing Materials is an organization tasked, among other duties, with setting standards for commercial glaze labeling. The standards are meant to ensure the glazes' ability to be safely used on eating surfaces. The labeling can take several different forms.

"Dinnerware safe" (food safe) glazes are marked as such. They are safe for use where food and drink will come in contact with the glaze if

the glaze is properly applied and fired. However, the glaze should be fired to its correct temperature with most glaze manufacturers recommending the placement of a pyrometric cone near the glazed pots to ensure this temperature requirement. "Dinnerware safe" (food safe) glazes should not be mixed together as their separate non-leaching qualities might be compromised.

Glazes marked "non toxic" that produce a textured or crackled surface should not be used for any pottery with an eating surface, as food or drink will produce bacteria that can grow in the recessed areas of the glaze.

Commercial glazes are also marked "not for spray application," which means that the glaze when atomized will create health and safety problems if inhaled. Glazes marked HL/CR (health label cautions required seal) of the Art and Craft Materials Institute, Inc. are certified for use when appropriate cautions are observed. The glaze can be used by potters who understand the cautions and safety advice listed on the glaze label.

Each commercial glaze manufacturer will have a complete description of the glaze warning label information. Due to new Federal regulations, this information must be available on the glaze container label. Significantly, a glaze manufacturer will not guarantee the finished properties of the glaze, since the method of application and the firing conditions can affect the final fired stability of the glaze. It is also recommended that anyone selling functional pottery using commercial glazes is responsible for complying with FDA guidelines for lead release. Overall, the best recommendation would be to test any glaze through an independent nationally certified glaze-testing laboratory before advertising any statements on the glaze's safety for use on dinnerware.

Additional testing can be done in the field of organics, pesticides, and herbicides, but these are expensive tests and are not generally required for pottery glazes. Significant omissions are the metal cobalt and vanadium, which are not regulated at present; however, Alfred Analytical Laboratory can give recommendations on safe release levels with unlisted metals as well as what metals should be tested in a given glaze formula.

Costs

Each time the ASTM leachate test is performed it costs $10.00. For each metal, the charge is also $10.00. For example, one cup tested costs $10.00 to perform the leachate test; if two cups are tested, $20.00. If two metals are to be tested on one cup, the leachate is $10.00 and the two tests are $20.00, for a total of $30.00. Two cups, two metals each cost $60.00. Checks should be sent with the sample cup. Many potters send a representative sample cup from their production kiln and do not request return of the cup, which can reduce the total cost of testing by not including return postage.

Chapter 17

"The Potter's Health & Safety Questionnaire"

A professional potter from Massachusetts, Angela Fina, originally suggested the concept behind "The Potter's Health & Safety questionnaire." Several years ago she had attended a NCECA (National Council on Education for the Ceramic Arts) convention and informally asked potters if they ever had an illness or knew of anyone having an illness that could be directly related to their pottery activities. Since this national event draws potters of all ages from throughout the country that either teach ceramics or are practicing potters, the population constitutes a fairly wide statistical sampling of the people involved in ceramics. After several days of surveying potters' responses to these two questions and the lack of reports of serious illness, it was thought a more scientific approach would be the best course of action to truly understand what risks potters encounter when working with ceramic materials. At that point, the only information relating to potters having problems with raw materials or studio hazards came from word of mouth.

With Angela Fina's suggestion, a list of twenty-one questions was devised that would hopefully cover several health and safety areas associated with the use of ceramic materials by potters. Much has been investigated and written about the effects of clays, feldspars, flint, and other ceramic related raw materials on workers in industry and mining. However, statistical information gathered from a search of the medical literature and OSHA does not relate to a potter working in their studio. The duration and concentrations of exposure rates do not accurately portray how potters use the materials in their studios, schools, or manufac-

turing operations. The uncharted area of ceramic raw materials and safety issues as pertaining to potters has to be explored and reported. The primary goal of "The Potter's Health & Safety Questionnaire" was to compile statistical data based on a population of potters.

The methodology of the questionnaire tried to establish a wide representative sample of potters. Several strategies were employed to achieve this goal. The one page questionnaire contained twenty-one questions and was designed for a fast and efficient completion by people working with clay. The questions were simply stated and several preliminary test questionnaires were field tested and revised for ease of completion by recipients. The goal was to obtain the highest response rate possible about how potters use clay and glaze materials. While no single device can elicit a wide range of accurate information on such a broad encompassing topic, hopefully this data will be the beginning of a more complete study of ceramic materials as they affect potters.

The questionnaire was dispersed through several different methods: word of mouth, pottery guilds, craft centers, schools, email notices to potters, internet postings, magazine notices, and at the March 2000 NCECA in Denver, Colorado. Also, several ceramics suppliers throughout the United States handed out the questionnaires to their customers. Another goal of the questionnaire was to obtain as diverse a sample of potters, male and female, from different areas of the country, various ages, different educational backgrounds, varying experience levels in ceramics, health histories, and studio safety practices. While no single survey can hope to reach a complete population in every area of the ceramics community, the scope of the survey was increased due to a high response rate over a two-year period. From this information, certain trends and assumptions can be deduced. From 1999 through 2001, 1,958 questionnaires were dispersed with 316 returned responses. The respondents represented 39 states, Japan, and Canada.

The following is the response by percentage to each question asked to all participants.

The Potter's Health & Safety Questionnaire

Please consider filling out the questions listed below. We as potters are concerned with our health and safety when using ceramic materials. The information you supply will be relevant in determining future safety recommendations in the field of ceramics. (circle all that apply)

1. Are you a
   a. teacher 41.4%
   b. professional potter 30.9%
   c. hobbyist 9.9%
   d. other 17.8%

2. Education
   a. high school 7.9%
   b. college 45.4%
   c. graduate school 46.4
   d. other 0.3%

3. Where do you work in ceramics?
   a. school 40.7%
   b. craft center 8.0%
   c. private studio 45.0%
   d. other 6.3%

4. How many hours per week are you in the ceramics studio?
   a. 1-10 hrs. 14.8%
   b. 11-20 hrs. 23.2%
   c. 21-40 hrs. 35.6%
   d. 41+ hrs 26.5%

5. Do you produce
   a. functional pottery 38.5%
   b. sculpture 12.0%
   c. both 40.9%
   d. other 8.6%

6. Age?
   a. 18-39 27.7%
   b. 40-49 30.0%
   c. 50-59 29.0%
   d. 60 + 13.3%

7. Sex
   a. male 32.2%
   b. female 65.8%

8. What injury(s) have you experienced that are a result of your ceramics activities?
   a. none 37.8%
   b. hand injury 28.5%
   c. skin sensitivity 11.0%
   d. back injury 12.7%
   e. eye injury .3%
   f. respiratory injury 2.1%
   g. leg injury 0%
   h. other 7.6%

9. Do you use protective goggles when looking into the kiln?
   a. always 35.5%
   b. occasionally 31.0%
   c. never 30.3%

10. How often do you clean your studio?
    a. daily 27.9%
    b. weekly 41.8%
    c. monthly 16.8%
    d. other 13.5%

11. Do you use protective gloves when unloading a hot kiln?
    a. always 70.9%
    b. occasionally 21.3%
    c. never 7.8%

12. Do you smoke?
    a. yes 6.6%
    b. no 93.0% if yes, how many packs per day
    c. less than 1 pack 1.8%
    d. 1 to 2 packs 73.2%
    e. 2+ packs 1.8%
    f. former smoker how many packs per day 23.2% (see appendix)

13. Do you wear a respirator when mixing dry ceramic materials?
    a. always 62.2%
    b. occasionally 26.9%
    c. never 10.5%

14. What is your greatest health concern when working with ceramic materials, kilns, wheels, mixers, pug mills, or any ceramic related equipment or activity?
  a. carpal tunnel syndrome 20.9%
  b. repetitive strain arm/hand 13.1%
  c. back injury 23.9%
  d. respiratory injury 33.7%
  e. eye injury 2.4%
  f. leg injury 0%
  g. other 6.1%

15. Do you know of anyone who has an illness or injury that can be directly related to working with clay or glaze materials?
  a. no 51.5%
  b. yes, what illness or injury? 48.5% (see appendix)

16. Have you ever had any fears of your work in ceramics being associated with any chronic illness or disease?
  a. yes 48.5%
  b. no 51.5% if yes, specify which illness (s) (see appendix)

17. Do you feel you have enough information on health and safety issues related to your ceramics activities?
  a. yes 58.3%
  b. no 41.7%

18. How many years have you worked with clay?
  a. less than 5 yrs. 10.0%
  b. 5-10 yrs. 21.7%
  c. 11-20 yrs. 21.4%
  d. 21- 30 29.8%
  e. 31+ 17.1%

19. Do you mix your own clay body from raw materials?
  a. yes 28.0%
  b. no 71.6%

20. Do you mix your own glazes from raw materials?
  a. yes 91.5%
  b. no 8.5%

21. Have you had any health problems when using lusters?
  a. yes 100.0%
  b. no

(optional information)

Summary and Analysis of Responses From All Participants

The following summary and analysis is drawn from a statistical review of the data. While it is recognized that any suppositions made from the data are subjective, the raw data is open to review by other researchers. The complete questionnaire, including appendix, is available through NCECA (National Council on Education for the Ceramic Arts, National Office, 77 Erie Village Square, P.O. Box 777, Erie, CO 80516-0777).

The majority of responses in descending order were from teachers, professional potters, and those marked *others*, with the hobby populations of potters having the least representation in the survey. Almost equally divided were responses from potters having undergraduate and graduate degrees. The majority of potters work in their private studios or schools. Most potters worked between 21 to 40 hours, with the second highest group working over 41 hours in ceramics. Both groups represented an extremely high number of dedicated people involved in ceramics. A majority of potters produced both functional and sculpture oriented pieces with slightly greater numbers producing only functional ceramic ware. This represents a diverse approach to working with clay and glazes by potters making functional and non-functional forms. Potters were almost equally divided in three age groups, 18-39 years, 40-49 years, and 50-59 years, with a lesser percentage over 60 years of age. Twice as many women responded to the survey as did men. Whether there are greater numbers of women involved in ceramics or they are more diligent in answering surveys is unknown.

When asked if potters had encountered an injury when working in their studios, one third reported no injury with the next group reporting hand injury followed by back injury. This would seem a logical outcome of long hours when working with clay, the very nature of which requires labor-intensive repetitive motion. Similar injuries are often found in factory workers, bricklayers, farmers, and, oddly, dentists. To prevent one type of potter's occupational injury, protective goggles with special filters are used when looking into a firing kiln. They protect the eyes from infrared and ultraviolet light waves emitted at high temperature during the firing process. One third of the general population of potters always used goggles, one third did occasionally, and one third never used goggles. The effects of prolonged exposure to this type of eye damage are less immediate than other forms of injury and subsequently potters are either not aware of injury or they are aware of potential injury and choose not to take precautions. The actual amount of eye damage is not known.

Another area of potential occupational injury or hazard is the level of ceramic material in the workplace. The area of concern is inhalation of micron size particles from dry clay and/or glaze materials. A majority of potters clean their studios weekly, with the next group cleaning their studios daily, followed by a smaller group cleaning monthly. As in potential eye damage from infrared and ultraviolet light, damage to the lungs may not immediately cause health problems. However, in industrial workers and miners it can result in silicosis and/or aluminosis after years of exposure to micron size particles of silica and alumina. Weekly cleaning of the studio by potters seems to be arrived at for several reasons. Daily cleaning can be considered too time consuming if the situation does not warrant it, whereas monthly cleaning can be too long an interval, allowing for ceramic materials to build up on floors and work surfaces. These decisions are made on an individual subjective basis based on several factors: the potter's personal level of cleanness and health habits, the potter's past learning experience with clean-up procedures, or his or her level of understanding regarding potential health problems in using ceramic raw materials.

What can be learned from the groups of potters who took their valuable time and effort to complete the questionnaires and send them in for tabulation? Female teachers and female professional potters supplied more information than any other group. As recorded by the high percentages of potters with college and graduate school educations, as a group they would be predisposed to realize the potential importance of information gained from the questionnaire. In short, they would be the faction most likely to see the benefit of spending the time to complete the questionnaire. Schools and private studios remain the places most likely to encourage the pursuit of ceramics and that is where most potters work. A high response rate from potters in private studios would be logical since they would be the ones most directly affected by

unsafe and unhealthy work environments. Potters working in schools would be highly motivated to see the benefit of research in health and safety issues.

It is not unusual to find teachers and professional potters spending long hours in their studios. Potters over sixty were the smallest group reporting, possibly because there are fewer potters working in such a labor-intensive activity as they enter advanced age. Potters were equally represented in younger ages, which assumes there was a wide level of interest in the survey.

The three most common injuries in the studio were hand, skin, and eye, with the highest single group reporting no injuries. This is significant in two ways: either serious life threatening injury is not occurring, or it is present, but potters have not discovered the illness at this date. One third of the potters do not use protective goggles when looking into a firing kiln, possibly because the damaging effects to the retina accumulate over a period of time and are not apparent on a day-to-day basis. Comparing this delayed possible damage to eyesight with the immediate damage from burns reveals most potters will wear protective gloves when unloading a hot kiln.

Potters truly seem to be health conscious due to the fact that the overwhelming majority do not smoke, which logically follows that most do wear respirators when mixing dry materials. Potters seem most concerned with the likelihood of getting respiratory illness, back injury, and carpal tunnel syndrome. The survey did not cover what procedures if any they are using to prevent back injury or carpal tunnel syndrome, but it appears they do take precautions against respiratory illness by the high percentage of respirator use. Along this line of inquiry, when asked if they knew anyone with an illness or injury directly related to their pottery experience one half did not. This response can be interpreted a few different ways. Either fellow potters are getting injured or sick and others do not know about their condition, or working with ceramic materials is not as problematical as some people believe.

Those potters who did report knowing someone with an injury or illness reported back injuries, back problems, tennis elbow, cancer, carpal tunnel syndrome, respiratory illness, silicosis, tendonitis, wrist injury, and lung cancer. While the reported illnesses range from mild to potentially life-ending, it cannot be proven from the responses whether or not the illness was in fact caused by activities in ceramics. The overall amount of responses in the serious category of illness was statistically very low. However, any report of a major illness should be thoroughly investigated. An additional inquiry into this segment of responses would be a future step in the process of determining the toxicity of ceramic materials. At this time, there are no statistics available to compare the general population's health profiles with potters' health profiles.

When asked what fears potters had of any illness or injury, almost half reported no concerns for their health and safety. The other half expressed fears in the following areas: cancer, lung cancer, respiratory illness, and silicosis. It is interesting to note, aside from silicosis, these could be the same concerns and fears of the general population of non-potters. Again more than half of the potters stated they felt they had enough information on health and safety issues, which corresponds closely with half of the potters not having health concerns. The question that this survey could not answer is, "What percentage of potters with health concerns actually have or will have health problems in the future, and will they be based on exposure to ceramic related activities?"

A high percentage of potters have now been working in the field of ceramics for five to thirty-one plus years. During this time, most potters have recognized and considered what health and safety measures are worth taking, and what activities are low risk and do not need a high level or any level of concern or protection. Significantly, all of the potters who used lusters noted health problems. Unfortunately, there was only one question on lusters in the survey, and the extent of severity of this problem could not be explored. An inquiry into luster use would be a logical area for in-depth research.

Potters surveyed, for the most part, do not mix their own clay bodies, but the overwhelming majority do mix their own glazes. This indicates a high level of thought as to the labor-intensive process of making pots or sculpture. Making your own clay is often compared to starting a business (making clay) in order to supply your other business (making pots). It takes people some time to figure out a more efficient use of their time is not to make clay but to make pots. The numbers of potters mixing their own glazes in conjunction with the high amount of hours worked and the long duration of experience in ceramics denotes a sophisticated and experienced approach to ceramics. As a group, their level of professionalism and expertise speaks to a knowledgeable advanced level of achievement. Professionals with the same characteristics in other more traditional fields are noted for their judgment, and the same standards can be applied to potters as to their health and safety knowledge.

Responses by Subgroups

Summary and Analysis of Responses from Teachers

Teachers as a subgroup had the highest level of formal education. The majority of teachers had a graduate school education with the next highest percentage having an undergraduate education. This is not surprising as this would be a self-selected group, considering the requirements of their profession. High levels of formal education would be expected.

Most teachers made functional pottery or sculpture at their schools with the next highest percentage working in their studios. Craft centers only represented a small portion of work places for teachers. The cost of assembling materials and equipment for working with ceramic materials can be expensive. It would follow that since teachers have the opportunity to work at school that many would do so. The largest group of teachers worked 21 hours to 40 hours. Considering that making pottery or sculpture was not their full-time occupation, the amount of time teachers devoted to ceramics represents a serious commitment. As with the general population of potters, most teachers produced both functional and sculptural ceramic pieces, followed by a group producing only functional pottery.

Most teachers responding were women 50 to 59 years of age with the second highest grouping 40 to 49 years old. When asked what injuries they have experienced as a result of working in ceramics, one third stated none with the next largest group reporting hand injuries followed by back injury. Correspondingly, both types of injury are reflected in the general population of potters. Again the nature of handling ceramic materials and the long hours worked are represented in the similar types of injury among various groups.

As for safety devices, one third of teachers do not use protective goggles when looking into a kiln. Conversely, two thirds either use them all the time or occasionally. Teachers reported using protective goggles at approximately the same percentages in the same usage categories (always, occasionally, never) as the general population of potters, which indicates there is little or no difference as to how they regard this type of safety device. Almost two thirds of teachers wear protective gloves when unloading a hot kiln, followed by occasional use of gloves. The lowest percentage in the group does not use any protective gloves. The same principles apply as in the general population of potters, meaning it is just common sense to wear protective gloves when unloading a hot kiln.

The majority of teachers clean their studios weekly with the next group cleaning daily. The smallest percentage cleans their studios monthly, which corresponds to the general population of potters answering the survey.

As in the general population of potters, the overwhelming majority of teachers do not smoke. Again, higher education can influence this number of non-smokers, since they would be more aware of the proven dangers of smoking. Similar responses to health issues and potential lung damage can be noted with more than half of the teachers using a respirator when mixing dry ceramic materials followed by one third using respirators occasionally.

When teachers were asked their greatest health concern, one third stated respiratory injury with the next group reporting back pain followed by carpal tunnel syndrome. The general population reported slightly more concern with carpal tunnel syndrome than teachers, possibly because they are doing more throwing or using forming techniques that require repetitive hand motion. Teachers were also asked if they knew of anyone having an illness or injury that can be directly related to working with clay or glazes, and almost half reported no knowledge of direct illness or injury. Teachers that report knowledge in this area stated carpal tunnel syndrome, back/arm pain, cuts, respiratory problems, and silicosis (disease could not be medically verified in the survey). All of the reported illnesses and injuries were reported in

extremely low percentages. The general population of potters reported approximately the same percentages of known illnesses.

When asked if they ever had any fears of a work-related illness or injury, half of the teachers reported no concerns, with the remaining half's concerns being divided among cancer, lung disease, respiratory illness, and silicosis. All heath concerns were reported in very low percentages. Over half of the teachers felt they had enough information on health and safety issues relating to ceramics. Again, this percentage is the same in the general population of potters.

The majority of the teachers have worked in ceramics between 21 and 30 years, with the next group having over 31 years experience. Both groups represent a significant commitment to the pursuit of clay and their responses to the survey questions revealed how long-duration experience with clay affects people.

Approximately two thirds of the teachers do not mix their own clay body formulas, but an overwhelming majority does mix their own glazes from raw materials. Clay mixing is a labor-intensive activity, and most people working in all groups have decided instead to concentrate their energy on mixing their own glaze formulas. As in other groups, all teachers questioned reported health problems when using lusters.

Summary and Analysis of Responses from Professional Potters

Professional potters as a group attended graduate school in fewer numbers than the general population of potters, possibly because they chose to start their carriers earlier and felt they did not need the academic training of a graduate program. The majority of professional potters reported working in studio situations and this would logically follow, as most people who would consider themselves professional potters would also develop their own studios for more efficient production of their pots. This compares with the general population of potters who worked almost equally in schools and private studios. The highest percentage of professional potters reported working in their studios from 21 to 40 hours per week, which is slightly more than the general population of potters. This is unique in that non-professional potters work on par with professional potters, demonstrating both groups are highly committed to ceramics. More than half of the professional potters reported making functional pottery as compared with the general population of potters reporting slightly over one third producing functional pottery. In this respect, functional pots sell more consistently than sculptural forms and professional potters are just following the money.

The majority of professional potters were in the 40 to 49 year age group followed by the next highest percentage in the 50 to 59 year age grouping. Both groups represent a mature commitment to the vocation of ceramics. As expected, the labor intensive hard work of pottery making on the professional level has the lowest percentage in the 60+ age group. The low percentages in this age grouping are also reflected in the general population of potters. Among professional potters, twice as many are women, as in the general population of potters. It cannot be determined if there are more professional women in pottery or more professional women have taken the time to complete and turn in the questionnaire. One third of professional potters have reported no injury. Those that do report injury fall into the following categories: hand, back, knee, and respiratory injury. The last reported type of injury does not go into detail on what type or severity of respiratory injury. However, the overall types of injuries reported correspond to the general population or potters. Significantly, the reported injuries in both groups do not include cancer or heavy metal poisoning.

A more direct view of injury protection is the use of safety equipment. Almost half of the professional potters use protective goggles when looking into the kiln, as compared with almost one third use of protective goggles in the general population of potters. The higher number of professional potters using protective goggles reflects a greater understanding of the potential effects of long-term exposure to damaging infrared and ultraviolet light emitted from firing kilns. Professional potters, either through their own education on safety issues or the general sharing of information among their peers, recognize the need for eye protection.

When asked how often they cleaned their studios, professional potters cleaned on a daily basis and weekly basis slightly less than the general population of potters. Correspondingly they cleaned their studios more on a monthly basis than the general population of potters. The lower rate of studio clean up can indicate

several things. Professional potters work cleaner, they are less concerned with studio clean up, or they have not perceived any ill health effects from cleaning their studios at a lower rate than the general population of potters. It can also mean they are more concerned with turning out more pots to earn a living than cleaning their studios. If there are any noticeable effects from not cleaning their studios at as high a rate as the general population of potters, they have not been reported or noticed.

The same high percentage of professional potters and the general population of potters use protective gloves when unloading hot kilns. The use of protective gloves is the most constantly used safety item in all groups of potters. The results of not using protective gloves can be immediate, namely getting a harmful burn, so it follows that it makes practical sense to use protective gloves. In other areas of safety, the causes and their effects are not immediately apparent, and this is refelcted in the lower usage of other safety equipment.

Both professional potters and the larger general population of potters overwhelmingly do not smoke. This denotes a health conscious educated population in both groups. It would also seem both groups would be aware of other work-related health issues and take the proper protective precautions where necessary. The majority of both groups report high use of respirators. Professional potters' greatest health concerns when working with clay are based on respiratory injury followed by carpal tunnel syndrome, which roughly corresponds to the concerns of the general population of potters. Respiratory injury might be a slowly progressive event over years of exposure so it would make sense to be concerned when working in a clay studio. Carpal tunnel syndrome occurs when the nerves in the wrist rub up against the carpal tunnel bone resulting in numbness and/or pain. Throwing on the potter's wheel, wedging clay, or any other repetitive motion can bring on the syndrome. Both situations are present where potters work; however, concern over a potential health hazard does not translate into actual health problems. A follow up survey over a longer period of time will have to determine if these two health problems are developing in potters at a greater rate than in the wider general population.

When professional potters were asked if they knew of anyone with a chronic illness or disease related to ceramics activities, over half of them reported in the negative, which is a slightly higher response than in the general population of potters. Professional potters reported back injury, carpal tunnel syndrome, hip/knee injury, and wrist injury as injuries they have known about in other potters. All injuries reported would be consistent with heavy, long duration physical labor in any field. Professional potters reported, in greater numbers than the general population of potters, that they had fears of chronic illness or disease with working with clay and glazes. The reason for this is possibly because they have a greater knowledge of the potential health and safety problems that can be associated when working with clay. Surprisingly, both groups reported that they have enough information on health and safety issues in ceramics. This would seem contradictory, as both groups also report health concerns when working in ceramics. Whether such ambivalence is consistent in other fields in the wider population is not known.

Professional potters mix their own clay less frequently than the general population of potters, possibly because they have determined their time is more valuable making pots than starting another business (mixing clay) to supply their pottery business. As in the general population of potters, most professional potters do mix their own glaze formulas from raw materials. Professional potters that reported using lusters did have health problems, as did teachers and the general population of potters. Additional comments of professional potters ranged from requesting information on the use of respirators to problems with tendonitis. The highest percentages of professional potters have worked in ceramics from 21 to 30 years followed by potters working 11 to 20 years. Both groups and the numbers working in each group approximate the percentages in the general population of potters. The number of years worked represents a major commitment to the field of ceramics. This is clearly a highly seasoned group of craftspeople that have made major decisions in their life to pursue ceramics. This fact gives a high degree of respect for their opinions on how they protect themselves when working with clay.

Summary and Analysis from Low Experience Potters

The lowest numbers of potters responding are found to be working in ceramics less than 5 years. Most potters in the 5 year or less group clean their studios on a weekly basis as compared with a higher percentage of potters with 21 to 30 years experience cleaning their studios on a daily basis. Potters with 5 years or less experience also reported using protective gloves when unloading hot kilns. This would be just common sense regardless of the experience level in ceramics, as severe burns could result from not wearing gloves when unloading a hot kiln. This group also reports a high percentage of non-smokers, and they do wear respirators when mixing dry materials, possibly because of an awareness of potential lung disease in both activities. Health problems were reported when using lusters. Greater degrees of studio cleaning occurred in more experienced groups of potters, indicating an enhanced awareness of studio safety procedures. As one accumulates more years of experience working with clay and glazes there is a direct correlation with increased health concerns and correspondingly increased safety procedures in the ceramics studio.

Responses by Ages of Potters

Potters 18 years to 39 years of age

In the 18 to 39 years old age group, potters used protective kiln goggles when looking into the kiln less frequently on a constant basis than the general population of potters. Correspondingly, this age group cleans their studios daily at a lower rate than the general population of potters. They also have a lower use of protective gloves when unloading hot kilns. Potters in this group for the most part do not smoke, but within the group that does smoke the percentage is double that of the general population of potters. Namely, when younger potters smoke they do so at double the rate of older groups of potters. The younger group reported greater use of respirators when mixing dry ceramic materials as opposed to lower usage rates in the general or older population of potters. This reversal of safety procedure usage concerning respirators cannot be explained. The higher percentage of respirator use among the 18 to 39 year age group possibly occurs because they have been better educated in respirator use in the studio. Whether the lower incidence of safety procedures has to do with lack of knowledge or whether this relatively young age group is aware of the dangers and thinks it cannot happen to them personally is undetermined.

Potters 40 years to 49 years of age

A slightly higher percentage of the 40 to 49 year olds use protective kiln goggles than the general population of potters. Both the general population of potters and the 40 to 49 year old group are using kiln goggles at higher percentages than the 18 to 39 year olds. Approximately the same percentage of potters in the general population as in the 40 to 49 year olds clean their studios on a daily basis. Both groups clean their studios in greater percentages than the 18 to 39 year olds. Both the 40 to 49 year olds and the general population of potters overwhelming do not smoke, as compared with the 18 to 39 year olds who smoke at twice the rate of both groups. Respirator use in the general population of potters and the 40 to 49 year olds is identical, but oddly there are higher use rates in the 18 to 39 year olds. However, general trends indicate as potters mature they become more active in their safety and health procedures.

Potters 50 years to 59 years of age

Potters in this age group used protective kiln goggles and kiln gloves in higher percentages than the general population of potters, 18 to 39 year olds, and 40 to 49 year olds. The use of protective kiln goggles and kiln gloves increases as the age of the potters increases, reflecting a greater understanding and knowledge of eye safety procedures. Correspondingly, they also cleaned their studios on a daily basis at the highest rate of any age grouping of potters. Almost all potters in this age group did not smoke but those that did smoked less than the younger age groups of potters. Respirator use among this group was slightly above the 40 to 49 year olds, but was below the 18 to 39 year old age group. Again it is significant to note the youngest age group of potters has the highest rate of respirator use in the survey of all potters.

Potters 60 years of age and older

The oldest age group of potters used protective kiln goggles and gloves at the highest rate of any age group of potters. They also had the highest rate of non-smoking potters in any age grouping. The high rates indicate older potters generally demonstrate greater concern with health and safety when working in ceramics as it pertains to smoking. Oddly, they had the lowest rates of respirator use in any age group. Whether this means they are mixing less dry material in their studios, or they lack the knowledge to protect themselves from airborne particles is undetermined. They also cleaned their studios on a daily basis less than the 50 to 59 year old age group. This could be possible because they are using their studios less often than other groups of potters. Another interpretation of lax respirator use and lower rates of studio cleaning is that older potters were not educated in clean studio procedures and respirator use when they started their careers in ceramics. As in all other age groups this group had health problems when using lusters.

Responses by Where Potters Work

Schools, Craft Centers, Private Studios

Roughly one third of potters working in schools, craft centers, and private studios reported no injury when working in ceramics. Those potters that did report an injury had the highest amount of hand injuries in the private studio followed by the school setting. Skin sensitivity was reported highest in the school and craft centers with the lowest reported cases in the private studios. Lower rates in the private studios could have resulted in greater access to hand cream, more space for storage of personal items, or a higher level of potter education, as potters having their own studios might be more experienced in the field of ceramics. The lowest percentages of potters using protective kiln goggles and protective gloves was found in schools, which could be due to the recurrent problem of students not replacing the safety equipment in a central location. Another common problem in schools is the theft of supplies and equipment, resulting in the loss of use for other students.

Schools have the greatest numbers of potters cleaning their work areas on a daily basis; they also have the greatest number of potters using respirators on a full time basis. Private studios have the least number of potters cleaning their studios on a daily basis and the least number of potters using respirators. The use of respirators in the private studio is totally up to the individual potter's judgment. In many instances, unsupervised potters or those not subject to group pressure will not wear respirators or clean their studios. Alternately, the school situation provides through the teacher a set regimen for cleaning the pottery workplace. In most pottery classes, there is a standard clean-up period so the next group of students can use the room. The school structure would account for the high percentage of potters cleaning their work areas on a daily basis as opposed to the private studio situation, which is unsupervised and depends on the individual potter's judgment as to the level of cleaning needed.

Representative Sample of All Groups of Potters' Additional Comments Section of the Questionnaire

Potters felt the need to give additional information and comments about their health concerns or studio safety practices. A percentage of the additional comments section was devoted to potters who had problems with back pain or carpal tunnel syndrome. Respiratory illness or noticeable toxic effects from raw materials or kiln emissions were not represented by potters in the comments section of the questionnaire. Other than the comments listed below, many potters requested that they have access to the results of the survey.

- "I've had problems with my right wrist and fingers on and off over the years. Acupuncture and varying tasks helps. Also throwing with softer clay."

- "Already suffer from carpal tunnel, elbow injury, and respiratory problems. However, I would have taken precautions had I been informed of the potential for injury and perhaps avoided some damage."

- "Successful carpal tunnel surgery in 1982 on right hand. Left hand is only now exhibiting symptoms." (working in ceramics 21+ years)

- "Standing to throw has helped reduce lower back pain. I would recommend it to any full time potter."

- "I would like to see safety a part of the curriculum in MFA and undergraduate programs."

- "Although not caused by clay activities, I do have back problems that are enhanced with my work in clay."

- "Old potters I know are very healthy mentally and physically, except for those who smoke or those who have other illnesses like cancer, A.L.S., heart disease—normal horrors of old age."

- "I think teachers and professors need to be specifically targeted with safety and health information, since their opinions and habits will mold those of all of their students."

- "I use a HEPA vac to clean. I think it's very important."

- "I need specific safety and cleaning standards to get our custodial staff to clean properly." (high school teacher)

- "Although I take safety seriously, many of my peers do not. I think that the first person you learn ceramics from will instill the amount of respect for safety you will have. We just need to develop safe habits."

- "It would be nice to know if most people who suffer repetitive-stress injuries are wheel throwers or hand builders. Our working techniques vary so widely."

- "Last year I had repeated bouts of hives, which were finally resolved by an allergist as *skin sensitivity*. I didn't connect it to clay work but to dryness and altitude."

- "I wear a full face respirator when luster glazing, utilizing specific cartridges. A separate respirator (1/2 mask) is used when mixing dry materials or handling chemicals."

Conclusion

Hopefully, "The Potter's Health & Safety Questionnaire" will be the start of other more extensive surveys in the field of ceramics. Potters represent a small segment of the ceramics population and an even smaller segment of the general population. Safety in the ceramics workplace, whether it is in a school, private studio, or craft center, is of the uppermost importance. It is of equal or greater importance to ensure that functional pottery is safe for use by the public. The primary objective is to acquire a baseline of knowledge on how raw materials and studio practices affect potters. Once that is accomplished, potters can apply that knowledge to produce safe pots in safe studios. However, most of the current available information concerning ceramic safety and raw materials is obtained through word of mouth information, and/or industrial/mining statistics. There are several inherent problems with each source of information.

Anecdotal knowledge relates to an individual potter's experience with the material or safety practice. The limitation on this type of knowledge along with combining other potters' self knowledge comes about when there is no larger base of data for comparison. Often one potter's experience with a raw material or safety procedure will not have common elements that other potters can apply to their situation. The accuracy of such individual information can be subject to errors in several different ways. There could be errors in an observed cause and effect, and inaccuracies in transferring the information to other potters. Using such information presents a problem in that there is also no central gathering system for raw data and its interpretation. If one potter stirs a liquid glaze with their hands and develops a skin rash and reports the glaze caused the problem, could the rash be caused by other factors? A wider systematic survey of many potters will offer a more accurate indication of a potential glaze problem. A properly constructed survey can also determine if certain types of glazes cause difficulties or if there are outside factors causing the problem.

The other area of available information relates to statistics kept by government agencies and private businesses. Industry and mining statistics relating to ceramic materials and safety practices are for the most part not relevant to where and how potters use their materials. The exposure levels and duration rates that are commonly found in industrial operations are much higher than for potters. Does this mean all information gathered from industry is invalid? No, but greater accuracy on potential ceramic toxic qualities can be achieved by surveying potters who actually use the raw materials at different rates and durations than industry. Can a miner working in an industrial setting for thirty years with raw materials be compared to a potter working in their studio? How much extrapolation is involved in interpreting industrial toxicology data when compared with how a potter would use the same material in their studio? Regrettably, at this time, with the limited knowledge of how potters are affected by raw materials and kiln emissions, it is impossible to state how accurately extrapolation of industrial data reflects potters' actual experiences. A detailed investigation on how potters use raw materials might offer a basis for evaluating a revised set of safety procedures.

"The Potter's Health & Safety Questionnaire," while not complete in the scope of information it elicits from potters, offers a beginning in an ongoing effort to fill in the blank areas of knowledge. The initial information from the survey indicates potters as a group are very dedicated to their craft, spending long hours in their private studios, schools, and craft centers. Their safety procedures and knowledge of raw material handling practices increases with age and time spent in the ceramics field. The majority of potters do use protective kiln gloves, since not using gloves can cause immediate burns when reaching into a hot kiln. Education in safety practices is reflected in the high use of respirators in schools. As a group, potters do not smoke, which indicates a high degree of general health consciousness, which they apply to their craft. The concept of a ceramics safety education should be applied to potters working in private studios and craft centers. What is most interesting in the survey is the health problems associated with the use of ceramic lusters. Unfortunately, the limited scope of the survey could not follow up on this activity. Future investigations will have to address this most important issue, as all the potters who used lusters reported some type of health problem.

Chapter 18

Risk Assessment

The health issue that has surrounded talc is just one of the many ceramic raw material warnings that deserve thorough investigation. While this type of examination is a time consuming process, it does result in an enhanced understanding of the relative risk concerning the use of each raw material. In the final analysis, the potter will have to make an informed decision on whether to use a raw material or to find an appropriate substitute.

In the past, raw material warnings were based on insufficient or incomplete scientific evidence or more frequently on data that had been extrapolated from industrial exposure and duration rates of a raw material, which do not correspond to the potters' experience with the raw material. For example, high rates of exposure and long durations of exposure to silica dust in mining operations can cause silicosis in workers. This is a well-known fact that has been proven by epidemiological studies in various industries. Can we then go on to say that lower rates of exposure and shorter durations of exposure will not cause silicosis in potters? Exactly what reduced level of exposure will be considered safe to potters? Is that level the same for all potters? Are there other factors that might enhance the toxic reaction, such as smoking or diet? The answers to such questions will, to some degree, affect the choices we make as potters. However, even though some questions cannot be answered at this time, a plan can be enacted where the consistent use of air cleaners, vacuums, respirators, and studio clean up procedures can enhance the safety margin in our favor.

Raw material warnings are also based on word of mouth stories that leave the listener with a powerful emotional impression. We have all heard anecdotes of potters developing a serious illness attributed to the use of a raw material. Such stories by definition are selective, as we do not hear many tales of people in good health that have been using raw materials for years.

An anecdotal story appeals directly to our way of thinking and processing information, which is described in *Voodoo Science* by Robert Park. *Voodoo Science* is based on psychologist James Alcock's descriptions of our brains as belief engines. It begins when we associate two events that take place. For example, if event B happens followed by event A, then the next time A occurs, the brain expects B to begin again. Our ancestors found this method of thinking useful. If they ate a piece of fruit and then got sick, they avoided that fruit in the future. This survival factor in our brain wiring could not separate causal connections from coincidence. The fact that our current brains are still hardwired for this effect makes us vulnerable to believe in stories of a potter getting sick when he or she came in contact with a raw material. Statistical evidence, medical studies, and testing are needed to validate such information. The scientific procedure gives us the tools to separate causal connections from coincidence. The same principles of scientific investigation and independent testing should be applied to the subject of health and safety issues in the field of ceramics.

The potter can react in a number of ways to recurrent raw material warnings. Some potters are overloaded with dire predictions about toxic materials, and they shut down listening. Other potters realize there could be some type of potential risk with raw materials and take conservative safety measures based on the information they have obtained from several sources. A few potters have taken a *prudent avoidance* policy. *Prudent avoidance* is a term coined by Granger Morgan of Carnegie Mellon University, which essentially means if there is *any possibility* of a toxic substance, avoid it. While this policy on the face of it sounds like good advice, it totally bypasses the relative risk of using a specific raw material. It also does not allow for any proportionality to the situation. Using a prudent avoidance policy could mean keeping away from men with guns, or it could suggest not driving a car because of the potential for accidents in this widespread activity. In the first example, it might be prudent and proportional to the perceived risk to keep away from men with guns. In the second case, we all know that there is a possibility of being in a car crash, but we evaluate the activity and accept the risk. We keep the risk in proportion and take sensible safety measures to reduce the risk further (seat belts, good car maintenance, no drinking, paying attention to the road, etc.), but we still decide the reward of mobility is greater than the risk of a crash.

The potter can assume any one of these reactions to the potential toxicity of a given raw material. This is a personal choice we make in our everyday lives with other risk/reward events. In some instances, we base our decision on emotional reactions that do not involve scientific facts or statistical studies. We make a decision on an emotional basis that might or might not be accurate, such as staying out of the ocean because of sharks. There is a strong instinctual fear of being eaten by a sharp-toothed creature. However, the fact is that driving the family car to the beach poses a statistically greater danger to our lives than a shark attack. In short, we assign a degree of risk to each situation based on emotion or intellectual information we obtain. While the examples given are not directly related to going into your studio and making pots, evaluating situations on a risk/reward basis is something we do everyday.

I am always on guard when reading articles or books that state a raw material is "a possible carcinogen." That does not mean I disregard the information immediately, but now I have to look behind the statement and research facts and past studies of the material. "Possible" is a red flag that means you have to take on the responsibility of looking into a claim of toxicity further and get more information. Richard Wilson, a Harvard physicist illustrated *possible* as: if someone tells you there is a cat walking down Main Street you might think it is strange, but it's possible, and you would not question the tale. If the story is that a tiger is running down Main Street, it would still be possible, but you might want some proof. If the story states a brontosaurus was running down Main Street, you would think someone was mistaken and probably saw something else. All three stories are possible, even the last, but I don't think many of us would waste too much time on checking out the brontosaurus report. What does this all mean? Simply, *possible* can be an open-ended term and not a conclusion. As the Main Street story illustrates, there are many degrees of *possible*. Each potter must determine the level of confidence he or she has in the information gathered. Potters must also be open to reviewing the topic in the future to see if new facts have been discovered, which they can then use to amend their decisions on using the material.

I strongly believe the best policy is to broadly educate yourself in the use of ceramic materials and pottery equipment. Potters should be reading and attending workshops, lectures, and demonstrations with the goal of attaining a body of knowledge that will enable them to handle ceramic materials in a safe manner. At that point, the potter must go on to adopt the appropriate health and safety measures to ensure a low risk ceramic environment.

Chapter 19

Conclusion

I have been a ceramics consultant for over 25 years and have made pottery since 1966. Someone once said, "A consultant is someone who takes the watch off your wrist and then tells you the time." I sincerely hope that I offer more than that to people who seek my advice. Every day individual potters, ceramics supply companies, and ceramic manufacturers call with varied technical questions. One topic that clients ask about is the toxic potential of the materials they work with on a daily basis. While each circumstance is different, I feel a profound responsibility to offer the best advice, given the situation and materials they are encountering in their working environments. Clients are depending on an "expert" to give an unambiguous reply to a health and safety question. Through this text I have chosen to write down what I tell people every day. Hopefully, it will offer relevant information that can be of use to potters.

As an added factor concerning this book, I realized with every sentence that the written word does carry a presumption of accuracy. There is clearly a difference in the potential risk to potters when giving information on technical issues versus health issues. We all tend to listen to "experts" and take what they say as accurate. As potters, we face too many diverse issues to research them all individually, and our training and education often does not allow us to know every conceivable topic under investigation. We depend on the advice of others who have studied a specific body of information to help us arrive at our decisions. The whole topic of safety in the ceramics studio can be evaluated from many directions, resulting in conflicting recommendations based on each expert's viewpoint and evaluation of the data. I will not leave it up to the reader to guess my viewpoint on the health risks associated with ceramic materials. *Potters working with ceramic raw materials and firing their kilns encounter low risk toxicity and health factors, provided they follow the appropriate safety guidelines.* While this general statement does not begin to cover a specific potter working in his or her studio, I do believe it does begin to place the activity of working with clays and glazes in the proper perspective.

Everyone has a hidden or apparent bias on the issues of health and safety in the field of ceramics. An honest approach when researching the subject is to recognize a preconceived opionion or influence, while still keeping an open mind to new information. If conflicting data is found on a particular point, it has to be balanced against an existing body of knowledge. In the scope of researching the data available for this book, I certainly think it would have been more interesting and dramatic to have reported a group of potters experiencing a severe toxic reaction with a raw material; however, what I discovered was fairly dull and mundane. The information and recommendations I have reported will not make newspaper headlines but will offer an effective strategy for working with clay, glazes, and kiln firing. *Practicing good housekeeping procedures consistently and using common sense produces a safe working environment.*

An important part of the book is "The Potter's Health & Safety Questionnaire," which is only the first step in eliminating the blank areas in our knowledge on how to operate safe ceramics studios. We often hear from potters working in the field of ceramics, "I've made pots for more than twenty years, and it hasn't hurt me yet," balanced by reports of how looking into a kiln can cause cataracts or the potential dangers of ingesting ceramic materials. Somewhere between these two points, there is useable accurate information. "The Potter's Health & Safety Questionnaire" is the first of many steps to arrive at practical answers on how clay, glazes, and kilns affect us as potters.

Acknowledgments

I wish to thank the following people who gave me their time and expertise in supplying information and advice.

Jim Fineman, potter, who helped with a review of the technical information and editing.

Mr. Larry Sussberg, President, Ceramic Supply, 7 Route 46 West, Lodi, NJ 07644 was very supportive and supplied safety products for testing. Ceramic Supply has been instrumental in offering ceramics safety workshops to potters in the Northeast.

Ms. Bethany Clark, Research Assistant, Jeff Zamek Ceramics Consulting Services, Northampton, Mass. was outstanding in her efforts locating published information on barium carbonate. Her efficiency and dedication contributed greatly to the chapter on barium carbonate.

Ms. Donna L. Kurkul, Medical Librarian, Richard H. Dolloff Medical Library, The Cooley Dickinson Hospital, Northampton, Mass. I would like to thank Donna for her time and effort searching the data for information on barium toxicology.

Lauren Proctor, M.D., Amherst, Mass. was very helpful in advising in the direction and scope of research concerning barium carbonate ingestion.

Bruce Cowan, M.D., Easthampton, Mass. who was most interested in my research and directed my efforts in obtaining the relevant medical information.

Paul Berman, M.D., Easthampton, Mass. contributed his time in helping focus my search for toxic reactions of barium carbonate in the general population.

Mr. Jerry Cartlidge, (retired) Alfred University, College of Ceramics, Engineering Division, Alfred, NY. It was a pleasure to work with Mr. Cartlidge again after so many years. His knowledge of testing procedures was most valuable in understanding ceramic materials.

Ms. Cynthia Edney, Analytical chemist, Alfred University, College of Ceramics, Engineering Division, Alfred, NY. spent considerable time locating and interpreting current barium release test data for the chapter on barium carbonate.

Mr. Jerry A. Cook, Technical Director, Chemical Products Corporation, Cartersville, Ga. Thank you for supplying data and information on barium carbonate sales in the pottery industry.

Mr. Bruce E. Connolly, Public Services Librarian, Scholes Library of Ceramics, NYS College of Ceramics at Alfred University, Alfred, NY. Thank you for your efforts finding and locating past articles on barium carbonate. Bruce has always demonstrated an exceptional ability to locate ceramics related source materials often with short notice.

Mr. Rudy Kottemann, Chemical Products Corporation, Cartersville, Ga. helped me turn raw information on raw materials into readable text.

Alfred University, College of Ceramics, Art & Design Division, Engineering Division, Alfred, NY. Thanks to the teachers and support staff who have given their time and effort in training potters.

Thank you to the staff of Dalloz Safety Equipment.

Ms. Sharon Platt, Marketing Communications, Dalloz Safety Equipment

Mr. Todd Young, 3M sales representative, Occupational Health and Environmental Safety Division, supplied information on respirators.

Mr. William D. Jordan, c.s.p. Environmental Health and Safety Officer, Massachusetts College of Art, Boston, Mass. who offered informative details on the safety systems located at the college.

Ms. Elaine Aldrich, Library Assistant, Dolloff Medical Library at Cooley Dickenson Hospital, Northampton, Mass. who researched raw material toxicology.

Ms. Marge Westerfield, Librarian, Dolloff Medical Library at Cooley Dickenson Hospital, Northampton, Mass. who researched raw material toxicology.

Nancy Balin, MD, F.A.C.S., Northampton, Mass. provided a detailed explanation of eye disorders and the safety factors that can be employed to prevent potential eye injury.

Mr. Mike Shelto, President of RMS Industries, Box 773, Rocky Hill Conn., 06067 provided technical information on Uvex industrial protective glasses (Cobalt Blue #5) for protection against infrared and ultraviolet radiation.

Mr. Dave Koch, Senior Technical Specialist, Dalloz Safety Group, P.O. Box 622, Reading, PA 19603 was most informative about Dalloz products, (800) 977-9177. Thank you for supplying information on shielded headgear and face protection equipment.

Ms. Michelle Breen, Technical Specialist, Dalloz Safety Group. Thank you for supplying technical data on safety shields.

Mr. Kirk Van Pelt, Technical Specialist, Dalloz Safety Group supplied additional information on the Wilson Safety Shields and safety procedures.

Mr. Dave De Vries, Director of Practices and Standards, American Society of Safety Engineers, was very generous with his time and expertise in directing my research in the areas of preventing infrared and ultraviolet hazards.

Mr. Jeff Goss, a professional potter located in Stowe, Vt., was of great help in offering his practical advice on clothes for the ceramics studio. Jeff has been making pots for more than thirty five years and his information was greatly appreciated.

Mr. Richard Bunchamper, Professor of Ceramics, Keane College, Elizabeth, NJ, offered technical support in the health and safety factors related to college ceramics studio equipment.

Mr. Chuck Plosky, Professor of Ceramics, Jersey City State College, Jersey City, NJ, was very helpful in suggesting practical studio clean up techniques.

Mr. Bob Woo, Pelham, Mass., professional potter, with more than thirty years experience in making pots gave valuable information on safety procedures used in his pottery studio.

Mr. Jim Bailey, President of Bailey Ceramic Supply, was very helpful in supplying information on his company's safety equipment.

Mr. Steven Branfman, Owner of the Potters Shop Book Store. Thank you for your contribution of Raku tong and face shield photographs.

Mr. Tim Frederich, The Edward Orton Jr. Ceramic Foundation, was very helpful and informative with technical information on the manufacture and use of Orton pyrometric cones and kiln venting.

Ms. Donna Jaehrling, Lab Safety Supply Inc., supplied information on Material Safety Data Sheets.

Ms. Claudia Ciano-Boyce, Ed.D and Ms. Lynn Shelley-Sireci, Ph.D tabulated "The Potter's Health & Safety Questionnaire."

Mr. Tomas Gothers, Laboratory technical director, Massachusetts College of Art/Ceramics Dept. who took photos and supplied information on studio clean up procedures and ceramics room venting.

Ms. Constance Baugh, who let me photograph her pottery studio in operation.

Mrs. Mary Ellen Harvey, a potter who inspired me to write directly and succinctly. Mary Ellen had developed an innovative "folk art" original way with clay. Her spirit and energy were always present in her pots.

Mr. Frank Tucker, Tucker's Pottery Supplies, Inc. supplied information on safety products.

Mr. Bill Newman, Southern Pottery Equipment & Supplies, has contributed information on kiln safety gloves.

Mr. Graham Turnbull, Standard Ceramic Supply Company, was most helpful in offering information on his companies low fire, no talc clay body.

Edouard Bastarache M.D. (Occupational & Environmental Medicine) has contributed research on eye injuries due to radiation.

Mr. John Cowen, President of Sheffield Pottery, Inc. was most helpful with information on his company's safety products for potters.

Mr. Timothy R. Pfiffner, President Great Lakes Clay & Supply, allowed me to use information on his company's safety products.

Ms. Christine Winokur, President Kickwheel Pottery Supply, Inc., offered health and safety information published on her company's web site.

Mr. Dean E. Venturin, Director, Health, Safety and Environmental Areas, Unifrax Corporation, supplied information on several of his company's refractory ceramic fiber products.

Mr. Roland Hale, President of Alfred Analytical Laboratory, was very informative in explaining the procedures used when testing glazes for heavy metal release.

Sources

The Alfred Analytical Laboratory, 4964 Kenyon Road, Alfred Station, NY, 14803, (607) 478-8074, fax (607) 478-5324, email ats@infoblvd.net, has been testing glazes for potters and is a nationally certified laboratory.

The American Academy of Orthopaedic Surgeons lists information on carpal tunnel syndrome on their Web site at orthoinfo.aaos.org.

Bailey Ceramic Supply, Inc., P.O. 1577, Kingston, NY 12402, (800) 431-6067, fax (845) 339-5530, www.BaileyPottery.com.

Edouard Bastarache M.D.(Occupational & Environmental Medicine), author of "Substitutions for Raw Ceramic Materials," lives in Quebec, Canada and has a colorful history. He studied surgery, internal medicine, and neuroendecrine physiology and has been a consultant in occupational and environmental medicine for 25 years. At the same time as his medical studies, he studied ceramics under Julien Cloutier at La Boutique d'Argile (The Clay Shop) and later taught at the same school. Bastarache now lives in the Sorel-Tracy region of Quebec, near the St. Lawrence river.

Ceramic Supply of NY/NJ, 7 Route 46, West, Lodi, NJ 07644, (973) 340-3005, www. 7ceramic. com.

The Edward Orton Jr. Ceramic Foundation, 6991 Old 3C Highway, Westerville, Ohio 43082, (614) 895-2663, fax (614) 895-5610, www.ortonceramic.com.

Great Lakes Clay & Supply, 120 S. Lincoln Ave., Carpentersville, Ill. 60110, (800) 258-8796, fax (847) 551-1083, email tpfiffner@greatclay.com.

Kickwheel Pottery Supply, Inc. 6477 Peachtree Industrial Blvd., Atlanta, Ga. 30360, (770) 986-9011, www.kickwheel.com. Safety information available from http://kickwheel.com/KPSproductsafety.html.

"The Kiln Safety booklet." by The Edward Orton Jr. Ceramic Foundation, 6991 Old 3C Highway, Westerville, Ohio 43081, (614) 895-2663, fax (614) 895-5610. The Edward Orton Jr. Ceramic foundation has manufactured high quality pyrometric products since 1896. Orton also offers kiln accessories and temperature controllers.

Lab Safety Supply Inc., 401 S. Wright Road, PO Box 1368, Janesville, Wis. 53547-1368. Supplied booklets titled "Preparing, Understanding and Using Material Safety Data Sheets." MSDS Employee information chart No. 13805. Call (800) 356-0783 for current pricing.

Laguna Clay Company, 14400 Lomitas Avenue, City of Industry, Calif. 91746, (626) 330-0631, www.lagunaclay.com.

McCann, Michael. *Artist Beware*. Watson Guptill.

Mr. Steve Branfman, owner of The Potters Shop, 31 Thorpe Road, Needham, Mass. 02494, (781) 449-7687, email PottersShop@aol.com, supplied photos of Raku tongs and face shield. The Potters Shop bookstore has the widest selection of books on ceramics with a very helpful and knowledgeable staff.

Park, Robert. *Voodoo Science*: *The Road from Foolishness to Fraud*. Oxford University Press, 2000.

Rhodes, Daniel. *Clay and Glazes for the Potter*. 3d ed. Revised and expanded by Robin Hopper. Iola, Wis.: Krause Publications, 2000. Supplied information on salt glaze reactions.

Sheffield Pottery Supply, Inc., US Rt. 7 Box 399, Sheffield, Mass. 01257, (413) 229-7700, www.sheffield.pottery.com.

Southern Pottery Equipment & Supplies, 2721 West Perdue, Baton Rouge, La. 70814, (225) 932-9457, fax (225) 932-9446.

Standard Ceramic Supply, Division of Chem-Clay Corporation, P.O. Box 4435, Pittsburgh, Pa. 15205-0435, (412) 276-6333, fax (412) 276-7124, www.standardceramic.com/clay.

Tucker's Pottery Supplies Inc., 15 West Pearce St., No. 7 Richmond Hill, ON Canada L4B 1H6, (905) 889-7705, www.tuckerspottery.com.

Unifrax Corporation, 2351 Whirlpool Street, Niagara Falls, NY 14305-2413, (716) 278-3800, www.unifrax.com. "New Magnesium Silicate Fiber Isofrax^{TM} is a soluble alternative to refractory ceramic fiber (RCF)" paper by Dean E. Venturin, Director, Health, Safety, and Environment.

Williams, Gerry and Peter Sabin, Sarah Bodine, eds. *Studio Potter Book*. Van Nostrand Reinhold Co., 1979.

Articles by the Author

"Adjusting Glazes for Color and Opacity." *Ceramic Industry Magazine, Dec. 2001.*

Suggestions Column. *Ceramics Monthly, Dec. 2001.*

"The Potter's Health & Safety Questionnaire." *National Council on Education for the Ceramic Arts*, newsletter, Fall 2001 newsletter.

"Substitutions for Gerstley Borate." *Ceramics Monthly, Oct. 2001.*

"Additives for Clay Bodies." *Ceramics Industry Magazine, Sept. 2001.*

Suggestions Column, *Ceramics Monthly*, June/July/Aug. *2001.*

"Black Friday." *Ceramics Monthly, May 2001.*

"Opening Doors." *Ceramics Monthly,* April 2001.

"The Economics of Raw Materials." *Ceramic Industry Magazine,* March 2001.

"Solutions for Common Health and Safety Issues in the Ceramics Studio." *The Crafts Report,* Jan. 2001.

Text on Soda Vapor firing and photo. Included in *Clay and Glazes for the Potter*, 3ed. by Daniel Rhodes, pgs. 311-313, 295.

"Venting Electric Kilns." *Pottery Making Illustrated,* Winter 2000.

"Potter's Health & Safety Questionnaire." *NCECA News,* Winter 2000.

"Preventing S-Cracks." *Pottery Making Illustrated,* Fall 2000.

"No More Gerstley Borate," *Ceramics Monthly,* March 2000.

"Suggestions Column." *Ceramics Monthly,* Feb. 2000.

"Getting Stuck." *Ceramics Monthly,* Jan. 2000.

Editorials: Health & Safety Recommendations for Raw Materials, Is Barium Carbonate Safe? *Potters Guide, 1999.*

"Functional Pottery Sets." *Pottery Making Illustrated,* Winter 1999.

"Studio Safety." *Pottery Making Illustrated,* Fall 1999.

"Glaze Crawling." *Ceramics Monthly,* Sept. 1999.

"Eye Protection for Potters." *Pottery Making Illustrated,* Summer 1999.

"Respirators for Potters." *Pottery Making Illustrated.* Spring 1999

What Every Potter Should Know. (book) Jeff Zamek, Ceramics Consulting Services. Krause Publications, March 1999.

"Material Substitutions for Clay Bodies." *Ceramics Monthly,* Feb.1999.

"Additives for Glazes and Clay Bodies." *Ceramics Monthly,* Dec. 1998.

Suggestions Column, *Ceramics Monthly,* Dec. 1998.

"Ordering Raw Materials." *Ceramics Monthly,* Oct. 1998.

"Studio Safety: Assessing Risks." *Pottery Making Illustrated,* Summer 1998.

Suggestions Column, *Ceramics Monthly,* June 1998.

"Gerstley Borate and Colemanite." *Ceramics Monthly,* June 1998.

"Production: Mistakes to Avoid." *Pottery Making Illustrated,* Spring *1998.*

"The Perfect Clay Body?" *Ceramics Monthly,* March 1998.

"Education: A Lifetime of Learning." *Pottery Making Illustrated,* Winter 1998.

"Raw Material Substitutions for Glazes." *Ceramics Monthly,* Nov. 1998.

"Marketing: 12 Steps to Success." *Pottery Making Illustrated,* Oct.1997.

"Avoiding Common Problems." *The Firing Line,* Winter/Spring 1997.

"Is Barium Carbonate Safe?" *Ceramics Monthly,* Sept. 1997.

"Why Clay and Glazes Melt." *Ceramics Monthly,* June 1997.

"Avoiding Common Problems." *Ceramics Monthly,* Sept. 1996.

"Weighing the Benefits of Wet vs. Dry Clay." *Clay Times,* June 1996.

"Five Steps to Stop Glaze Shivering." *Ceramics Monthly,* Oct.1995.

"Eight Steps to Stop Crazing." *Ceramics Monthly,* April 1995.

"How to Buy Supplies." *Ceramics Monthly,* May 1991.

"Economics and Raw Materials." *Ceramics Monthly,* Jan. 1989.

Suggestions Column. *Ceramics Monthly,* Sept. 1985.

Suggestions Column. *Ceramics Monthly,* March 1985

"Methane Gas and Sewer Sludge: New Routes to Energy Efficiency in Firing Clay." *The Studio Potter,* December 1984, Vol. 13 No.1.

"Methane and Paper Sludge." *Ceramics Monthly,* June 1983.

"Sodium Vapor Firing." Alfred University, College of Ceramics, Alfred, NY, Part 1, June 1973, Part 2, April 1974.

"Alternative to Salt Glazing." *Craft Horizons,* June 1973.

Index